AF883916

CHILD PSYCHOLOGY

Edited & Compiled by
Dr. Sinku Kumar Singh
M.P.E., M.Phil, NET, Ph.D. (FELLOW)
Shri Sant Sawta Mali Gramin Mahavidhyalaya,
Phulambri
Aurangabad, Maharashtra

K.S.K. **Publishers and Distributors**
7/26, Basement, Ansari Road, Darya Ganj,
New Delhi-110002

Published by:

K.S.K. Publishers and Distributors

7/26, Basement, Ansari Road, Darya Ganj, New Delhi-110002.

Ph.: (O) 011-65190343, 43551324, 42564726
(M) 9811088729, (Fax) 011-42564726
(Res.) 47091605

E-mail: *khelsahitya1@rediffmail.com*

Web: *www.khelsahitya.com*

© 2016 Author

ISBN - 978-81-89983-27-7

PRINTED IN INDIA 2016

All Rights Reserved.

No part of this publication may be stored in a retrieval system, transmitted or reproduced in any way, including but not limited to photocopy, photograph, magnetic or other record, without the prior agreement and written permission of the publisher.

Laser Typeset by:
JAIN MEDIA GRAPHICS
Delhi-110035.

Printed by:
ASIAN OFFSET PRINTERS
Delhi

Price: Rs. 700/-

Preface

Child study is a very complex field; human beings, and children, specifically, are very complex. Consequently, simple answers and solutions to problems are very often too simple. A short example helps make the point. Most of us have had the unfortunate experience of having problems with our car. We take the car to the mechanic and explain the problem. The mechanic diagnoses the problem and attempts to solve it. We get the car back, and very often the problem is still there! Why is this all-too-familiar example relevant? The reason is, compared to children, cars are VERY SIMPLE! If well-trained professionals have difficulty with this relatively simple entity, think of the difficulty involved in "figuring out" children, who are vastly more complex than even the most complex car.

Our best hope for gaining insight into children and their worlds is through the systematic study of the varied contexts in which they live and function. This is best accomplished through training in a variety of methods following the scientific method. After a phenomenon is recognized, we should generate hypotheses, or educated hunches, that we think might be causing or related to the phenomenon. These hunches should then be tested, systematically, until we arrive at a satisfactory answer. Furthermore, seemingly similar phenomena may have different causes and consequences with different children, thus the process should be repeated under slightly varying conditions.

Our message, in short, is that there are very few simple answers and solutions to working with children. Indeed, we are skeptical of such simple answers. Your best guide in the venture of working with children is an understanding of theory and methods in child study. This book provides that basis. Our underlying belief is that sound theory and empirical research are needed to guide effective work with children. Consequently, this book is organized such that different theories and methods for studying children are presented. Our aim is to provide students with a repertoire of theoretical and research skills that will be useful in their work. Students should view the theories and methods as a "tool kit" that can be applied to various situations.

Child Psychology reflects the increasingly sophisticated and varied research methods used to examine the highly complex interactions contributing to children's cognitive, emotional, and social development. The volume provides an invaluable and practical resource for students and instructors on a wide variety of courses, and for researchers and professionals working in the field of child development. This text addresses the basics of developmental psychopathology in a clear manner, with enough detail to facilitate a real understanding of the concepts and their relevance to clinical work with children. This introductory undergraduate text on child and adolescent psychopathology adopts a developmental psychopathology approach to understanding child disorders. The author examines the emergence of disorders over time, pays special attention to risk and protective factors that influence developmental processes and trajectories, and examines child psychology in the context of normal development.

Rachana Sharma

Contents

1

Introduction

Child Psychology, study of children's behaviour—including physical, cognitive, motor, linguistic, perceptual, social, and emotional characteristics—from birth through to adolescence. Child psychologists attempt to explain the similarities and differences among children and to describe normal as well as abnormal behaviour and development. They also develop methods of treating social, emotional, and learning problems and provide therapy privately and in schools, hospitals, and other institutions. Two critical problems for child psychologists are ---(1) to determine how environmental variables (such as parental attitudes) and biological characteristics (such as health) interact and influence behaviour, and (2) to understand how behavioural changes influence one another.

Both Plato and Aristotle wrote about children. Plato believed that children are born with special talents and that their training should stress those talents. His views are consistent with modern thinking about individual differences and education. Aristotle proposed methods for observing children's behaviour that were forerunners of modern methods. For many centuries thereafter, little interest was shown in the development of children because they were regarded only as miniature adults. In the 18th century the French philosopher Jean-Jacques Rousseau seemed to echo

Plato when he stated that children should be free to express their energies in order to develop their special talents. His view suggests that normal development occurs best in a nonrestrictive, supportive environment. Similar concepts are popular today.

Scientific Study

In the 19th century, Charles Darwin's theory of evolution provided an impetus for the scientific examination of child development. His emphasis on the survival behaviour of different species stimulated an interest in observing children to identify the various ways that they adapt to things, and in learning about the inheritance of human behaviour. These studies were of limited scientific value because they lacked objectivity and often failed to describe adequately the behaviours being observed, making validation impossible.

Scientific research in child development flourished from the early 1900s. One major stimulus was the introduction (1916) by the American psychologist Lewis Terman of the test known today as the Stanford-Binet Intelligence Test. This test led to a number of studies about children's intellectual development. In the 1920s scientists at more than a dozen leading American universities began large-scale observational studies of children and their families; all used the longitudinal method, in which the same children are observed and tested over a specific time period.

The American psychologist Arnold Gesell established a research institute at Yale University in the 1920s for the sole purpose of studying children. He developed the technique of analysing children's behaviour from film, frame by frame. Gesell also made much use of the cross-sectional method, in which different children are observed at each of several age levels. The accumulated results of all the major studies reported over a period of 20 years provided information about patterns and rates of child development, as well as age norms for a wide variety of behaviours. These norms are used by both professional workers and parents to assess children's development. One problem with the observational studies was that they emerged from an interest in evolution and genetics. Consequently, environmental influences were largely dismissed as unimportant and were excluded from the work on intelligence.

Environmental Studies

About the time that the observational work was flourishing, other researchers were writing about the role of the environment in children's development and behaviour. Sigmund Freud, who emphasized the effects of environmental variables on development, particularly stressed the importance of parental behaviour during infancy. To this day, Freud's theory continues to influence child psychologists. The American psychologist John B. Watson also stressed the role of the environment in shaping children's development. His views were consistent with those of behaviourism, an approach to psychology that had a great impact in the 1950s on research about children.

Although behaviourists emphasize environment, they almost totally deny the influence of biological variables on development. Their basic assumptions are that the mind of a newborn child is a blank slate, or *tabula rasa;* all behaviours are determined by environmental events; and differences among children are the result of those environmental variables. Behaviourists encouraged experimental studies and were responsible for moving child psychology into the mainstream of psychology. Although they contributed much to the study of children, their concepts eventually were viewed as being too narrow.

In the early 1960s attention was focused on the work of the Swiss psychologist Jean Piaget, who since the 1920s had been writing about children's cognitive development. Piaget called himself a genetic epistemologist—one who studies the origins of human knowledge—and his theories led to more advanced work in child psychology. This work involves both experimental and observational methods and, in accounting for behaviour, integrates biological and environmental variables. Thus, current studies have their origins in Darwin's theory of evolution but also incorporate Watson's concern for the influence of the environment.

Developmental Theories

A theory of development should reflect an attempt to relate behavioural change to chronological age; that is, diverse behavioural characteristics should be related to specific stages of growth. The rules governing the transitions between these growth states also must be identified. The dominant developmental theories are Freud's theory of personality development and Piaget's theory of perception and cognition. Both explain human development in terms of interactions of biological determinants and environmental events. Freud's theory is based on the concept that a healthy personality requires the satisfaction of instinctual needs. In Freudian theory the personality is composed of the id, ego, and superego. The id is the source of instinctual drives. The role of the ego is to cope with the demands of the id while remaining within the rules of society, which in turn are represented by the superego.

The physical focus of instinctual needs changes with age, and the periods of different focus are called stages. Infants, for example, achieve maximum id satisfaction from sucking; this is called the oral stage. Children progress through four stages, ending with adult sexuality. Freud clearly integrated biological and environmental variables in his theory. Piaget believed that from birth humans are active learners who do not require external incentives. He proposed that cognitive development occurs in four stages:

- Stage I, sensorimotor intelligence (birth-2 years), takes the child from unrelated reflexive movements to behaviour that reflects knowledge of simple concepts.

- Stage II, preoperational thought (2-7 years), is characterized by an increasing use of abstract symbols as reflected in imaginative play.
- Stage III, concrete operational thought (7-11 years), involves relatively sophisticated problem-solving behaviour and attainment of adult thought.
- Stage IV, formal operational thought (12 years and older), is characterized by the ability to develop hypotheses and deduce new concepts.

CHILD DEVELOPMENT

The various aspects of child development encompass physical growth, emotional and psychological changes, and social adjustments. A great many determinants influence patterns of development and change.

Heredity and Environment

It is generally agreed that patterns of child development are determined by the joint interaction of genetics and the environment, although sharp disagreements occur about the relative importance of an individual's genetic makeup. Research on this problem involves the use of separately reared monozygotic (identical) twins. Their behaviours are compared for similarities and differences, and the results are then compared with behaviours of twins reared together.

If genetics is critical, the twins reared apart will be as similar in most respects as those reared together. (These studies usually assume that when twins are reared apart, their environments are different in important ways, an assumption that is not always true.) Except in instances of massive environmental deprivation, the patterns and rates of physical and motor development appear to be genetically controlled.

Research also indicated that both genetic and environmental variables contribute to intellectual behaviour. A genetic component also exists in personality characteristics such as introversion and extroversion, activity level, and predisposition to psychoses. Many advances have been made in identifying the genetic causes of mental disorders, but more research is needed to understand better how genetic mechanisms operate among normal children.

Physical Growth

On the average, a newborn baby weighs 3.4 kg (7.5 lb) and is 53 cm (21 in) long, with the head disproportionately larger than the lower part of the body. As the child grows, increments in height are greatest from birth to three years; thereafter they are relatively constant until adolescence. The growth spurt at adolescence is far less than during infancy. Weight increments are also large during the first three years but are equally large during adolescence. Research shows that growth rates are influenced by the health of the child. Rates of development decelerate during illness; after an illness is cured, however, growth rates accelerate until children attain their appropriate height and weight.

Motor Activities

Dramatic changes occur in motor skills from birth through the first two years. At birth infants are capable of extensive uncoordinated movements. One feature of the early motor behaviour of infants is the large number of reflexlike actions. These actions appear for a short time after birth and then disappear. For example, when the palm of the hand is stroked lightly the fingers involuntarily close, forming a fist; this is called the palmar reflex.

From these early movements, distinct sequential patterns of motor development occur. Walking, which occurs on the average between 13 and 15 months, emerges from a sequence of 14 earlier stages. Research shows that the rate of acquisition of motor skills is innately determined and that the acquisition of these skills is not influenced by practice. Severe restrictions on motor activities, however, will alter both the pattern and rate of development. After basic motor skills are acquired, children learn to integrate their movements with perceptual skills, especially spatial perception. This process is critical for the achievement of eye-hand coordination and for the higher-level skills required for many sports activities.

Language

The ability to communicate and to understand language is one of the main achievements of human beings. An amazing feature of language development is the speed with which it is acquired: The first word is spoken at about 12 months; by two years of age most children have vocabularies of about 270 words, and this increases to 2,600 words at the age of six. It is almost impossible to determine the number of sentence constructions that can be generated within a single language. Children, however, use syntactically correct sentences by the age of three and highly complex constructions by the age of five.

This extraordinary phenomenon cannot be explained by means of simple learning theory. The American linguist Noam Chomsky postulated that the human brain is especially constructed to detect and reproduce language; the mental system does not require formal learning and will function perfectly when language is available to the child. Although developmental psycholinguists do not agree with all of Chomsky's concepts, they do accept the idea of special mental language systems. Today theorists are concerned with the relationship between cognitive growth and language. It is now assumed that language reflects children's concepts and develops as their concepts expand.

Personality Formation

Theories of personality are attempts to describe how people behave in satisfying their physical and psychological needs. An inability to satisfy such needs creates a personal conflict. Personality formation is viewed as the process by which children learn how to avoid conflict when possible and how to cope with conflict when it inevitably occurs. Overly restrictive or overly permissive parents limit their children's options in avoiding and coping with conflict.

A normal response to overwhelming conflict is to revert to a defence mechanism such as rationalization—for example, denying that one ever had a specific objective or goal, it being obvious that they had previously had one. Although everyone uses defence mechanisms at some time, they should not become a person's sole means of coping with conflict. A child with a balanced, integrated personality feels accepted and loved and has been allowed to learn a number of appropriate coping mechanisms.

Intelligence and Learning

Intelligence may be defined as the ability to manipulate abstract verbal concepts effectively. This definition is reflected in the types of questions asked on intelligence tests for children. Two well-known tests—the Stanford-Binet and the Wechsler Intelligence Scale for Children, Revised—are used to index children's mental growth and to predict learning performances. Because school learning seems to depend on the ability to reason verbally, the content of intelligence tests seems appropriate; some relationship does indeed exist between intelligence-test performance and school achievement. Predictions based on tests are imperfect, however, because intelligence tests do not measure motivation and because knowledge about the skills needed for school learning is incomplete. It has also been argued that intelligence tests are sometimes inappropriate when used with children from ethnic minorities, who may not understand or respond appropriately to certain items because of language difficulties or cultural differences. Thus, test scores must be interpreted with great care, as with all forms of psychological testing.

Family Relationships

The attitudes and values of parents and their behaviour towards their children clearly influence patterns of development. Likewise, children's characteristics influence parental attitudes and behaviours; disabled children, for example, require more attention and are likely to cause more parental anxiety than do children without disabilities.

Extensive studies have established that parental behaviour towards children varies widely—ranging from restrictiveness to permissiveness, warmth to hostility, and anxious involvement to calm detachment. These variations in attitudes produce different patterns in family relationships. Parental hostility and permissiveness, for example, are associated with highly aggressive, non-compliant children. Warm, restrictive behaviour by parents is associated with dependent, polite, and obedient children. Punishment techniques also influence behaviour. For example, parents who often use physical punishment tend to have children who rank above average in their use of physical aggression. It appears, then, that one of the ways children acquire patterns of behaviour is by imitating their parents.

Social Relationships

Social relationships among infants involve mutual interest without interaction. This is known as parallel play. Beginning with the years before school, relationships among children the same age and roughly equal status—the peer group—become increasingly sophisticated social systems influencing their values and behaviour. The transition to the adult social world is aided by the organization of peer groups with a leader, members with varying strengths and weaknesses, and a recognition of the need for cooperative behaviour. Peer-group conformity reaches a peak when children are about 12 years of age. Conformity never disappears, but its manifestations among adults are less obvious. The members of peer groups change with age. Preadolescent groups tend to be homogeneous—that is, members are usually of the same sex and come from the same area. Among older children, social relationships are more likely to be based on shared interests and values.

Socialization

The process by which children learn acceptable and unacceptable behaviour is called socialization. Children are expected to learn, for example, that extreme physical aggression, stealing, and cheating are unacceptable, and that cooperation, honesty, and sharing are acceptable. Some theories suggest that socialization is achieved only through imitation or through a process of rewards and punishments. Current theories, however, stress the role of cognition, or perceiving, thinking, and knowing; thus, mature socialization requires that a person explicitly or implicitly understand the rules of social behaviour that function in all situations.

Socialization also includes understanding concepts of morality. The American psychologist Lawrence Kohlberghas demonstrated that moral thinking exists on three levels. At the lowest level, a rule is obeyed in order to avoid punishment. This level characterizes the thought of very young children. At the highest level, a person has a rational understanding of universal moral principles necessary for society's survival. Of course, the understanding of such concepts is often inconsistent with behaviour and research has shown that moral behaviour varies with each situation and is not predictable.

Current Trends

Child psychologists continue to be interested in the interaction of biological traits and environmental events that influence behaviour and development; in the role of cognition in socialization, especially in adapting to sex roles; and in understanding the processes of cognition. Psychologists now generally agree that biological risk factors—such as low birth weight, oxygen deprivation before or during birth, and physical and psychological handicaps—are important in behaviour and development. Extensive longitudinal studies are under way to determine how risk factors affect children's experiences, and how differences in these experiences affect their behaviour. This research will provide methods for helping children with risk factors to develop more successfully.

The role of cognition in children's sex-role learning and stereotypical thinking is also being examined. Although a few general sex differences have been established—for example, girls often excel in verbal ability, and boys often excel in mathematical ability—it is not clear how innate traits and environmental events interact to produce these differences. Sex roles have long been rigidly defined in society, but cultural pressures are slowly breaking down these stereotypes so that members of each sex can more easily change or adapt behaviours to fit specific situations.

Much current work involves identifying the cognitive components (such as memory and attention span) used in problem-solving activities. Researchers in developmental psychology are also trying to identify the processes that occur in the transition from one level of thought to the next. Another area of investigation is the cognitive components in reading and arithmetic. It is hoped that this research will lead to improved methods of teaching academic skills and more effective remedial teaching.

2

Child Development Stages

Child development stages describe theoretical milestones of child development. Many stage models of development have been proposed, used as working concepts and in some cases asserted as nativist theories.

Age	Motor	Speech	Vision and hearing	Additional Notes
4-6 weeks				Smiles at parent
6-8 weeks		Vocalizes		
3 months	Prone:head held up for prolonged periods. No grasp reflex	Makes vowel noises	Follows dangling toy from side to side. Turns head round to sound	Squeals with delight appropriately. Discriminates smile.
5 months	Holds head steady. Goes for objects and gets them. Objects taken to mouth	Enjoys vocal play		
6 months	Transfers objects from one hand to the other. Pulls self up to sit	Double syllable sounds such as 'mumum' and 'dada'	Localises sound 45cm lateral to either ear	May show 'stranger shyness'

(Cont...)

	and sits erect with supports. Rolls over prone to supine. Palmar grasp of cube			
9-10 months	Wiggles and crawls. Sits unsupported. Picks up objects with pincer grasp			Apprehensive about strangers
1 year	Stands holding furniture. Stands alone for a second or two, then collapses with a bump		Looks for toys dropped Drops toys, and watches where they go	Cooperates with dressing, waves goodbye, understands simple commands
18 months	Can walk alone. Picks up toy without falling over. Gets up/ down stairs holding onto rail. Begins to jump with both feet. Can build a tower of 3 or 4 cubes and throw a ball	Babbles tunefully Babbles 2 or 3 words repeatedly 'Jargon'. Many intelligible words		Demands constant mothering. Drinks from a cup with both hands. Feeds self with a spoon. Most children with autism are diagnosed at this age.
2 years	Able to run. Walks up and down stairs 2 feet per step. Builds tower of 6 cubes	Joins 2-3 words in sentences		Parallel play. Dry by day

(Cont...)

3 years	Goes up stairs 1 foot per step and downstairs 2 feet per step. Copies circle, imitates cross and draws man on request. Builds tower of 9 cubes	Constantly asks questions. Speaks in sentences		Cooperative play. Undresses with assistance. Imaginary companions
4 years	Goes down stairs one foot per step, skips on one foot. Imitates gate with cubes, copies a cross	Questioning at its height. Many infantile substitutions in speech		Dresses and undresses with assistance. Attends to own toilet needs
5 years	Skips on both feet and hops. Draws a man and copies a triangle. Gives age	Fluent speech with few infantile substitutions in speech		Dresses and undresses alone
6 years	Copies a diamond. Knows right from left and number of fingers	Fluent speech		

Did you know that our children are in the business of learning? Learning is to gain knowledge, understanding, or skill. An even broader definition of learning is "any permanent change in behavior that occurs as a result of a practice or an experience." This makes what we teach our children even more important as it has the potential to have a lasting affect in their behavior. Children are a bundle of ideas and thoughts. If you ever really look at your child you will see that these thought patterns are much different from that of an adult and can certainly be expressed in much different ways. In order to understand the process of learning it is important to know the physical changes that take place.

Physical Specifications

Age	Average length/ height(cm)	Length growth	Average weight	Weight gain	Respiration rate(per minute)	Normal body temperature	Heart rate (pulse)(per minute)	Visual acuity (Snellen chart)
1-4 months	50-70 cm	2.5 cm per month	4-8 kg	100-200 g per week	30 to 40	35.7-37.5 °C		
4-8 months	70-75 cm	1.3 cm per month	(doubling birth weight)	500 g per month	25 to 50			20/100
8-12 months	Approx. 1.5 times birth length by first birthday		9.6 kg. Nearly triple the birth weight by first birthday	500 g per month	20 to 45	35.7-37.5 °C (96.4-99.6 °F)	80 to 110	20/60
12-24 months	80-90 cm	5-8 cm per year	9-13 kg	130-250 g per month	22 to 40			
2 years	85-95 cm			1 kg per year	20 to 35			

(Cont...)

		7-13 cm per year	12-15 kgabout 4 times birth weight					
3 years	95-100 cmNearly double birth length	5-8 cm per year	13-17 kg	1.4-2.3 kg per year	20 to 30	35-37 °C	90 to 110	20/40
4 years	101.6- 114cm	5cm-6.5cm per year	14.5-17kg	1.8-2.3kg per year	20-30	36.6-37.4°C	90 to 110	20/30
5 years	105-115 cm	5-6.5 cm per year	17-21 kg	1.8-2.3 kg per year	20-30		90 to 110	20/20
>5 years	105-120 cm	5-7 cm per year	17-22 kg	2 kg per year				

Specifications Sorted by Reached Age

Creative development could very well be seen as how the child learns in its environment through experimenting in different ways of doing everything.

1-4 Months

Physical

- Head and chest circumference are nearly equal to the part of the abdomen.
- Head circumference increases approximately 2 cm per month until two months, then increases 1.5 cm per month until four months. Increases are an important indication of continued brain growth.
- Continues to breathe using abdominal muscles.
- Posterior fontanel closes by the second month.
- Anterior fontanel closes to approximately 1.3 cm.
- Skin remains sensitive and easily irritated.
- Legs may appear slightly bowed.
- Cries with tears.
- Eyes begin moving together in unison (binocular vision).

Motor Development

- Rooting and sucking reflexes are well developed.
- Swallowing reflex and tongue movements are still immature; continued drooling and inability to move food to the back of the mouth.
- Grasp reflex gradually disappears.
- *Landau reflex* appears near the middle of this period; when baby is held in a prone (face down) position, the head is held upright and legs are fully extended.
- Grasps with entire hand; strength insufficient to hold items. Holds hands in an open or semi-open position.
- Muscle strength and control improving; early movements are large and jerky; gradually become smoother and more purposeful.

- Raises head and upper body on arms when in a proneposition.
- Turns head side to side when in a supine (face up) position; near the end of this period can hold head up and in line with the body.
- Upper body parts are more active: clasps hands above face, waves arms about, reaches for objects.

4-8 Months

Physical

- Head and chest circumferences are basically equal.
- Head circumference increases approximately 1 cm per month until six to seven months, then 0.5 cm per month; head circumference should continue to increase steadily, indicating healthy, ongoing brain growth.
- Breathing is abdominal; respiration rate depending on activity; rate and patterns vary from infant to infant.
- Teeth begin to appear, with upper and lower incisors coming in first. Gums may become red and swollen, accompanied by increased drooling, chewing, biting, and mouthing of objects.
- Legs may appear bowed; bowing gradually disappears as infant grows older.
- Fat rolls ("Baby Fat") appear on thighs, upper arms and neck.
- True eye color is established.

Motor Development

- Reflexive behaviors are changing:
- Blinking reflex is well established
- Sucking reflex becomes voluntary
- Moro reflex disappears
- When lowered suddenly, infant throws out arms as a protective measure.

- Swallowing reflex appears and allows infant to move solid foods from front of mouth to the back for swallowing.
- Picks up objects using finger and thumb (pincer grip).
- Reaches for objects with both arms simultaneously; later reaches with one hand or the other.
- Transfers objects from one hand to the other; grasps object using entire hand (palmar grasp).
- Handles, shakes, and pounds objects; puts everything in mouth.
- Able to hold bottle.
- Sits alone without support, holding head erect, back straightened, and arms propped forward for support
- Pulls self into a crawling position by raising up on arms and drawing knees up beneath the body; rocks back and forth, but generally does not move forward.
- Lifts head when placed on back.
- Can roll over from back or stomach position.
- May accidentally begin scooting backwards when placed on stomach; soon will begin to crawl forward.
- Looks for fallen objects by 7 months
- Plays 'peek-a-boo' games
- Cannot understand "no" or "danger"

8-12 Months

Physical

- Respiration rates vary with activity
- Environmental conditions, weather, activity, and clothing still affect variations in body temperature.
- Head and chest circumference remain equal.
- Continues to use abdominal muscles for breathing.
- Anterior fontanel begins to close.
- More teeth appear, often in the order of two lower incisors then two upper incisors followed by four more incisors and two lower molars but some babies

may still be waiting for their first.

- Arm and hands are more developed than feet and legs (cephalocaudal development); hands appear large in proportion to other body parts.
- Legs may continue to appear bowed.
- "Baby Fat" continues to appear on thighs, upper arms and neck.
- Feet appear flat as arch has not yet fully developed.
- Both eyes work in unison (true binocular coordination).
- Can see distant objects (4 m to 6 m (15 to 20 feet) away) and points at them.

Motor Development

- Reaches with one hand leading to grasp an offeredobject or toy.
- Manipulates objects, transferring them from one hand to the other.
- Explores new objects by poking with one finger.
- Uses deliberate pincer grasp to pick up small objects, toys, and finger foods.
- Stacks objects; also places objects inside one another.
- Releases objects or toys by dropping or throwing; cannot intentionally put an object down.
- Beginning to pull self to a standing position.
- Beginning to stand alone, leaning on furniture for support; moves around obstacles by side-stepping.
- Has good balance when sitting; can shift positions without falling.
- Creeps on hands and knees; crawls up and down stairs.
- Walks with adult support, holding onto adult's hand; may begin to walk alone.
- Watches people, objects, and activities in the immediate environment.
- Shows awareness of distant objects (4 m to 6 m (15 to 20 feet) away) by pointing at them.

- Responds to hearing tests (voice localization); however, loses interest quickly and, therefore, may be difficult to test informally.
- Follows simple instructions.
- Reaches for toys that are out of reach but visible
- Recognizes objects in reverse
- Drops thing intentionally and repeats and watches object
- Imitates activities like playing drum

Psychological Development

- Related Elements in Society: Law (legitimizes and provides boundaries for autonomy)

  If denied independence, the child will turn against his/her urges to manipulate and discriminate. Shame develops with the child's self-consciousness. Doubt has to do with having a front and back — a "behind" subject to its own rules. Left over doubt may become paranoia. The sense of autonomy fostered in the child and modified as life progresses serves the preservation in economic and political life of a sense of justice.

Ego quality: Will

When a child reaches ages one through three, Erikson explains, the child is developing a sense of autonomy . During this age, the toddler discovers he/she is no longer attached to the primary caregiver but is a separate individual. Autonomy is the independence a toddler strives for from caregivers. Toddlers' autonomous behavior is a way of forming their own identity away from their caregivers. This stage is a time where a toddler has the "will" to become independent. Shame and doubt are likely to occur when the toddler is not given any choices or boundaries because the toddler is determined to become independent. The strong will of a toddler may cause conflict between child and caregiver. Many parents are unaware of how to properly establish healthy boundaries for the toddler while allowing the child to develop their independence. Parents who are assertive and too demanding may find themselves in a power struggle with their toddler.

Preschool (3 to 5 Years)

- Psychosocial Crisis: Initiative vs. Guilts
- Ego quality: Purpose
- Related Elements in Society: ideal prototypes/roles Initiative adds to autonomy the quality of undertaking, planning, and attacking a task for the sake of being active and on the move. The child is learning to master the world around him or her, learning basic skills and principles of physics; things fall to the ground, not up; round things roll, how to zip and tie, count and speak with ease. At this stage the child wants to begin and complete his or her own actions for a purpose. Guilt is a new emotion and is confusing to the child; he or she may feel guilty over things which are not logically guilt producing, and he or she will feel guilt when his or her initiative does not produce the desired results.

The development of courage and independence are what set preschoolers, ages three to six years of age, apart from other age groups . Young children in this category face the challenge of initiative versus guilt . As described in Bee and Boyd (2004), the child during this stage faces the complexities of planning and developing a sense of judgment. During this stage, the child learns to take initiative and prepare him or herself towards roles of leadership and goal achievement. Activities sought out by a child in this stage may include risk-taking behaviors, such as crossing a street on his or her own or riding a bike without a helmet; both examples involving self-limits. Within instances requiring initiative, the child may also develop negative behaviors. These behaviors are a result of the child developing a sense of frustration for not being able to achieve his or her goal as planned and may engage in behaviors that seem aggressive, ruthless, and overly assertive to parents; aggressive behaviors, such as throwing objects, hitting, or yelling, are examples of observable behaviors during this stage.

School Age (5 Years to Teens)

- Psychosocial Crisis: Industry vs. Inferiority
- Ego quality: Competence
- Related Elements in Society: division of labor

To bring a productive situation to completion is an aim which gradually supersedes the whims and wishes of play. The fundamentals of technology are developed. To lose the hope of such "industrious" association may pull the child back to the more isolated, less conscious familial rivalry of the oedipal time.

"Children at this age are becoming more aware of themselves as individuals." They work hard at "being responsible, being good and doing it right." They are now more reasonable to share and cooperate. Allen and Marotz (2003) also list some perceptual cognitive developmental traits specific for this age group: Children understand the concepts of space and time, in more logical, practical ways, beginning to grasp, gain better understanding of cause and effect and understand calendar time. At this stage, children are eager to learn and accomplish more complex skills: reading, writing, telling time. They also get to form moral values, recognize cultural and individual differences and are able to manage most of their personal need and grooming with minimal assistance (Allen and Marotz, 2003). At this stage, children might express their independence by being disobedient, using back talk and being rebellious.

Toddlers (12-24 Months)

Physical

- Weight is now approximately 3 times the child's birth weight.
- Respiration rate varies with emotional state and activity.
- Rate of growth slows
- Head size increases slowly; grows approximately 1.3 cm every six months; anterior fontanelle is nearly closed at eighteen months as bones of the skull thicken.
- Chest circumference is larger than head circumference.
- Rapid eruption of teeth; six to ten new teeth will appear.
- Legs may still appear bowed.
- Toddler will begin to lose the "Baby Fat" once he/she begins walking.
- Body shape changes; takes on more adult-like appearance; still appears top-heavy; abdomen protrudes, back is swayed.

Motor Development

- Crawls skillfully and quickly.
- Stands alone with feet spread apart, legs stiffened, and arms extended for support.
- Gets to feet unaided.
- Most children walk unassisted near the end of this period; falls often; not always able to maneuver around obstacles, such as furniture or toys.
- Uses furniture to lower self to floor; collapses backwards into a sitting position or falls forward on hands and then sits.
- Enjoys pushing or pulling toys while walking.
- Repeatedly picks up objects and throws them; direction becomes more deliberate.

- Attempts to run; has difficulty stopping and usually just drops to the floor.
- Crawls up stairs on all fours; goes down stairs in same position.
- Sits in a small chair.
- Carries toys from place to place.
- Enjoys crayons and markers for scribbling; uses whole-arm movement.
- Helps feed self; enjoys holding spoon (often upside down) and drinking from a glass or cup; not always accurate in getting utensils into mouth; frequent spills should be expected.
- Helps turn pages in book.
- Stacks two to six objects per day.

COGNITIVE DEVELOPMENT

- Enjoys object-hiding activities
- Early in this period, the child always searches in the same location for a hidden object (if the child has watched the hiding of an object). Later, the child will search in several locations.
- Passes toy to other hand when offered a second object (referred to as "crossing the midline"-an important neurological development).
- Manages three to four objects by setting an object aside (on lap or floor) when presented with a new toy.
- Puts toys in mouth less often.
- Enjoys looking at picture books.
- Demonstrates understanding of functional relationships (objects that belong together): Puts spoon in bowl and then uses spoon as if eating; places teacup on saucer and sips from cup; tries to make doll stand up.
- Shows or offers toy to another person to look at.
- Names many everyday objects.

- Shows increasing understanding of spatial and form discrimination: puts all pegs in a pegboard; places three geometric shapes in large formboard or puzzle.
- Places several small items (blocks, clothespins, cereal pieces) in a container or bottle and then dumps them out.
- Tries to make mechanical objects work after watching someone else do so.
- Responds with some facial movement, but cannot truly imitate facial expression.
- Most children with autism are diagnosed at this age.

Language

- Produces considerable "jargon": puts words and sounds together into speech-like (inflected) patterns.
- Holophrastic speech: uses one word to convey an entire thought; meaning depends on the inflection ("me" may be used to request more cookies or a desire to feed self). Later; produces two-word phrases to express a complete thought (telegraphic speech): "More cookie," "Daddy bye-bye."
- Follows simple directions, "Give Daddy the cup."
- When asked, will point to familiar persons, animals, and toys.
- Identifies three body parts if someone names them: "Show me your nose (toe, ear)."
- Indicates a few desired objects and activities by name: "Bye-bye," "cookie"; verbal request is often accompanied by an insistent gesture.
- Responds to simple questions with "yes" or "no" and appropriate head movement.
- Speech is 25 to 50 percent intelligible during this period.
- Locates familiar objects on request (if child knows location of objects).
- Acquires and uses five to fifty words; typically these are words that refer to animals, food, and toys.

- Uses gestures, such as pointing or pulling, to direct adult attention.
- Enjoys rhymes and songs; tries to join in.
- Seems aware of reciprocal (back and forth) aspects of conversational exchanges; some turn-taking in other kinds of vocal exchanges, such as making and imitating sounds.

Social

- Less wary of strangers.
- Helps pick up and put away toys.
- Plays by themselves
- Enjoys being held and read to.
- Often imitates adult actions in play.
- Enjoys adult attention; likes to know that an adult is near; gives hugs and kisses.
- Recognizes self in mirror.
- Enjoys the companionship of other children, but does not play cooperatively.
- Beginning to assert independence; often refuses to cooperate with daily routines that once were enjoyable; resists getting dressed, putting on shoes, eating, taking a bath; wants to try doing things without help.
- May have a tantrum when things go wrong or if overly tired or frustrated.
- Exceedingly curious about people and surroundings; toddlers need to be watched carefully to prevent them from getting into unsafe situations.

Psychological

(J. Chasse, 2008) Psychosocial stimulation is vital during the toddler years. Play begins to become interactive. Toddlers begin to learn and exhibit independence, but ironically they enjoy sharing this discovery with others. Another important advancement is active social play with adults including mirroring and repeating. Songs, rhymes, and finger plays (eg. itsy bitsy spider, little teapot, etc.) are a great way to encourage and stimulate this area of development.

Two Year Old

Physical

- Posture is more erect; abdomen still large and protruding, back swayed, because abdominal muscles are not yet fully developed.
- Respirations are slow and regular
- Body temperature continues to fluctuate with activity, emotional state, and environment.
- Brain reaches about 80 percent of its adult size.
- 15 baby teeth almost finished growing out

Motor Development

- Can walk around obstacles and walk more erect
- Squats for long periods while playing.
- Climbs stairs unassisted (but not with alternating feet).
- Balances on one foot (for a few moments), jumps up and down, but may fall.
- Often achieves toilet training during this year (depending on child's physical and neurological development) although accidents should still be expected; the child will indicate readiness for toilet training.
- Throws large ball underhand without losing balance. Holds cup or glass (be sure it is unbreakable) in one hand. Unbuttons large buttons; unzips large zippers.
- Opens doors by turning doorknobs.
- Grasps large crayon with fist; scribbles enthusiastically on large paper.
- Climbs up on chair, turns around and sits down.
- Enjoys pouring and filling activities-sand, water, styrofoam peanuts.

- Stacks four to six objects on top of one another.
- Uses feet to propel wheeled riding toys.

Cognitive

- Eye-hand movements better coordinated; can put objects together, take them apart; fit large pegs into pegboard.
- Begins to use objects for purposes other than intended (may push a block around as a boat).
- Does simple classification tasks based on one dimension (separates toy dinosaurs from toy cars).
- Stares for long moments; seems fascinated by, or engrossed in, figuring out a situation: where the tennis ball has rolled; where the dog has gone, what has caused a particular noise.
- Attends to self-selected activities for longer periods of time. Discovering cause and effect: squeezing the cat makes her scratch.
- Knows where familiar persons should be; notes their absence; finds a hidden object by looking in last hiding place first. (This is what Piaget termed object permanence, which usually occurs during the sensorimotor stage of Piaget's childhood theory of cognitive development)
- Names objects in picture books; may pretend to pick something off the page and taste or smell it.
- Recognizes and expresses pain and its location.

Language

- Enjoys being read to if allowed to participate by pointing, making relevant noises, turning pages.
- Realizes that Language is effective for getting others to respond to needs and preferences.
- Uses fifty to three hundred different words; vocabulary continuously increasing.
- Has broken the linguistic code; in other words, much of a two-year-old's talk has meaning to him or her.

- Receptive Language is more developed than expressive Language ; most two-year olds understand significantly more than they can talk about.
- Utters three- and four-word statements; uses conventional word order to form more complete sentences.
- Refers to self as "me" or sometimes "I" rather than by name: "Me go bye-bye"; has no trouble verbalizing "mine."
- Expresses negative statements by tacking on a negative word such as "no" or "not": "Not more milk."
- Repeatedly asks, "What's that?"
- Uses some plurals; tells about objects and events not immediately present (this is both a cognitive and linguistic advance).
- Some stammering and other dysfluencies are common.
- Speech is as much as 65 to 70 percent intelligible.

Social and Emotional

- Shows signs of empathy and caring: comforts another child if hurt or frightened; appears to sometimes be overly affectionate in offering hugs and kisses to children
- Continues to use physical aggression if frustrated or angry (for some children, this is more exaggerated than for others); Physical aggression usually lessens as verbal skills improve.
- Temper tantrums likely to peak during this year; cannot be reasoned with while tantrum is in progress.
- Impatient; finds it difficult to wait or take turns.
- Enjoys "helping" with household chores; imitates everyday activities: may try to toilet a stuffed animal, feed a doll.

- "Bossy" with parents and caregivers; orders them around, makes demands, expects immediate compliance from adults.
- Watches and imitates the play of other children, but seldom joins in; content to play alone.
- Offers toys to other children, but is usually possessive of playthings; still tends to hoard toys.
- Making choices is difficult; wants it both ways.
- Often defiant; shouting "no" becomes automatic.
- Ritualistic; wants everything "just so"; routines carried out exactly as before; belongings placed "where they belong."

Three Year Old

Physical

- Growth is steady though slower than in first two years.
- Adult height can be predicted from measurements of height at three years of age; males are approximately 53% of their adult height and females, 57%.
- Legs grow faster than arms,
- Circumference of head and chest is equal; head size is in better proportion to the body.
- "Baby fat" disappears as neck appears.
- Posture is more erect; abdomen no longer protrudes.
- Slightly knock-kneed.
- Can jump from low step
- Can stand up and walk around on tiptoes
- "Baby" teeth stage over .
- Needs to consume approximately 6,300 J (1,500 calories) daily.

Motor Development

- Walks up and down stairs unassisted, using alternating feet; may jump from bottom step, landing on both feet.

- Can walk on one foot, balance momentarily.
- Can kick big ball-shaped objects.
- Needs minimal assistance eating.
- Jumps on the spot.
- Pedals a small tricycle.
- Throws a ball overhand; aim and distance are limited.
- Catches a large bounced ball with both arms extended.
- Enjoys swinging on a swing (not too high or too fast).
- Shows improved control of crayons or markers; uses vertical, horizontal and circular strokes.
- Holds crayon or marker between first two fingers and thumb (tripod grasp), not in a fist as earlier.
- Can turn pages of a book one at a time.
- Enjoys building with blocks.
- Buildsa tower of eight or more blocks.
- Enjoys playing with clay; pounds, rolls, and squeezes it.
- May begin to show hand dominance.
- Carries a container of liquid, such as a cup of milk or bowl of water, without much spilling; pours liquid from pitcher into another container.
- Manipulates large buttons and zippers on clothing.
- Washes and dries hands; brushes own teeth, but not thoroughly.
- Usually achieves complete bladder control during this time.

Cognitive Development

- Listens attentively to age-appropriate stories.
- Makes relevant comments during stories, especially those that relate to home and family events.
- Likes to look at books and may pretend to "read" to others or explain pictures.
- Enjoys stories with riddles, guessing, and "suspense."
- Speech is understandable most of the time.

- Produces expanded noun phrases: "big, brown dog."
- Produces verbs with "ing" endings; uses "-s" to indicate more than one; often puts "-s" on already pluralized forms: geeses, mices.
- Indicates negatives by inserting "no" or "not" before a simple noun or verb phrase: "Not baby."
- Answers "What are you doing?", "What is this?", and "Where?" questions dealing with familiar objects and events.

Social Development

- Stacks objects in sized order and can make a pyramid
- Seems to understand taking turns, but not always willing to do so.
- Friendly; laughs frequently; is eager to please.
- Has occasional nightmares and fears the dark, monsters, or fire.
- Joins in simple games and group activities, sometimes hesitantly.
- Often talks to self.
- Uses objects symbolically in play: block of wood may be a truck, a ramp, a bat.
- Observes other children playing; may join in for a short time; often plays parallel to other children.
- Defends toys and possessions; may become aggressive at times by grabbing a toy, hitting another child, hiding toys.
- Engages in make-believe play alone and with other children.
- Shows affection toward children who are younger or children who get hurt.
- Sits and listens to stories up to ten minutes at a time; does not bother other children listening to story and resents being bothered.
- May continue to have a special blanket, stuffed animal, or toy for comfort.

Four Year Old

Physical Development

- Head circumference is usually not measured after age three.
- Requires approximately 1,700 calories daily.
- Hearing acuity can be assessed by child's correct usage of sounds and *Language also, by the child's appropriate responses to questions and instructions.

Motor Development

- Walks a straight line (tape or chalk line on the floor).
- Hops on one foot.
- Pedals and steers a wheeled toy with confidence; turns corners, avoids obstacles and oncoming "traffic."
- Climbs ladders, trees, playground equipment.
- Jumps over objects 12 cm to 15 cm (5 or 6 inches) high; lands with both feet together.
- Runs, starts, stops, and moves around obstacles with ease.
- Throws a ball overhand; distance and aim improving.
- Builds a tower with ten or more blocks.
- Forms shapes and objects out of clay: cookies, snakes, simple animals.
- Reproduces some shapes and letters.
- Holds a crayon or marker using a tripod grasp.
- Paints and draws with purpose; may have an idea in mind, but often has problems implementing it so calls the creation something else.
- Becomes more accurate at hitting nails and pegs with hammer.
- Threads small wooden beads on a string.
- Can run in a circle

Cognitive

- Can recognize that certain words sound similar
- Names eighteen to twenty uppercase letters. Writes several letters and sometimes their name.
- A few children are beginning to read simple books, such as alphabet books with only a few words per page and many pictures.
- Likes stories about how things grow and how things operate.
- Delights in wordplay, creating silly Language.
- Understands the concepts of "tallest," "biggest," "same," and "more"; selects the picture that has the "most houses" or the "biggest dogs."
- Rote counts to 20 or more.
- Understands the sequence of daily events: "When we get up in the morning, we get dressed, have breakfast, brush our teeth, and go to school."
- When looking at pictures, can recognize and identify missing puzzle parts (of person, car, animal).

Language

- Uses the prepositions "on," "in," and "under."
- Uses possessives consistently: "hers," "theirs," "baby's."
- Answers "Whose?", "Who?", "Why?", and "How many?"
- Produces elaborate sentence structures: "The cat ran under the house before I could see what color it was."
- Speech is almost entirely intelligible.
- Begins to correctly use the past tense of verbs: "Mommy closed the door," "Daddy went to work."
- Refers to activities, events, objects, and people that are not present.
- Changes tone of voice and sentence structure to adapt to listener's level of under-standing: To baby brother,

"Milk gone?" To Mother, "Did the baby drink all of his milk?"

- States first and last name, gender, siblings' names, and sometimes own telephone number.
- Answers appropriately when asked what to do if tired, cold, or hungry. Recites and sings simple songs and rhymes.

Social Development

- Outgoing; friendly; overly enthusiastic at times.
- Moods change rapidly and unpredictably; laughing one minute, crying the next; may throw tantrum over minor frustrations (a block structure that will not balance); sulk over being left out.
- Imaginary playmates or companions are common; holds conversations and shares strong emotions with this invisible friend.
- Boasts, exaggerates, and "bends" the truth with made-up stories or claims of boldness; tests the limits with "bathroom" talk.
- Cooperates with others; participates in group activities.
- Shows pride in accomplishments; seeks frequent adult approval.
- Often appears selfish; not always able to take turns or to understand taking turns under some conditions; tattles on other children.
- Insists on trying to do things independently, but may get so frustrated as to verge on tantr ıms when problems arise: paint that drips, paper airplane that will not fold right.
- Enjoys role-playing and make-believe activities.
- Relies (most of the time) on verbal rather than Physical aggression; may yell angrily rather than hit to make a point; threatens: "You can't come to my birthday party"

- Name-calling and taunting are often used as ways of excluding other children.
- Establishes close relationships with playmates; beginning to have "best" friends.

PSYCHOLOGICAL

Initiative Vs. Guilt. During this third stage, the "play age," or the later preschool years (from about 3½ to, in the United States culture, entry into formal school). During it, the healthily developing child learns: (1) to imagine, to broaden his skills through active play of all sorts, including fantasy (2) to cooperate with others (3) to lead as well as to follow. Immobilized by guilt, he is: (1) fearful (2) hangs on the fringes of groups (3) continues to depend unduly on adults and (4) is restricted both in the development of play skills and in imagination.

FIVE YEAR OLD

PHYSICAL

- Head size is approximately that of an adult's.
- May begin to lose "baby" (deciduous) teeth.
- Body is adult-like in proportion.
- Requires approximately 7,500 J (1,800 calories) daily
- Visual tracking and binocular vision are well developed.

MOTOR DEVELOPMENT

- Walks backwards, toe to heel.
- Walks unassisted up and down stairs, alternating feet.
- May learn to turn somersaults (should be taught the right way in order to avoid injury).
- Can touch toes without flexing knees.
- Walks a balance beam.
- Learns to skip using alternative feet.
- Catches a ball thrown from 1 m (3 feet) away.

- Rides a tricycle or wheeled toy with speed and skillful steering; some children learning to ride bicycles, usually with training wheels.
- Jumps or hops forward ten times in a row without falling.
- Balances on either foot with good control for ten seconds.
- Builds three-dimensional structures with small cubes by copying from a picture or model.
- Reproduces many shapes and letters: square, triangle, A, I, O, U, C, H, L, T.
- Demonstrates fair control of pencil or marker; may begin to colour within the lines.
- Cuts on the line with scissors (not perfectly).
- Hand dominance is fairly well established.

Cognitive

- Forms rectangle from two triangular cuts.
- Builds steps with set of small blocks.
- Understands concept of same shape, same size.
- Sorts objects on the basis of two dimensions, such as color and form.
- Sorts a variety of objects so that all things in the group have a single common feature (classification skill: all are food items or boats or animals).
- Understands the concepts of smallest and shortest; places objects in order from shortest to tallest, smallest to largest.
- Identifies objects with specified serial position: first, second, last.
- Rote counts to 20 and above; many children count to 100.
- Recognizes numerals from 1 to 10.
- Understands the concepts of less than: "Which bowl has less water?"
- Understands the terms dark, light, and early: "I got up early, before anyone else. It was still dark."

- Relates clock time to daily schedule: "Time to turn on TV when the little hand points to 5."
- Some children can tell time on the hour: five o'clock, two o'clock.
- Knows what a calendar is for.
- Recognizes and identifies coins; beginning to count and save money.
- Many children know the alphabet and names of upper- and lowercase letters.
- Understands the concept of half; can say how many pieces an object has when it's been cut in half.
- Asks innumerable questions: Why? What? Where? When?
- Eager to learn new things.

Language Development

- Vocabulary of 1,500 words plus.
- Tells a familiar story while looking at pictures in a book.
- Defines simple words by function: a ball is to bounce; a bed is to sleep in.
- Identifies and names four to eight colours.
- Recognizes the humor in simple jokes; makes up jokes and riddles.
- Produces sentences with five to seven words; much longer sentences are not unusual.
- States the name of own city or town, birthday, and parents' names.
- Answers telephone appropriately; calls person to phone or takes a brief message
- Speech is almost entirely intelligible.
- Uses "would" and "could" appropriately.
- Uses past tense of irregular verbs consistently: "went," "caught," "swam."
- Uses past-tense inflection (-ed) appropriately to mark regular verbs: "jumped," "rained," "washed."

Social Development

- Enjoys and often has one or two focus friendships.
- Plays cooperatively (can lapse), is generous, takes turns, shares toys.
- Participates in group play and shared activities with other children; suggests imaginative and elaborate play ideas.
- Shows affection and caring towards others especially those "below" them or in pain
- Generally subservient to parent or caregiver requests.
- Needs comfort and reassurance from adults but is less open to comfort.
- Has better self-control over swings of emotions.
- Likes entertaining people and making them laugh.
- Boasts about accomplishments.

Physical

- Weight gains reflect significant increases in muscle mass.
- Heart rate and respiratory rates are close to adults.
- Body may appear lanky as through period of rapid growth.
- Baby teeth beginning to be replaced by permanent ones, starting with the two upper front teeth
- 20/20 eyesight; if below 20/40 should see a professional.
- The most common vision problem during middle childhood is myopia, or nearsightedness. (Berk, 2007).
- Uses 6,700 J to 7,100 J (1,600 to 1,700 calories) a day.

Motor Development

- Gains greater control over large and fine motor skills; movements are more precise and deliberate, though some clumsiness persists.
- Enjoys vigorous running, jumping, climbing, and throwing est.

- Has trouble staying still.
- Span of attention increases; works at tasks for longer periods of time, though
- Can concentrate effort but not always consistently.
- Understands time (today, tomorrow, yesterday) and simple motion (things go faster than others).
- Recognizes seasons and major activities done in the times.
- Has fun with problem solving and sorting activities like stacking, puzzles and mazes
- Enjoys the challenge of puzzles, counting and sorting activities, paper-and-pencil mazes, and games that involve matching letters and words with pictures.
- Recognizes some words by sight; attempts to sound out words
- In some cases the child may be reading well.
- functioning which facilitates learning to ride a bicycle, swim, swing a bat, or kick a ball.
- Making things is enjoyed.
- Reverses or confuse certain letters: b/d, p/g, g/q, t/f.
- Able to trace objects.
- Folds and cuts paper into simple shapes.
- Can Tie Laces, string (like shoes).

LANGUAGE

- Can identify right and left hands fairly consistently.
- Holds onto positive beliefs involving the unexplainable (magic or fantasy)
- Arrives at some understanding about death and dying; expresses fear that parents may die.
- Talks a lot.
- Loves telling jokes and riddles; often, the humor is far from subtle.
- Experiments with slang and profanity and finds it funny.
- Enthusiastic and inquisitive about surroundings and everyday events.

- Able to carry on adult-like conversations; asks many questions.
- Learns 5 to 10 words a day; vocabulary of 10,000-14,000.
- Uses appropriate verb tenses, word order, and sentence structure.
- Uses Language rather than tantrums or Physical aggression to express displeasure: "That's mine! Give it back, you dummy."
- Talks self through steps required in simple problem-solving situations (though the "logic" may be unclear to adults).
- Has mood swings towards primary caregiver depending on the day
- Friendship with parent is less depended on but still needs closeness and nurturing.
- Anxious to please; needs and seeks adult approval, reassurance, and praise; may complain excessively about minor hurts to gain more attention.
- Often can't view the world from another's point of view
- Self-perceived failure can make the child easily disappointed and frustrated.
- Can't handle things not going their own way
- Does not understand ethical behavior or moral standards especially when doing things that have not been given rules
- Understands when he or she has been thought to be "bad"; values are based on others enforced values.
- May be increasingly fearful of the unknown like things in the dark, noises, and animals.

3

The Origins of Child Behaviour

The development of the child does not begin at birth. When he is born, the infant is already a highly organized individual, capable of a considerable number of elaborate activities. The behavior of the newborn is the result of an orderly process of growth in which the original germinal material develops, becomes differentiated, and is modified. To achieve a through understanding of a child's behavior, it is necessary to trace the development of his characteristics from their origins in the prenatal period.

An account of the origins of child behavior must begin with a description of the nature and variations of the germ cells by which the child is related to his ancestry. Many aspects of individual development can be understood only in relation to heredity. From this beginning, the course of individual prenatal growth must be traced through the stages of fertilization, embryonic development, and fetal growth to birth. A large amount of reliable information has long been available concerning the prenatal growth of the structure of the individual. Recently, much interest has been given to the prenatal development of function and behavior. This last approach endeavors to trace the reactions of the individual, as well as his form, from their real beginning.

The observational attack on the early development of behavior promises to throw considerable light on an age-old psychological problem, that of "the original nature of man." Some speculative writers on this topic seem to have assumed that the innate characteristics of man spring into existence miraculously and without pre-existing cause. Traits that were manifested later in life were often erroneously thought of as "inherent" or "potential" in the less mature organism in which they had not yet appeared. Abandoning these conceptions, scientists have sought instead to describe the precise course of behavior from its very beginning. By careful observation of the time of the appearance and of the nature of the development of structures and functions, more truth can be ascertained than by any amount of theorizing about supposedly ultimate origins.

HEREDITY

Germ Cells. The characteristics of an organism are determined jointly by the material from which it is formed and by the conditions under which it develops.

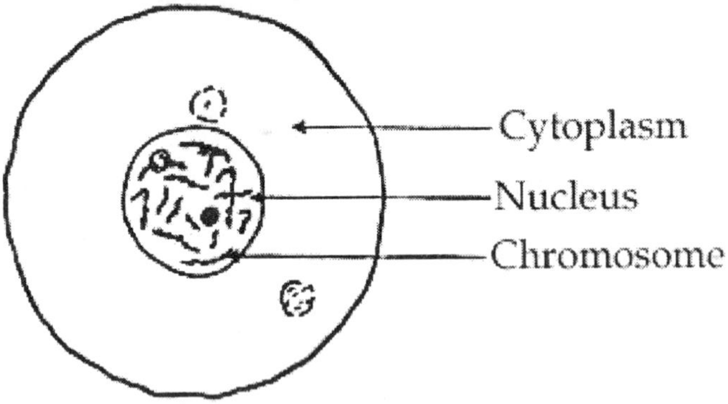

FIG. *Structure of a typical cell—- cells have a great diversity of shapes, but all have* cytoplasm, *a* nucleus, *and* chromosomes.

Although psychology is concerned primarily with the facts of individual development, the importance of the original material must not be ignored. In all species that reproduced bisexually, including man, the individual begins his existence as a single cell, the fertilized germ cell. This is form by the union of two original germ cells, one from each parent. The structure of a typical cell may be seen in Figure above. The external ring is the *cytoplasm*, a mass of relatively undifferentiated protoplasmic material. Within is the more differentiated *nucleus*, which contains long threadlike bodies, the *chromosomes*, which are of special interest in the study of heredity. Each chromosome consists of a linear string of exceedingly minute particles, the *genes*, which are believed to be the principal carriers of heredity traits. The existence of the genes was at first inferred from the operation of heredity, but they have since been observed directly.

In the fertilized germ cell and in all of the body cells that are derived from it during the course of development, the chromosomes occur in pairs. Each gene of a chromosome is paired with a corresponding gene in the adjacent chromosome. In the human species, there are twenty-four such pairs of chromosomes. One chromosome of each pair comes from the maternal germ cell and one from the paternal. Each of the separate parental germ cells, therefore, contains half of the normal number of chromosomes and each supplies, in a sense, half of the heredity of the offspring.

In both parents, the germ cells develop in the reproductive glands, dividing from existing cells by the usual process of cell division, or mitosis. Just before the final stage of development of a germ cell, a peculiar type of division occurs in which half of the chromosomes go to one of the resultant cells, and half to the other. One further division then takes place, the one complete germ cell producing four cells, each with half of the usual number of chromosomes. In the maternal production of germ cells, only one of these four, the *ovum*, remains large and capable of subsequent development. The other three smaller cells of the last division are the *polar bodies*, which are not functional. In the paternal germ cell division, however, all four of the cells development into *spermatozoa*, each capable of fertilizing an ovum.

The ovum and spermatozoan differ considerably in the less essential aspects of structure. The ovum is large as compared to other body cells, while the sperm is among the smallest. The ovum is round and inactive; the sperm elongated and extremely motile. The ovum carries a large bulk of cytoplasm and some yolk which assists in nourishing the embryo, but the sperm has a minimum of cytoplasm. Each, however, contains the twenty-four single chromosomes, which are of the greatest importance in determining the course of development.

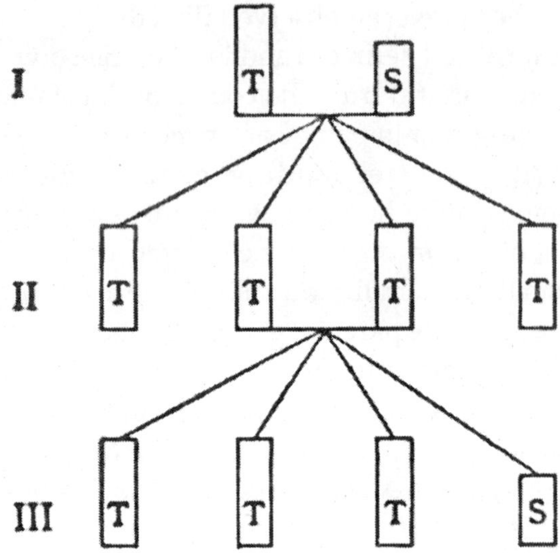

FIG. Mendelian Haredity When the tall and short varieties of peas were crossed, the offspring (II) were all tall. In generation III, the 3 to 1 ratio occurs.

In the process of fertilization the maternal and paternal chromosomes join to form the normal paired arrangement. The characteristics of the individual are determined by the combined effects of these paired chromosomes. The two sets of determiners, however, interact in a number of complex ways. The manner in which the genes operate in influencing the traits of the individual constitutes the laws of heredity.

Mendelian Heredity. The simplest principles upon which the modern study of heredity is based were discovered in 1866 by Gregor Johann Mendel, a monk at Brünn, now in Czechoslovakia. Experimenting with cross-pollinated lines of plants, Mendel noted that if two varieties of peas that were characteristically tall and short were crossed, the offspring (generation II) were all tall. Upon propagating these, the plants of generation III appeared in the now famous Mendelian ratio of three tall to one short. These facts are indicated in Figure last page. Since the tall characteristic is the only one to appear in generation II, and is in the majority in generation III, it is termed dominant, while the short trait is recessive.

Modern genetics explains the Mendelian type of inheritance by the concept of paired genes, as shown in Figure. Let us suppose that the second gene from the top, as represented in the figure, is the determiner for tallness, indicated by its blackness. The white gene indicates the absence of the tall characteristic, or the determiner for shortness. In generation II, each offspring, receiving one chromosome of the pair from each parent, has a paired dominant and recessive, hence the dominant trait appears. The chromosome pair containing two dominant determiners is known as *duplex* with respect to this trait, that containing one as *simplex,* and that containing none as *nulliplex.* In generation III, the four possible combinations of paternal and maternal contributions give one duplex, two simplex, and one nulliplex. Only in the last does the recessive trait appear overtly, hence the three to one ratio.

The so-called Mendelian ratio does not cover all cases, however. One common observation that is widely used in the experimental work of geneticists is the *back-cross,* made by mating a simplex and a nulliplex. An observation of practical importance may be made from even these very simple genetic studies. It is sometimes said that heredity means "resemblance to parents." This is inexact and often misleading statement. Thus in the type of heredity, generation II resembles one parent but not the other, while one fourth of the offspring of generation III resemble neither parent! In the back-cross, half of the offspring resemble one parent and half are like the other. It is clear that the traits of offspring cannot be predicted from observations of the parents alone, but only from a knowledge of the germ cells of the parents. In some plants and lower animals this can often be determined by tracing the variations in offspring through many generations. With the human species it is impossible in most instances to have adequate knowledge of the germ cells for practical prediction.

Other Principles of Heredity. A number of observations concerning heredity do not conform to simple Mendelian principles. One of the best studied of these exceptions is *sex-linked* inheritance. In a female germ cell two chromosomes exist, known as the *x* chromosomes, which behave according to ordinary principles. The corresponding pair in the male is an *x* chromosome and a *y* chromosome, the *y* chromosome showing a singular ineffectiveness as a determine of traits. Hence a single recessive defect in the *x* chromosome of the male cause the undesirable trait to appear, since it is not paired with a normal dominant. A defect in the male of generation I does not appear in generation II, and the descendants of his sons are free from it. But the daughters in generation II are "carriers" of the trait, and if paired with normal males will transmit it to half their sons. Among human characteristics, red-green colorblindness and hemophilia, a tendency to excessive bleeding, show some signs of sex-linked heredity. They are consequently much more prevalent in males than in females.

Another complication in genetics arises from the fact that *the same defect may be caused by different genes*. The *same* defect may occur in the maternal parent due to another defective pair, represented as the fourth. Since the defective genes do not coincide in any of the offspring, none of them will show the defective trait overtly. This element in heredity is the basis of the common belief that the union of closely related persons will result in defective offspring, which is not always true. Related persons have rather similar germ cell organization, and any defect that is offspring present is likely to be due to the same genes. Unrelated persons, who have a greater chance of having their defects in different genes, are less likely to transmit them to their offspring. Excellences as well as defects are due to genes, however, and inbreeding may result in the emphasis of good traits as well as of undesirable ones.

Still another factor that renders predictions by heredity more hazardous is the phenomenon of *crossing-over*. A pair of chromosomes sometimes becomes twisted, and then interchanges genes. When each of these separate chromosomes subsequently combines with those of the other parent, new combinations of hereditary possibilities become established. At first, crossing-over perplexed biologists, for it resulted in strange non-Mendelian ratios of trait occurrence among offspring. Later, it became the basis for the discovery of the relative positions of genes in the chromosomes, for adjacent genes cross over together more frequently than do remote ones. Crossing-over follows orderly principles, and can be expected in definite percentages of cases in certain insects that have been investigated exhaustively.

Blended Inheritance. Much of the simpler research in heredity ignores quantitative differences in the degree of existence of various traits. Characteristics are discussed as though they were either present or absent, which is a sufficiently close approximation of the truth in many instances. Other and, on the whole, more important traits appear in a uniform gradation. These include skin color, height, and practically all mental traits, such as intelligence. Blended or continuous traits can be explained by principles of heredity which require only a little extension of the laws so far described.

A relatively simple example of a blended trait occurs in a certain variety of wheat.

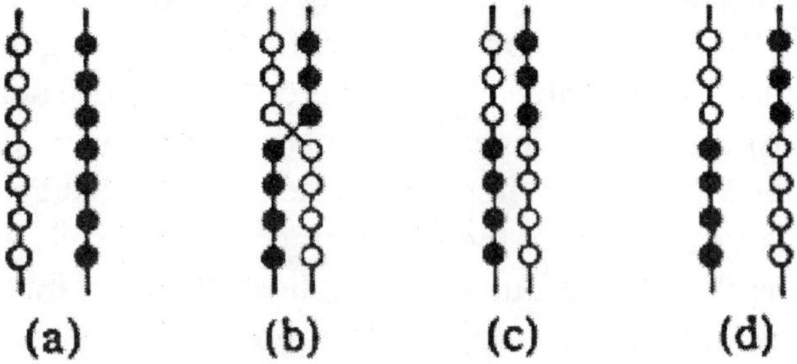

FIG. Crossing-Over The normal chromosomes (a) overlap and come together (b). In (c) and (d) the two lines of genes on each side are represented as having joined, making a new combination.

If the two positive genes are A and A′, and their respective absences are *a* and *a*′, then each parent can contribute four varieties of determiners: *AA*′, *Aa*′, *aA*′, and *aa*′. There are sixteen possible combinations of these when paired, as follows:

AA′ *Aa*′ *aA*′ *aa*′

AA′: *AA*′/*AA*′ *AA*′/*Aa*′ *AA*′/*aA*′ *AA*′/*aa*′

Aa′: *Aa*′ *AA*′ *Aa*′ *Aa*′ *Aa*′ *aA*′ *Aa*′ *aa*′

aA′: *aA*′ *AA*′ *aA*′ *Aa*′ *aA*′ *aA*′ *aA*′ *aa*′ *aa*′: *aa*′/*AA*′ *aa*′/*Aa*′ *aa*′/*aA*′ *aa*′/*aa*′

Thus are found one offspring with four determiners, four with three, six with two, four with one, and one with none, which is the required ratio. Blended inheritances in animal species, such as skin color in human beings, can adequately be accounted for by the hypothesis that several genes may affect a given trait. In fact, the number of interacting genes must be very large. In the earlier days of the study of heredity it was often incorrectly assumed that each gene determined one characteristic, a so-called "unit character." This is now known to be a gross oversimplification. About fifty genes affect the eye structure of the intensively studied fruit-fly, *Drosophila*. It is probable that even more contribute to complex human characteristics. A hundred or so cooperating genes could account for all known human variations in height or intelligence, even assuming that heredity were the only causal factor underlying these traits.

Hereditary Determiners and Environmental Influences. A common misconception of heredity holds that the genes determine certain characteristics absolutely, regardless of the conditions under which the organism develops. This assertion is not true. Hereditary traits are those which develop from the germinal material under average, conditions of environment. There is ample evidence that characteristics which appear in the typical Mendelian ratios in usual environments will not appear at all when circumstances of growth are altered. Conversely, some defects behave as typical inherited traits under abnormal conditions, but do not develop when environments are normal. An example of the latter case may be taken from the widely studied fruit-fly. If certain strains of the eggs of *Drosophilia* are hatched under conditions of excessive cold, supernumerary legs will be produced. The occurrence of this abnormality follows Mendelian principles. If the eggs of this line of descent are hatched under normal conditions of warmth, however, the extra legs will be absent. If eggs not carrying the genes for the legs defect are hatched, the defect will not occur, even when developed in the cold. As Jennings points out, both heredity and environment are necessary to produce this characteristic. If the eggs with the defective gene hatched in the clod are *A*, those with defective gene hatched in warmth are *B*, and those without the defective gene are *C*; only *A* will show the defect. The difference between *A* and *C* is due to "heredity"; the difference between *A* and *B* to "environment." The same difference that is due to heredity in one instance may be due to environment in another. Many other instances illustrating this point have been demonstrated in a variety of animals.

The genes, then, are merely packets of chemicals from which the individual develops. The course of the growth of these original materials is influenced by environmental conditions, resulting in the characteristics of the mature organism. Since any change in the germinal material may cause a modification of the resultant animal, all traits are determined by heredity. Also, since changes in conditions of development may affect any characteristic, all are influenced by environment. Only when the action of heredity is emphasized by holding environmental factors constant, can its action be observed clearly.

Human Heredity. The preceding sections have emphasized the fact that most of our knowledge of heredity is based on observations of plants and lower animals. The human species, on the whole, is poor material for experimental work in this field. In the first place, humans breed too slowly. Three generations of men consume a hundred years, whereas three generations of rats can be bred in eighteen months. A second reason for the inadequacy of direct human data is the large number and complex arrangement of the human chromosomes. On the basis of the various combinations of man's twenty-four pairs of genes alone, there are 282,429,536,481 possible kinds of human individuals. If the phenomenon of "crossing-over" takes place in humans, as is probable, the number is vastly greater than this. A third, and perhaps greatest, difficulty in the exact study of human heredity is the complexity of the human environment. No other organism makes such deliberate attempts to mould the traits of its young, nor is another animal so receptive to modification. Because of these complexities, most data concerning heredity have to be obtained from simpler organisms, but there is no doubt that the same general principles operate in the case of man.

For a number of complex blended traits such as stature, intelligence, and tendencies to, emotional behavior, it has been possible to determine approximately the relative contributions of heredity and of various environmental factors. For these characteristics to exist at all requires both nature and nurture, but they are affected in various degrees by the several features of environment. Some recognition is given to the naturenurture problem in subsequent chapters in which the particular characteristics of the child are considered.

The Prenatal Development of Structure

The course of prenatal development is perhaps the most remarkable transition in animal life. During this period, the simple fertilized ovum develops into a complex and differentiated multicelled human structure. This growth takes place in two principal ways, first, through increases in the number of cells by cell-division, which is accompanied by progressive differentiation of function, and second, by an increase in the size of many individual cells. The prenatal phase of development may be divided conveniently into three parts. The first two weeks constitute the *germinal* period during which the individual retains an egg-like organization. The second or *embryonic* period is one of rapid change from ovular form to a structure that is characteristically human in appearance. This phase ends at about the eighth week of development. In the third or *fetal* period which extends to birth, further growth and differentiation occur. During this last phase the organism becomes capable of responding to stimuli, because his behavior as well as his structure becomes organized.

The Germinal Period. The ovum and sperm usually meet in the upper part of the uterine tube, where fertilization occurs. During the next two weeks the fertilized ovum remains about the same size since it receives little or no external nourishment, but marked changes in its internal structure occur. The single cell divides into two cells, these into four, then into eight and so on, until a globular cluster of many cells is formed. Cell differentiation occurs to a certain extent even at this earliest stage, for some of the cells are larger than others and some divide more rapidly. Soon a small cavity forms within the mass of cells and develops until an outer layer and a separated inner cluster of cells may be noted. The outer layer subsequently develops into accessory tissues that serve to protect and nourish the embryo. Only a part of the inner group develops eventually into the child. Further differentiation is soon observed in the inner cluster. Two other cavities appear within it, between which is a flat layer of cells constituting the *germinal disk* from which the embryo forms. During the earlier part of the germinal period, the fertilized ovum is unattached and free-moving. By the end of the second week it becomes implanted in the tissues of the uterus of the mother. From this time the developing child exists parasitically, receiving nourishment from the mother and growing rapidly in size.

The Embryonic Period. The period of development from the third to about the eighth week is one of rapid change. At the beginning of this stage, the germinal disk is noted between two cavities in the inner mass of cells, the amniotic sac and the yolk sac. The cells lining these two cavities differ in character and in their subsequent course of development. Those toward the amniotic sac constitute the *ectoderm* from which the nervous system and the skin develop. Those lining the yolk sac are *entoderm* cells. In embryonic life they are nutritive in function, and develop into the digestive and respiratory tracts. By an interaction of these two layers of cells, a third layer develops between them, the *mesoderm.* From these cells are derived the skeletal and muscular systems of the body. The three-layered germ disk is at first flat or only slightly convex but soon thickenings and ridges develop in it parallel to a principal axis, and it gradually becomes elongated and tubular. Throughout this period the "primitive segments" appear along the back of the embryo, later developing into vertebrae and trunk muscles. The head is very large as compared to the rest of the body. Just below it are the branchial arches which later form structures of the lower face and neck. The heart is very prominent and begins to function as early as the third week.

The limb buds appear during this time and develop into recognizable arms and legs. During the six weeks of the embryonic stage, the individual has increased in mass 20,000 times (2,000,000 per cent), but he has attained a length of only about twenty-five to thirty millimeters and a weight of about two grams. Still, the eight-week embryo has the typical form of a human being, and would not be mistaken for any other animal.

The manner in which the differentiation of the parts of the embryo is accomplished is not fully known. The position of cells in the original globular mass is an important influence. If the position of cells is changed, they will in many instances develop altered characteristics. Thus, if certain cells left in their original position normally would develop into skin, they may be made to develop into eye tissues by transplanting them to the eye region. There is evidence that certain chemical substances in the early embryo, termed *organizers,* may guide the differential development of cells. When these organizers are applied to other than their original portions of the embryo, anomalies occur. The differences in degree of metabolic activity in various parts of the organism which establish *physiological gradients* have also been held to account for differentiation. Even in the most fundamental development of structure, certain *environmental influences* may affect the nature of development. In certain lower organisms, applications of light, electric fields, X-rays, gravity, and chemical influences have been found to affect even the direction of the axis around which the embryo develops. Prenatal growth is not, therefore, just "by nature," but is influenced both by the cell structure and by the conditions of development.

The Fetal Period. The remainder of the prenatal period, about eight lunar months, is known as the *fetal* stage. It is marked by rapid growth which occurs during the early part of the period largely by an increase in the number of cells, and during the latter part by an increase in their size. At birth the child's body is seven times as long as at three months. Sitting height is approximately six times as great at the end of this period as at its beginning. The rate of growth is greater during the earlier fetal period than during the later months. The rate of growth is expressed as the ratio of the increase during a period to the status at the beginning of the period. For example, the per cent of growth in height during a month is given by:

Not only do the sizes of various parts of the young human being change markedly during the fetal period, but the relative *proportions* also change in large degree. From the third to the fourth lunar month, the total length more than doubles. From the beginning to the end of the ninth month, however, the increase is only one-tenth. By the close of the ninth month, head height and head circumference are six times as large as at the beginning of the third month. Height of the pelvis, transverse diameter at the hips and length of lower extremity, however, grow relatively more during the later than during the earlier period. From the third to the ninth month they increase by eight or ten times.

The Development of the Nervous System. Because of its relationship to behavior, the development of the nervous system during the prenatal period is of especial interest to psychology. The fundamental pattern of the nervous system is laid down early in the embryonic period. The first groove in the ectoderm folds inward to make the *neural tube*. The greater art of length of this tube develops into the spinal cord, while the upper part becomes further differentiated as the brain. As early as the fifth week the principal brain structures, including the medulla, the cerebellum, the mid-brain, and the end-brain, are distinguishable as enlarged nodes at the top of the neural tube. By the third month the brain has acquired all of its principal structural features. The higher brain centers, however, do not function effectively until about the time of birth.

The neural cells are first differentiated from other body cells at the upper or head end of the neural tube. These send shoots downward along the tube, proceeding, as Child has contended, from an area of high metabolism to one of lower metabolism, or, in other words, down a physiological gradient. As these fibers pass other cells in the neural tube on their way downward, the latter are stimulated to send out processes at right angles to the axis, between the primitive segments. The axial fibers become the connecting portions of the nervous system; those at right angles become the sensory and motor neurones. The nerves, therefore, grow out of the central nervous system, and the branching character of the system is established. The development of neural structure, in general, precedes that of the muscles and of sensory receptors. For example, nerves start growing out to an arm or leg stump before the muscles there are yet developed. During the entire fetal period there is great *neural overgrowth*, the neural structures formed being far in advance of their present requirements. This fact has great significance for learning and the development of intelligence.

The *sensory mechanisms* also develop during the prenatal period. The structural changes that precede the development of vision begin very early, probably in the second week, and gradually develop until some time after birth. The ear also develops enough to be functional at birth as is shown by studies of its anatomical development. The olfactory mechanisms are sufficiently mature to function in the case of infants born one month prematurely. Taste buds appear early, probably during the third fetal month. The muscular and deep pressure senses, and the skin senses function very early, as may be seen in the account of the development of behavior.

Laws of Structural Development. Embryologists have long noted that the development of vertebrate embryos tends to proceed from the head or cephalic portion to the posterior or caudal portion.

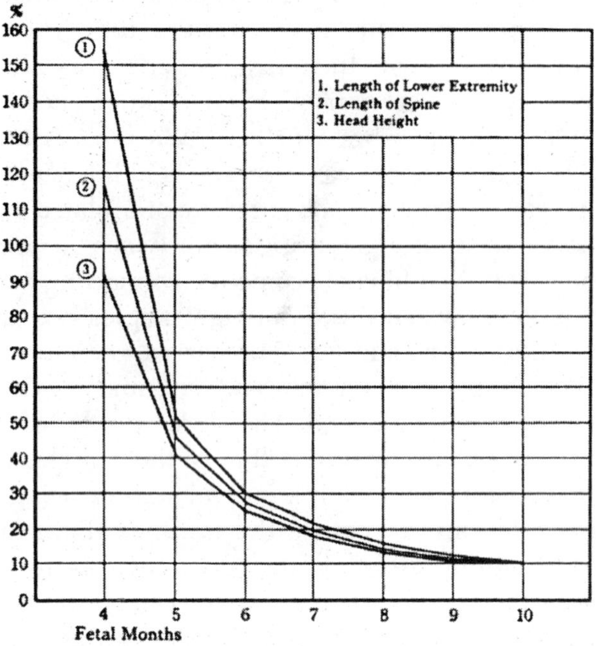

FIG. *Percentage Growth During The Fetal Period (Scammon and Clakins.)*

This principle has been termed the "law of cephalo-caudal development" or the "law of developmental direction." Jackson and Scammon have stated this law as follows: "While each part (of the body) passes through its own cycle of changes, these changes as a whole tend to follow what is known as the *law of developmental direction;* for it is generally found that development (including growth and differentiation), in the long axis of the body, appears first in the head region of the body and progresses toward the tail region." Thus, the arm buds appear and develop before the legs, and the head is quite mature before the legs attain their final shape. In the *late* stages of development the slowest growth is in vertical height of the head, next slowest in growth of the spine, and most rapid in growth of the lower extremities. This means that in the *earlier* period of the first three months, the head has already attained the greatest proportion of its mature size, and the legs the least.

Another developmental law is that structures along the axis (proximal) mature earlier than those farther on either side (distal). This *law of proximo-distal development* is as well demonstrated in the human embryo as that of cephalo-caudal development. Both of these laws will be found significant in tracing the beginnings of function as well as of structure.

The Prenatal Development of Function

The Development of Motor Responses. A knowledge of the prenatal development of behavior assists greatly in understanding the nature of the newborn child. It has been known for a long time that the fetus makes many movements while still in the uterus. Using the stethoscope, the physician can detect these movements as early as from the fourteenth to the sixteenth prenatal week, and usually they are felt by the mother shortly afterward. The beating of the fetal heart, which begins in the third week, reaches sufficient magnitude to be heard by the external stethoscope by the eighteenth week. Considerable interest has been attached to movements of the chest and thorax of the fetus, resembling breathing movements, which may be felt through the mother's body. According to one view these responses are related to the development of the rhythmic action of the respiratory centers of the central nervous system. By another interpretation, they supplement the work of the fetal heart, while a third theory regards them as preparing the organism for true breathing which begins after birth, by strengthening the neuromuscular mechanisms of respiration. Movements of the digestive organs, such as the peristaltic movements, may occur as early as the seventh week. Some responses of the later fetal period may be determined by observing the prematurely born. Contractions of the stomach and periodic stomach tonicity are found among the very premature. Crying occurs among premature infants born in the sixth fetal month.

More exact date on the development of fetal behavior have been obtained by applying definite stimuli to fetuses in various stages of maturity and noting the resulting responses. This type of research is most easily carried out with larval stages of lower animals such as amphibians which develop from a transparent egg and are readily observable throughout the period of growth. Especially notable among such studies are those of G.E. Coghill on *Amblystoma*, a small salamander, which lead to several generalizations applicable to man. The fetal stages of mammals are more difficult to investigate, but several investigators have made thorough studies of the development of the rat, cat, guinea pig, and opossum. The usual method has been to remove fetuses of known fertilization ages into saline baths of normal blood temperature and to observe reactions to various stimuli. Fewer observations, by essentially the same method, have been made of early nonviable human fetuses which were operatively removed to preserve the mother's life. Our best information on the prenatal development of the child comes from the last-named source.

An understanding of the course of development in higher animals and man is greatly facilitated by reviewing the stages of maturation of certain functions in the simpler organism, *Amblystoma*, on which Coghill performed his pioneer experimental work. The description of the development of locomotion in *Amblystoma* is instructive. Up to a certain stage the little organism is *non-motile* and does not respond to tactual stimulation, although the separately developed muscle segments can be stimulated electrically. The *early flexure* stage appears rather suddenly, during which period a touch on the side of the head will produce a bending of the head, usually away from the stimulus. The lower part of the body is not yet sensitive.

With further maturity, the bending response extends down the entire body, producing the *coil reaction*. Soon afterward the "*S-reaction*" is seen. In this, a second flexure of the head in a direction opposite to the first starts before the completion of the coil, throwing the organism into an S-shape. *Swimming* occurs when the S-reactions are made with sufficient vigor and rapidity to cause locomotion. Perhaps more significant is the later development of the land locomotion of *Amblystoma*. At first, the legs move only as part of a whole-body reaction, as if the animal were repeating the swimming movement, but on stilts. Gradually the legs become more capable of independent action, the fore legs preceding the hind legs in maturation. First, the legs become able to move as a whole, relatively independently of the rest of the body. Then, in succession, independent movements of the knees, the feet, and the toes appear. Coghill makes the generalization, which is, as we shall see, applicable to man, that the earlier movements involve a massive action of the entire body. Maturation consists of the progressive differentiation of more specific movements which are "carved out" of the primarily integrated pattern of behavior.

The data on the development of the human fetus include a number of sporadic observations by several physicians, and two organized programs of research, those of Minkowski in Switzerland and of Hooker in America. The observations of the latter were recorded by motion pictures, allowing a careful and leisurely analysis of the reactions elicited. It was found that the development of responses of the human fetus to slight tactile stimulation started in the eighth week, and progressed to about the fourteenth, when almost all of the specific reflexes of the new-born, except breathing, were represented. During this short six-week period, therefore, human behavior appears and reaches a remarkable degree of maturity.

The first reactions observed in the human fetus are not dissimilar to those of Amblystoma. To a light tactual stimulation of the neck, the response is a lateral flexion to the opposite side. The arms and legs move only passively with the bodily musculature. By nine and a half weeks of age, this response becomes extended down the body. The cheek is now the most sensitive area, and the response includes not only head and trunk flexion but also a turning movement of the shoulder and rump. At eleven and one-half weeks, the elbow joint and the lower extremities are also involved in the complex response. This sequence is analogous to the downward extension of the total pattern of behavior described by Coghill in the case of *Amblystoma*.

From the twelfth to the fourteenth week the differentiation of motor responses proceeds rapidly. Specific mouth and facial reactions may be observed at this stage. Hand and finger movements appear, similar to the grasping reflex of the newborn. One twenty-two-week fetus feebly retained an object in its hand. All of the early generalized movements and more definite reflexes seem to operate only through neural centers of the spinal cord. From the fourth month onward, lower brain centers begin to control the nature of the responses, while the cerebral cortex, although formed, probably has little influence before the seventh month. The more essential and simpler patterns of motor response are thus laid down early, leaving the development of the higher centers, which are more important in later coordinated action and in learning, to the period just before birth.

Principles of Motor Development. Some general principles can be drawn from the observations of fetal development, in lower animals and man. The most important of these is the generalization stressed by Coghill, that *mass activity* precedes specific behavior in the course of development. Initially, the responses of the fetus are diffuse and non-specific. It reacts as a whole, and in an integrated manner from the very beginning. As maturation progresses, local activities appear by a process of differentiation or of *individuation*, as Coghill calls it. The parts of behavior thus develop from the whole, rather than the whole by the combination of parts, as was at one time believed. "The nervous system concerns itself first with the maintenance of the integrity of the individual, and only later makes provision for local reflexes." The same principle is applicable to the development of behavior after birth, as is shown later.

It is also notable that the development of functions follows two principles that also hold for the development of structure. Behavior development, in general, shows evidence of the *cephalo-caudal sequence*. The first responses in all animals are elicited in the upper region of the body, and progress downward. The principle of *proximo-distal* development is also apparent in the individuation of functions. At first the responses involve reaction mechanisms along the axis. The extremities respond, initially only in conjunction with the trunk, but eventually acquire a greater degree of independence and precision of action. This phase of development is not completed before birth but continues during the early postnatal years, as the child develops motor control and skill.

An interesting hypothesis advanced in various forms by Kuo, Holt, and others, calls attention to the possible rôle of environment and stimulation in the development of specific behavior, even before birth. According to this point of view, a reflex first occurs as part of a total pattern of reaction initiated by internal stimuli. If certain sensory stimuli are simultaneously present whenever a given reaction is made, a connection will be formed by the simplest mode of learning, the conditioned reaction. For example, the grasping reflex may be acquired because its stimulus, pressure on the palmar surface of the hand, occurs whenever a fist is clenched. Thereafter, the proper pressure will call forth a definite reaction of grasping. In this way, many reflexes may be *learned* before birth, by the same processes operating in postnatal learning.

Prenatal Sensory Development. The human fetus is sensitive to light cutaneous stimulation from the eight week onward, as the description of motor development has already revealed. Responses to pressure and to temperature also appear before birth. Skin sensitivities develop first in the neck and head region, and then progress to include the surface of the rest of the body. The fetus responds differently to mild stimuli than to intense ones, especially in the later phases of development. In response to a light touch or stroking, there is a tendency to move the stimulated part toward the stimulating object. If the stimulus is strong, on the other hand, the response is more violent and likely to be an avoiding one. The same types of reaction are seen after birth, when they constitute the basis of attraction and repulsion. It is believed that pain sensitivity is poorly developed even in late fetal life, since very intense stimuli that cause tissue injury call forth responses no different from those elicited by moderately strong stimuli. Responses to intra-organic stimuli are quite evident during the prenatal stage.

Eye movements may be evoked before birth, although not by retinal stimulation. These early movements are caused by changes of bodily position and seem related to equilibratory reflexes. Prematurely born infants may differentiate between light and dark, and show the iris reflex. The mechanisms for smell and taste are present in the prenatal stage, but receive no adequate stimulation until after birth. Smell reactions have been found in the prematurely born. Recent experimental work seems to indicate that the fetus may respond to loud sounds a month before birth. This may not be an auditory response, however, but one to tactually sensed vibration. To sounds of ordinary intensity the child is probably insensitive before birth and shortly after, because the external ear is closed and the middle ear filled with a gelatinous substance.

Views of Original Nature

Past Theories of Original Nature. Before the rise of the present interest in the objective observation of child development, many speculative explanations were proposed to account for the origins of behavior. Among these approaches the *instinct theory* and the *reflex theory* deserve consideration, as they still have some influence on popular thought concerning child nature.

The instinct theory held that a considerable number of complex forms of behavior were wholly or in large part native. Among the so-called instincts those of acquisitiveness, curiosity, gregariousness, constructiveness, and pugnacity were typical. The instinct theory stated that human beings carry out these types of activity because of original nature alone, because of inherent characteristics of the species. Among the criteria formerly used to determine if a tendency were instinctive, *universality* usually held a high place. If a trait appeared in all races and civilizations of man and was not obviously learned, it was usually considered to have come into existence just by the nature of things. Other frequently used criteria were that a trait was native if it *appeared in lower animals* as well as in man, and if it appeared without any opportunity for it to be learned.

The instinct theory is not favorably regarded today for several reasons. In the first place, a more careful observation of child development has shown many so-called instincts to be non-existent in man, their inclusion having been due to analogies drawn, from supposed animal behavior. The "hunting instinct" is an example of this class. A second objection is that some so-called instincts are far from purely native, but are dependent on definite training and, in fact, often difficult to teach. Cleanliness, sympathy, and constructiveness are illustrations of such tendencies. The final objection to the instinct theory is that it really explained nothing. Giving a trait the designation of "instinct" does not tell anything about its origin and development, but only asserts that it is present. The instinct theory therefore tended to prevent rather than to encourage further research in child nature. Because of these objections, the instinct hypothesis has been discarded from modern description of child and adult psychology.

Discarding the criteria and theories of the instinct approach, some of the pioneers in the objective study of child psychology concentrated on a determination of what traits are *present at birth*. Such characteristics, they believed, should properly be called native. The most commonly discovered specific forms of behavior present at birth were comparatively simple responses to limited stimuli, the reflexes. This view of original nature may conveniently be called the *reflex approach*. According to the early applications of this point of view, the reflexes were the elementary and native particles of behavior, and all more complex activity was built up by learned combinations or "chains" of these simple elements. Although the concept of the reflex is still very useful in psychology, more recent investigations have led to a considerable modification of the crude theory of original nature that was based on it.

Prenatal Growth and Original Nature. The studies of prenatal development that have been summarized in this chapter have influenced the concept of original nature greatly. Even behavior that is present at birth has a past history, and the embryological approach has been an attempt to make the course of this development clear. The two chief contributions of this point of view may now be restated briefly.

The embryological study of the development of function has emphasized the *primary integration* of behavior. The behavior of the child is not interpreted as consisting of a number of separate and unrelated reflex acts which are afterward put together. In its early development, the fetus first reacts as a whole. The reflexes that are present at birth are only fragments of this whole-behavior that have become differentiated in the early stages of development. The function of the nervous system as a correlator and organizer of behavior is emphasized, rather than as a connection mechanism operating between definite stimuli and responses.

A second valuable contribution of the embryological approach is the stress placed on the *continuity of development*. Birth is no longer regarded as the zero point in human conduct, but only as in incident occurring in a continuous process of growth and differentiation. This concept breaks down the absolute barrier between reflex and habit, and between "native" and "acquired." These principles are serviceable in the study of postnatal development as well as of prenatal growth. Modern psychology regards the child as an integrated and continuously growing organism, developing under the interacting influences of his own structural characteristics and of the environment about him, both before birth and afterward.

4

The Principles of Learning

DEVELOPMENT AND LEARNING

The Concepts of Maturation and Learning. The development of human behavior is a continuous process which starts long before birth, as was emphasized in the preceding chapter. It has been customary to isolate two principal factors basic to this process of development, which are usually termed maturation and learning. If the first appearance of an item of behavior is correlated with the observable growth or maturation of structure, the event is called maturational development, or simply *maturation*. For example, the contraction of a muscle group involved in a so-called reflex is said to be the natural result of the stimulation of certain sense organs, because the neural structures grow in such a way as to conduct the neural impulse from the sense organs to these particular muscles. Thus the capability of performing the reflex is attributed to the anatomical growth of the necessary structures, including the central nervous system.

On the other hand, some changes in behavior are ascribed to the effects of environmental situations. When a modification or adaptation of behavior is correlated with observable stimulating situations, the process is known as *learning*. The study of the bases of this phenomenon constitutes the principal subject matter of the present chapter.

Although maturation and learning are sometimes contrasted, certain striking similarities between the two processes give rise to the view that they are different aspects of the same thing. It is considered probable that there are unobservable anatomical changes in the central nervous system that accompany learning, and also unobservable stimulating situations which influence the intra-organic development usually ascribed to maturation. Accordingly, it is contended that the apparent distinction between the two processes is due only to the need for different terms to describe the conditions in different stages of development. During the prenatal period, the opportunity to observe the stimulations that affect the individual is limited. On the other hand, the minute changes in the mature nervous system, which probably accompany learning, are extremely inaccessible to observation. Hence, the hypotheses of maturation and learning are commonly used to describe earlier and later development, respectively. Whether these are distinct processes, or simply phases of the same process, cannot be settled here with finality. In either case, a study of the similarities between maturation and learning will promote a better understanding of the development of human behavior.

Prenatal Learning. The continuity of development is emphasized by the fact that maturation is not confined to the prenatal period, nor, learning to postnatal life, as might be supposed from the previous discussion. Peiper found by attaching a tambour recording apparatus to the mother's abdomen that the unborn child would not only respond to a loud sound, but if the sound was very loud and sudden the response was such a complex and vigorous movement that it might be called "fear." When the sound stimulus was repeated a number of times the reactions decreased in vigor and complexity and finally disappeared altogether. This reduction of the response was probably not due to fatigue, since the fetus usually failed to respond even to the second stimulus. Thus it had become habituated to the sound. It had *learned* not to respond.

This kind of diminution and disappearance of a particular response upon repetition of the stimulus is often called negative adaptation, but it is an example of learning, namely a modification of behavior as result of an external stimulating situation. A demonstration of the positive type of learning, of the augmentation or appearance of a reaction to a given stimulus as result of an appropriate situation has been attempted in the case of a human fetus. By means of tambours attached to the mother, Ray was able to record fetal reactions to a loud sound but not to a certain type of mechanical vibration applied to the mother's abdomen. After the vibration and the sound had been presented together a number of times, application of the vibration alone produced a movement of the fetus. Ray was not completely sure but that the fetus might have made this reaction to the vibration even if it had not been subjected to the training situation. According to Hull's view, however, the preliminary trials with the vibration alone offer some indication that the vibration was originally ineffective and that therefore the final responses to it were the result of learning.

Postnatal Maturation. Evidence that maturation occurs after birth is even clearer than are the indications that learning may occur before birth. Shirley followed the growth of twenty-three children from birth to one year of age (sixteen of them to two years of age), making repeated tests and observations at short intervals. Her results show that different abilities and forms of behavior appear and develop in a fairly definite order, and that this order is surprisingly similar for all of the babies, even for those who develop rapidly and for those who are not so precocious. For example, while one child may learn to pull himself up to a standing posture by hanging on to furniture before another child can walk when led by the hand, nevertheless each one can walk when led before he can get to his feet, even by pulling himself up. Also, each child can learn to climb upstairs earlier than he can climb down. Of course, there are exceptions to this general rule. Items of behavior which appear at very nearly the same age sometimes appear in one child in an order the reverse of that in another child or of that established by the average of all the children. Of all, the items for all the children, however, less than 15 per cent reversed the order of the group.

Correlations of each child's sequential order of development of 42 items of motor behavior with the order of the average child were all .93 or above, the majority of children having correlations of .97 or .98. Remembering that a correlation of 1.00 would indicate perfect agreement between the child's program of development and that of the group average, we see that these children all adhered very closely to the same program. The fact that this order of development is not correlated with any program of training imposed upon the children to induce the learning of particular items of behavior in any particular order means that the order itself is the result of maturation rather than learning. Gesell and his associates have observed similar constant sequential patterns of development of other forms of behavior. By comparison of premature, term, and postmaturely born infants they have found that the constancy of these patterns is not obliterated I even by variations in the fetal ages at which the babies are born. Thus an infant born one month prematurely may be expected, at the age of three months, to behave in many ways much like a typical two-month-old baby. Gesell and Thompson have shown experimentally that the effectiveness of learning itself depends upon the degree of maturation which has taken place up to the time the learning situation is presented. Thus, in the case of identical twins, one was given every encouragement to learn in a stair-climbing situation for six weeks up to age fifty-two weeks, and the other was trained only two weeks ending at age fifty-five weeks. At the end of training the one with little practice and greater maturation (age fiftyfive weeks) climbed the stairs in an average time of 12.9 seconds, whereas the other one (at age fifty-two weeks) required an average time of 26.4 seconds although she had had three times as much tutoring.

These examples illustrate the rôle of maturation in the acquisition of new, forms of behavior in postnatal life. Maturational development, however, like learning, also has its negative instances. In at least two instances, the loss of a reaction is correlated with the observable maturing of neural structure. The grasping reflex present at birth, and the Babinski reflex (extension of the toes in response to touch stimulation of the sole), both disappear, usually during the first six months. This is believed to be associated with definite stages of neural growth which occur at the same time as the loss of the reflex. Some disagreement is found as to whether the disappearance of these reactions is due to maturation, or to the learning of new responses that overlie the original behavior. The very confusion on this point, however, argues for the essential unity of maturation and learning.

Cephalo-Caudal Sequence. Just as in prenatal life, so in postnatal, functions appear and develop earliest in the head end of the infant, and progressively later in regions farther and farther removed from the head. This sequence in the development of sensory function is illustrated by the greater sensitivity of the skin on the upper part of the body. As the skin on the lower parts of the body becomes more sensitive, that on the upper parts becomes still more sensitive. The Shermans studied this by prodding infants with a harmless but supposedly painful needle. Before the infants were five hours old they had to be poked about ten times on the leg but only six or seven times about the head and neck before they would respond.

Two stimulations were sufficient in the head region at thirty-five hours of age, but not on the leg until the infants were twice that old. In regard to motor functions, authorities agree that these appear in the cephalo-caudal order. If the infant is placed on his stomach on a table, for example, he raises his head off the table by means of the neck muscles at an earlier age than that at which he can lift his chest. Shirley has shown that "reactions leading to an upright posture begin at the head and proceed down the neck and trunk to the legs"; that the baby has no control over his head and neck muscles at birth, but that he gains control of them before he can control the muscles of the lower portions of the body. The infant gains motor control of the eyes first, then of the muscles of the head and neck, then of the Shoulder, arm, and upper trunk, and later of the lower trunk and legs. The direction of the sequence is obvious and it is probably a maturational phenomenon, although the motor control itself undoubtedly is learned or at least facilitated by opportunities to practice.

Proximo-Distal Sequence. Voluntary control of muscles in the appendages is mastered with respect first to those muscles near the point of attachment and later those at the extremities. From the studies of Halverson and Castner it appears that when an infant four or five months old reaches for a small object, the performance is largely carried on by the muscles of the upper arm and shoulder, the hand being directed (at first without success) and carried passively towards the object by these more proximal muscles. When the arm muscles are first brought under sufficient control to put the hand on the object, the fingers are as yet too clumsy to pick it up except by closing the whole hand. Individual control of the separate fingers comes later, and this explains why the baby can pick up an object an inch square before he can pick up a pill. Thus there is a proximo-distal principle not only in prenatal structure and function, but also in postnatal development of voluntary motor coordination.

The latter involves both learning and maturation. Some authors attribute it entirely to maturation, but the fact that learning is operating is clearly shown by an experiment by Dennis and Denniss in which practice in reaching, grasping, etc., was restricted as much as possible except that minimum opportunities for these activities were offered at regular intervals to test their development. The result was that these infants did not develop reaching, grasping objects, sitting alone, and standing with help until they were older than the upper limit of the age at which these acts are performed by infants who have ordinary opportunities for practice.

Differentiation of Specific from General Behavior

There is another striking and important characteristic in which learning resembles maturation, and prenatal development resembles postnatal growth of behavior. This is the general-to-specific sequence, or the individuation of discrete acts out of larger undifferentiated modes of response. Just as in the case of the fetus, stimulation of the young infant produces vigorous general movements of the body as a whole rather than specialized responses of single organs. As maturation and experience with stimulation proceed, the infant progresses to more and more specific responses of local muscles. Some observers have overemphasized the very obvious random or unintegrated nature of these early responses, as if they were composed of a large number of specific reactions. But the response of the infant, like those of the fetus, is a total response in which single acts are to a considerable degree related to the whole and to some extent related to each other. This is particularly true during the first ten days of life. Pratt, Nelson, and Sun give the proper emphasis to both the uncoordinated and the integrated nature of these "general" responses. They point out that almost any group of receptors may be stimulated by almost any kind of stimulus and that almost any part of the organism may respond; that the part of the organism stimulated responds most strongly, whereas the more distant segments respond less frequently and less intensively. However, the response within any given segment is not necessarily well-coordinated. It should be noted also that the commonly known reflexes are more specific responses than those just described, but even these are accompanied by, or are involved in, a general response.

Development proceeds as a gradual increase in the specificity or decrease in the generality of responses, producing particular localized reactions to particular stimuli. At the same time that these reactions are becoming particularized, they are also becoming reorganized into patterns different from the pattern of the original general response. The reflex theory of learning concentrated on this latter process; its error was in ignoring the former. An example of this increasing specialization of response is the development of reaching. If a small object is presented to a four-month-old infant, he has a tendency to reach for it with both hands. Not only this, but the legs, head and in fact the whole body are thrown into activity, and the response is so poorly directed that he is very likely not to obtain the object at all. At About the age of six months, the response is more restricted to the hands and he is able to take the object. If a second object is now held out toward him, the infant will probably drop the one he already has, not yet having sufficient independent control of the hands to reach with the other hand while one is occupied. Gesell finds that 20 to 50 per cent of infants nine months old can even take a third cube without dropping either of two others already grasped. This implies the ability to make a different reaction to each of the cubes at the same time, and also the integration of these three acts into a single organized performance.

Control of the eye muscles a follows a program of specialization and coordination, which explains the fact that the baby can see large objects before the eye movements become specific enough to fixate the gaze on small objects. Not only behavior of the skeletal muscles but also emotional development proceeds from general to specific responses, so that anyone who thinks that he can distinguish fear, rage, anger, pain response, and exasperation from each other in the newborn baby is deceiving himself. The baby learns these emotions by gradually selecting certain parts of the original general emotion as an adjustment to a certain type of situation, and other combinations of parts of the original pattern for other types of situations. Mental and verbal learning also reveal the process of differentiation of specific from general responses. Even the formation of concepts, which is often called generalization, involves specialization as well. At first the baby responds to all objects in much the same way, and when he has attained sufficient differentiation to distinguish animals from other objects, he still does not distinguish one animal from another.

It is obvious that highly developed, coordinated behavior is composed largely of the specific reactions which result from the process of differentiation, and so it is only natural that infancy should be characterized as a period of learning by differentiation and later childhood as the period of learning by reorganization. We have already noted, however, that these two processes proceed simultaneously, even in infancy. The baby does not break his general behavior up into bits, and then put it back together in new forms. He begins to reorganize it as soon as he begins to particularize it. Infant learning is predominantly but not exclusively differentiation. The integrative factor becomes more and more prevalent until in childhood it is predominant. Differentiation, however, never ceases as long as learning continues. It is not his tender age itself that causes the baby to be a generalized actor, but the fact that he is meeting a new environment which demands adjustment. Just as he kicks, squirms, and moves his whole body in reaching for a bright object, or in just looking at it, so the school-boy in learning to write, squirms, bites his cheek, wraps his feet around the chair legs, and reacts with his whole body. As his behavior becomes confined more to the hand and arm muscles and the movements of the pen become smaller and more uniform from one letter to another, he is said to have learned to write. Even in adult life, generalized behavior is characteristic of the early stages of adjustment to new situations.

In the conditioned response, described in the next section, the reaction is at first general and occurs to a variety of stimuli. During the process of learning it becomes more specific and more restricted to a particular stimulus. Thus the sequence of behavior from the general to the specific is a universal law that applies both to maturation and to learning, and to prenatal and postnatal development.

The Conditioned Response

Many of the most important characteristics of learning may be examined by reference to experiments on the conditioned response. Originally, the conditioned response was a technique for studying certain modifications of animal and human behavior. More recently, many psychologists have used it as a principle or theory by which all learning may be explained. We shall examine briefly the conditioned response as a precise method of studying the development of behavior, incidentally pointing out some of the applications of the theory to the explanation of children's learning.

Conditioning. The most fundamental and elementary characteristic of the conditioned response is the fact that as a result of experience with an appropriate situation the individual responds to a particular stimulus with a form of behavior that he had not previously made to it. He may have made the same or a similar response to other stimuli, but making it to a new stimulus means that he has acquired a new form of behavior, since designation of behavior must include reference to the stimulus which provokes it. The appropriate situation for this learning is one in which the new stimulus occurs just before the desired response is made to some stimulus which is already effective. The process by which the subject comes to make the desired response to the new stimulus, or signal, is called conditioning.

In practice, the experimenter, or teacher, presents the signal along with or immediately before a Stimulus. Whatever reaction (perhaps unobservable) the child may make to the signal is still in progress when he reacts to the stimulus. Thus the two reactions are merely parts of a single unified response. Ordinarily it is necessary to repeat this procedure a number of times, but finally the subject responds to the signal even when the stimulus is not given to reinforce it. An example will make this clear. A bandage is adjusted around a five-year-old girl's forehead so that it can be quickly and easily pushed down over the eyes as a blindfold, and quickly pushed back up at any time. A pneumatic tambour is attached to the child's throat in such a way as to record any movements of the throat and chin on a strip of moving paper. As soon as the child is lying quietly and the apparatus is recording a straight line which indicates no throat movements, the bandage is slipped down over the child's eyes.

At the end of 10 seconds a bit of sweet chocolate is dropped into her mouth. As she swallows the chocolate, the apparatus records her throat activity as a fluctuation of the line on the paper. At the end of another 10 seconds the bandage is slipped off the eyes. After a rest period of 3 minutes the blindfold is again applied, followed 10 seconds later by more chocolate. The third or fourth time this procedure is repeated the record may show that the child has made a swallowing movement after the blindfold is applied but *before* the chocolate is given. Of course this may be an accident, since a child will swallow occasionally without food, as a response to the accumulation of saliva in the mouth. So the procedure is repeated once more and if the child swallows this time after the blindfold and before the chocolate, the experimenter is convinced that she is responding to the application of the blindfold. The blindfold is the signal, the chocolate is the stimulus, and the swallowing is a conditioned response, because it occurs now to the signal without the chocolate, whereas before it would not.

Mateer has done this experiment with fifty normal children between one and eight years of age, and similar experiments with fourteen children of low intelligence, some of them feebleminded. This means that some of them undoubtedly were conditioned by the very first trial. The similarity of conditioning to other forms of learning is indicated by the fact that, on the whole, the younger children and the feebleminded acquired the behavior less readily than the average. The reliability of these results needs to be verified by studies of larger numbers of children at each age and mental level.

Other experimenters have conditioned a variety of responses, including motor, glandular, emotional, and reflex behavior, using signals in various sense fields. While some responses seem to be very difficult to condition, most of them can apparently be conditioned to any signal whatever, provided the subject neither ignores it entirely, nor reacts to it so violently as to interfere with his response to the stimulus. The most suitable signal is one which simply attracts the subject's attention and seems to him to be a necessary or inevitable part of the stimulus itself. Neither of these characteristics is essential, however, as there is good reason to believe that conditioned responses are sometimes unintentionally established when the subject clearly perceives neither the signal nor the stimulus. The important points are that he should respond to both of them at the same time and that the part of the response provoked by the stimulus shall be more vigorous than the part provoked by the signal.

Generalization. The response is so integrated that when the stimulus is omitted the behavior does not revert back to that which was previously provoked by the signal alone, but is similar to the original response to the stimulus. After conditioning, the child is thus seen to respond to a part (the signal) of a complex stimulus-situation (signal plus stimulus) very much as if the whole situation were presented. Children as well as animals have often been observed to give the conditioned response repeatedly to some particular sound, sight, or object which was not intended by the experimenter. This is called a generalized conditioned response and is sometimes carelessly described by saying that the subject responds to a new signal to which he has not been conditioned, simply because of having been conditioned to the old signal. But the new signal is always significantly similar to the old one in some aspect, and it is this aspect which constitutes the real signal to which he was actually conditioned in the training situation.

Since a subject can be conditioned to almost any signal, he may become conditioned to almost any aspect of a stimulus situation (or a number of aspects at the same time), whether the experimenter is interested in this aspect or not. A case in point is that of a boy who was not originally afraid of a rat or a rabbit but who was conditioned to fear the rat by a fearful noise which occurred several times while he was handling it. When he subsequently showed fear in response to the rabbit and even to a fur coat, it became evident that not only the rat, but also the furriness, was a signal to which he had been conditioned. This experiment does not prove that the boy responded to something to which he had not learned to respond.

On the contrary, it reveals more exactly just what he had learned. Many so-called instincts and "innate" personality traits are undoubtedly not instinctive at all, but simply conditioned responses which have not been investigated. We think they are inborn because we do not know how or when they were learned. More complete scientific study of the learning process in animals and young children will reveal not only the source of much adult conduct and misconduct but also the means by which more desirable behavior and personality can be developed.

Another example shows that a response may generalize even to a signal which applies to an entirely different type of sense organ from the original signal, and that the necessary aspect of similarity between the two signals may be a matter of meaning or of some higher mental process. Seven-year-old children who had been conditioned to a flash of light as a signal would respond when the word "light" was spoken. They had evidently been conditioned to some idea, or verbal or neural symbol which they experienced along with the visual signal. This symbol was then effective, even when it was produced by an auditory sensory process. Realization that this symbol itself is a response of the organism and serves as a further stimulus, reveals the possibilities of truly complex behavior.

Children were conditioned also using the spoken word as a signal, and they responded to the actual light. That children can respond to their own responses, that conditioning generalizes from one sense modality to another, and especially that it may transfer from symbolic to sensory processes, enormously increase the complexity of the possibilities of the conditioned response theory. These facts extend the concepts of conditioning into the field of the intellectual processes, and give promise of a mechanistic understanding of even the most obscure facts of mental life.

Fading Versus Retention. If, after a conditioned response is formed, the training process is discontinued for a considerable length of time and the signal then presented, the response may occur as at the end of the training period (retention), or it may not occur (fading), or it may occur with reduced vigor (both retention and fading). Fading and retention, then, are reciprocal measures of the same process.

After Mateer had trained her subjects, she brought them back to the laboratory twenty-four hours later, and found that thirty-six of the fifty made throat movements to the signal, showing retention. Whether there was also some fading in these thirty-six cases could have been discovered by measuring the size of the movements and comparing this with the response at the end of training on the previous day.

In at least some of the fourteen cases which showed fading, there was also some retention of the effects of the conditioning, but not enough to produce the actual response. This retention is demonstrated by the fact that when the fourteen children were conditioned a second time, they required, on the average, a smaller number of trials than they had required in the original learning. It is easily apparent that retention and fading are analogous to memory and forgetting. The method of revealing small degrees of retention by conditioning the subject a second time is the same as the saving or relearning method, which must be used to measure memory if forgetting has gone so far that neither recitation nor recognition is possible. The maximum limits of retention have not been worked out, but undoubtedly depend upon the adequacy of the original practice and the subject's subsequent experience. Infants have been observed to retain a conditioned response for seven weeks, but how much longer they might have retained it under more favorable circumstances is not known.

Unconditioning. After the conditioned response had been restored to those children in whom it had faded, all fifty children of Mateer's experiment were blindfolded repeatedly without being fed. Except for the nine youngest ones, who cried for the chocolate and thus eliminated themselves from the experiment, this was kept up with each child for from three to twelve trials, until he could be blindfolded twice in succession without provoking the throat movements. This means that repetition of the signal without reinforcement by the chocolate stimulus was the undoing of the conditioned response. The undoing was not complete, however, for when the children were again trained with the chocolate they learned the conditioned response more quickly than before. Thus some retention may survive the unconditioning process just as it may survive the fading process, and this retention, too, can be measured by the relearning method.

Unconditioning has been observed by many experimenters working with various kinds of behavior and with various types of human and animal subjects. It is often called unlearning or experimental extinction, and is probably due to the same process as habituation or negative adaptation, to which reference was made earlier in this chapter. The number of trials required depends upon many factors, including the nature of the response, the age, intelligence, and physical condition of the subject, some important but unknown factors, and especially, the thoroughness with which the conditioned response was established before unconditioning is begun. The factor about which scientific knowledge is most reliable is the rapidity with which the unreinforced signal is repeated. If the interval between trials is short, a smaller number of trials is necessary.

Whether it is impossible to uncondition some conditioned responses is not definitely known, but in every case which seems impossible there are one or two probable explanations. First, the behavior may be so firmly established that the necessary number of trials, while not infinite, is beyond the resources of the experimenter or the subject. Second, the signal may be accompanied each time by some reinforcing stimulus which, unknown to the experimenter, makes the experiment a conditioning rather than an unconditioning situation. At any rate, if an undesirable response proves difficult to eliminate by mere repetition of the signal, the attempt should be abandoned, and the subject should be conditioned or reconditioned to make some other response to the signal, preferably one which interferes with the undesirable reaction. This can be done by reducing the intensity of the signal and following it each time with a strong stimulus for the desirable response. As the training progresses the signal can be gradually restored to its original strength.

M. C. Jones used this means to cure a three-year-old boy of an unfortunate fear. He was afraid of rabbits, white rats, dogs, and even of feathers. A cure had been attempted previously by the unconditioning method and this was largely successful, but the child had a relapse when frightened by a dog. So the reconditioning method was tried. The rabbit was put at a "safe" distance (reducing the intensity of the signal) and the child was given candy and other food (stimulus for pleasant response). This was repeated once or twice a day, and as the child enjoyed his food (the dominant reaction) the rabbit was moved closer and closer (increasing the intensity of the signal), until finally the boy was playing with the animal (reconditioned response). Also he was no longer afraid of rats or feathers (generalization of reconditioning). This method of treatment is a type of reeducation very important for mental hygiene in the home as well as the clinic. It must be intelligently controlled, however, and in the case of violent emotional reactions, only by a competent psychologist, lest the emotion be conditioned to the food, instead of the pleasure being conditioned to the rabbit.

Specialization and Individuation. It has already been pointed out that conditioned responses generalize to various signals and that the order of development of conditioning is from general to specific. It is not surprising that the conditioned response occurs in reaction to various signals, since aspects of these signals are present in the conditioning stimulus situation. Nor is it surprising that the response itself is nonspecific in character, since it is a total response to a number of these stimulating aspects acting at the same time.

On any particular trial the real stimulus is the total of all the effective characteristics of the subject's environment. As the training progresses, many of these characteristics vary unavoidably from trial to trial while some remain constant. The portion of the mass response which depends upon the constant characteristics becomes more firmly conditioned to these characteristics, while the portions which depend on the variable characteristics fade. Thus the former portion becomes progressively differentiated out of the mass, making the response more specific in character (individuation). Thus also, the range of signals which will provoke the response becomes limited to those which display the constant characteristics (specialization).

Marquis's experiment. The rising curve indicates the progress of conditioning as an increase in the percentage of trials on which the infants made feeding movements of the mouth (such as sucking) in response to the buzzer, which was sounded for five seconds before the bottle was presented each time. The babies were fed six times a day starting when they were twenty-four hours old and from two to five trials were given at each feeding by taking the bottle away and then giving it back after the buzzer had been sounded again. While the percentage of conditioned responses is very small for the first three days, the curves suggest that the conditioning process probably began during the first day of practice, before the infants were two days old. [24] The fact that the reduction in general activity was a part of the conditioning process was proved by comparison with the results of a control experiment in which other infants heard the buzzer at each trial but were not given their bottles immediately afterwards. In this case general activity did not decrease. Four infants were used in the control group and eight in the experimental group, although one of the latter did not learn, apparently because of poor physiological condition which affected his appetite.

Differential Conditioning. Specialization has not been adequately analyzed experimentally, because it is difficult to control the fading of reactions to the variable characteristics. When experimenters wish to make a response specific to a particular signal they have found it feasible to uncondition the response to other signals which contain the undesired but not the desired characteristics.

Other Principles of Learning

The description of the conditioned response, although only an abbreviated account, should be enough to dispel the notion that conditioning is limited to stimulus substitution in the case of simple motor and glandular reflexes. The conditioned response underlies many complex forms of human behavior, and many writers believe that it describes all learning adequately.

In order to understand learning more thoroughly, however, it is desirable to examine it from the point of view of a number of other principles and theories. Many of these are older inventions, and have been the basis for the determination of important experimental facts. Some of the principles of learning which follow are treated briefly, because they are readily available in standard, general textbooks.

Trial-and-Error Learning "When left to himself to get out of leggings and shoes, the child pulls and pushes various attachments until he strikes the right fastening or shoestring." Thus Wagoner describes the young, child's trial-and-error learning, pointing out also that he does not learn at once just what to do, but that after some trials, "like the cat of puzzlebox fame, he learns to escape immediately by doing the correct thing."

This is the way learning takes, place when definite instruction is not given, very often because neither the teacher nor the learner has any way of knowing just what stimulus to apply to the desired response. The principal characteristics of trial-and-error learning are that general behavior consisting of varied (random) activities occurs, and that the individuation of the correct response out of the general behavior takes place gradually throughout a series of trials. When studied scientifically, trial-and-error learning is usually measured in terms of (1) the reduction in the time required for each successive "escape," (2) the reduction in the number of random movements (errors), (3) the total number of trials necessary to attain a certain degree of skill, or (4) the number of trials necessary to reach a point beyond which further practice produces no further improvement. The measurements of the first or second type may be plotted in the form of a learning curve to show rate of improvement at each stage in the course of learning. Curves for a number of children are often averaged. This procedure obscures the differences in speed of learning between different children and also the fluctuations in speed of each child, but it permits comparisons of the learning of different tasks.

Measures of the third and fourth type provide means of expressing individual differences in learning, the third with reference to a standard quality of behavior and the fourth with reference to the maximum quality or limit of learning for each child. Since these maxima are different degrees of skill for different children, they too represent individual differences, but not in speed of learning. Since individual differences of any of these kinds may depend upon various factors such as age and intelligence, they may be classified according to different amounts of a factor, and plotted into a curve, an age curve, for example. These curves often resemble learning curves but should be distinguished from them. The number of trials which children require before gaining a certain degree of voluntary control of the winking "reflex" when the eye is threatened has been studied by Partridge.Since there is a sex factor as well as an age factor in this task, for boys usually learn it faster than girls of their own age, a separate age curve is presented for the girls.

Such large differences between the sexes, however, are not found in the learning of most performances, nor is either sex consistently better than the other. Even in learning to control the wink there may be no native sex difference. The boys, especially the older ones, probably had more incidental practice than the girls (as in boxing) before the experiment began.

Comparison of the curve on cutting with those on the maze shows that, whereas maze-learning is more rapid during the early stages of practice than during the more advanced stages, improvement on the cutting test proceeds at about the same rate throughout the experiment. The fact that this rate is about the same as the rate of improvement before the practice began suggests very strongly that the age or maturation factor is more important than learning in producing this improvement. It is by thus analyzing, classifying, and comparing the results of learning under various conditions that those conditions which influence learning are discovered. If all the factors were known and could be controlled, the learning would not need to proceed by trial and error.

Motivation. The factors which cause the child to proceed at all, to persist in trial and error until learning is accomplished, are called *motives*, and their operation in the learning process as well as their application by parents and teachers, *motivation*. This is such a comprehensive subject that a chapter is devoted to it later. Accordingly, it is passed over here with brief mention. Motives are of different kinds, varying all the way from the simple stimulus itself in the conditioned response situation, to an ambition to make something of oneself, or an interest in baseball, or in the welfare of mankind. A motive is sometimes defined as anything which induces action and is usually thought of as a secondary stimulus or condition which promotes learning by causing the individual to get himself into a learning situation or by increasing the amount of practice. In trial-and-error learning hunger may be a motive or drive, because it increases the amount of varied behavior and thus hastens the time when the correct response will be made. Hunger, thirst, and sexual tension are innate physiological drives to activity. Interest and desire are learned motives. Thus it is obvious that the results of learning may serve as motives for further learning.

Contiguity. One of the fundamental principles of learning is the law of contiguity. It means that, if the subject is to learn to make a certain response to a given stimulus, the latter must occur at the same time or very nearly the same time as some other stimulus which is already effective in provoking that response. This is necessary so that the original reaction to the first stimulus may become a part of the total response, which will persist after the second stimulus no longer accompanies the first one. The operation of this law is illustrated in the case of the conditioned response, in which the signal is presented together with or just before the stimulus. The law was first discovered in connection with ideas. If two ideas occur together, then (at some later date), whatever provokes one of these ideas will tend to provoke the other also, or one of the ideas itself mwill tend to provoke the other. The ideas are said to have become associated. Contiguity is thus the basis of the association of ideas as well as the basis of conditioning.

Intensity. After two ideas occur together, the recurrence of the one does not always bring the other to mind. The conditioned response sometimes appears after the signal and stimulus occur together once, and sometimes it does not. If the ideas are very vivid or strong, they are more likely to become associated and if the response is very vigorous of intense, it is more likely to be conditioned. This is the law of intensity. It may be stated in terms of the intensity of the stimulus, since more intense stimuli usually provoke more intense responses. Intensity is no doubt a part of the explanation of the fact that a very severe fright is more likely to condition a person to fear some object than is a mild scare. There is a limit, however, to the benefit derived from increasing the intensity of the stimulus, because an extremely intense stimulus usually evokes other responses than the one aroused by the stimulus of medium intensity, and these often interfere with the desired response.

The Law of Effect. Many experimental data seem to justify the conclusion that the more pleasant or satisfying the results of a response are, the more likely the response is to be learned or conditioned. Whether this is a fundamental law or only a superficial fact, that is, whether the satisfying effect of the response really influences the learning or only accompanies it, has not been definitely agreed upon by authorities. Many important facts indicate, however, that it should not be ignored by anyone entrusted with the training of children. After all, any theory of learning has two functions, the scientific and the technical. Its scientific purpose is to lead to hypotheses which can be tested experimentally to see if the theory itself is correct. Its technical purpose is to suggest applications to actual situations which may promote learning. If a certain application of the law of effect is beneficial, it should be employed, even though it is not a crucial test of the validity of the law.

The use of rewards and punishment is, of course, a very obvious application of this law. Another application is that the reward will be most effective when it is related to an actual motive; food, for example, being a good reward when one is hungry, knowledge when one is curious, etc. Also, the reward will be most effective when it is the natural result of the behavior to be learned, or at least when it follows closely the performance of the behavior. All these rules have been profitably applied by many teachers. A word of caution may be in order, however. The intensity of the pleasure produced is not always proportional to the quantity of the reward received, and since large quantities of a reward often destroy the motive (as food, for example, dispels hunger), it is often practical to apply small rewards so that the motive will remain active and promote learning in subsequent trials.

The Law of Exercise. This law has been stated and interpreted in many ways which have caused it to be criticized. "Practice makes perfect," for example, is obviously questionable since persistent errors and bad habits are probably as much the result of practice as are the "perfect" forms of behavior which they mar. "The more a response is made to a given stimulus, the more firmly it will be learned as a response to that stimulus" has been challenged because of the facts of unconditioning and negative adaptation and also because a response is sometimes repeated a large number of times and seems to become neither conditioned nor unconditioned.

Instead of the law of exercise Dunlap has proposed three laws which cover the three facts just mentioned, and which may be summarized briefly as follows: Repetition of a response to a stimulus (1), will cause it to be learned, (2) will cause it to be unlearned, or (3) will have, no effect on its learning, depending upon whether the conditions are favorable for learning, unlearning, or neither. The second one has been successfully applied to the breaking of many bad habits, success depending upon finding or supplying the adequate conditions. For this purpose use is sometimes made of the law of effect (making the result of the response unpleasant, or robbing it of, its satisfyingness), of suggestion, or of some opportunity for substituting another response for the bad habit.

If conditions are favorable for learning, however, practice will promote learning. In the conditioning experiment, contiguity of stimulus and signal is not only favorable but essential. Even when we provide and try to maintain favorable conditions for learning, conditions for unlearning may occur at various stages in the process of practice. These and other factors produce fluctuations which are found in practically all learning curves unless they are artificially obscured by averaging. Some have suggested that repetition is effective because it supplies cumulatively the intensity which is necessary but which it is impracticable or impossible to apply in a single trial; and that repetition itself does not prouce learning, but merely gives the real conditions of learning more chances to operate. At any rate, if one, trial produces a tendency toward learning, repetition of the situation will produce an accumulation of this tendency, whether it is a matter of learning to make some particular response or to substitute some other response in the place of it. The theory that unconditioning or negative adaptation is really the substitution of some other response has already been mentioned. On this basis it can be seen that repetition promotes learning in both the conditioning and the unconditioning situations, but that different responses are being learned in the two cases.

Integration. While attending to the details of analyzing the factors involved in learning one should not forget what was pointed out earlier, namely, that development, including learning, is characterized by integration and organization. Learning does not proceed by simple addition of separate responses. The responses do not remain separate; instead they influence the total response, so that the latter, far from becoming less unified, becomes more unified. The particular muscle contractions, movements, or ideas which are involved in the learning process may drop out and the same adjustment of the individual to his environment remain, or an even better adjustment result. The thing that is learned is the total response to a total situation. The degree of integration of the behavior, whether it be muscular or mental behavior, depends upon the development of the nervous system as well as upon previous learning.

In general, older children are capable of more complex and highly integrated as well as more highly differentiated behavior. Nor should it be supposed that a child's response to a certain situation is more complex than his response to another, just because an adult has analyzed the first into elements. No one supposes that the child's perception of water is any more or less complex than it would be if water were composed of a single element, or three, instead of two. And yet it was a long time before teachers realized that children could learn to read by responding to words, phrases, and sentences instead of letters, and that the "larger" habits really are simpler.

Integration and organization of behavior commonly proceed tediously, and yet some organizations are learned with such suddenness as to defy description of the process of learning. Many attempts have been made to explain these instances, some based on the laws of learning established by study of slower learning, some by hypothesizing a new principle, and some by merely giving a name to them. None of these attempts has been entirely successful but all of them should be encouraged except those of the third type. *Belongingness* has been proposed as a relationship between two things which causes them to be integrated into a whole by the learner.

There are only two tests of belongingness: (1) whether it is perceived by the experimenter, which is obviously irrelevant, and (2) whether the learner makes the integration. If the integration is made by one individual and not by another, then belongingness exists for one and not for the other. These differences in the operation of belongingness may possibly be explained in terms of the previous learning of the two individuals, and in terms of the characteristics of the two situations. Leading proponents of "belongingness" have recognized this, and have attempted more detailed analyses. Some of their followers, unfortunately, have used the term only as a name, which obscures the issue instead of clarifying it. Insight is the same sort of explanatory principle but is attributed to the individual instead of the situation. If one child puts two sticks together to make a longer stick, and another child does not, the one is said to have insight and the other to lack it. Obviously, for the one child the sticks belong together, and for the other they do not. If the terms are used as mere labels, "insight" and "belongingness" are thus only two modern ways of saying that the child does put the sticks together. The important problem is not which way to say it, but how the child learns it.

5

Infancy

In the preceding chapters, we have assayed to develop an appreciation of the niceties of heredity and of the birth process. Now we shall examine the child that has thus been brought into the world. The child at birth is often spoken of as the *neonate*. This term, like many others in the literature of childhood, differs in usage from one author to another. We shall here cut the Gordian knot, define our own time limits, and proceed. There seems to be ample precedent both in medical and in psychological literature for using the word *infant* in speaking of the first 2 years of life. We shall in the succeeding chapter refer to the *preschool* child as the child from 2 to 6 years of age. It should be understood that this arbitrary division is merely for purposes of organization. In reality it might be better, where possible to do so, to drop entirely the idea of periods in an individual's life. After all, life is a continuum and at no certain time does a child stop being an infant and become a preschool child.

Nothing mysterious happens to the child when he is 5, although some of the literature of the past might lead one to think that the first 5 (or 6 or 7 or what not) were the only years worth counting. Similarly, many of the distinctions in educational practice between the junior and senior high school are just as tenuous. One might go further and say that even old age is not, in reality, an imposition of great changes, but is rather just a strengthening or a weakening of physical, emotional, and intellectual patterns that have been accumulating throughout life. So long, then, as we understand that there are no sharp *psychological* lines of cleavage between one period of life and another, we may adopt *literary* distinctions with safety. We shall, therefore, limit our present discussion to some matters that belong primarily to the first two years of life. In the following chapter, we shall consider those that are ordinarily thought of as belonging to the preschool period. There can be no quarrel, however, with anyone who wishes to say that much of the material contained in this chapter might just as well have changed place with much that is to be found in the succeeding chapter.

Infancy and the Sciences

Still another point must be called to mind before going further, and that is the overlapping of the fields of pediatrics, sociology, and child psychology. At many points regarding the child, the sociological and the psychological lose their identity. Professional workers in these two fields have accustomed their thinking to this fact. Similarly, the psychological becomes the medical and the medical the psychological with little change of aspect. In the field of infancy, this is particularly true. Much of what we shall have to say about infancy will show the inextricable blending of these two disciplines. Even the motor and the intellectual are but two sides of the same shield, as we shall see in our consideration of the developmental norms of infancy.

Perhaps psychology owes infancy an apology at this point, since such a large amount of the psychological study of recent years has had a more or less cloistered value. Stabilimeters have taught us much about the movements that an infant makes in his sleep, but we still do not know why at times babies do not go to sleep in spite of apparently normal sleeping conditions. Researches have been made upon the role in later life of the development of the index finger of the infant, the appearance and disappearance of certain reflexes, the time of the appearance of tears, the age when the first social smile is noticed, and many other matters which have, *more or less* practical value. Nevertheless, the space of this entire book would not permit a discussion of the matters of importance concerning infancy and early childhood about which psychology is still woefully ignorant.

The Newborn Infant

Let us take a look at a newborn infant. He is not an homunculus—a man reduced to smaller size. The fact is that, if the parts of his body were to grow at equal rates of speed from birth to maturity, he would become a monstrosity. Because of a very wise provision of nature, the infant's head at birth is of terrific size in proportion to the rest of his body. The head, therefore, will not need to grow so much after birth as some other parts of the body, because it has such a good running start. The reason for this is apparent enough when we consider the vital necessity of the functions presided over by the brain. Rand, Sweeny, and Vincent say: "One quarter of the weight of the adult brain is attained by birth, one half in the first nine months and about three quarters by the end of the second year and 90 per cent by six years."

Another striking characteristic of the head of the newborn child is the relatively small amount which is face. Many painters of the Madonna and Child have not recognized these infant peculiarities. The head at birth, furthermore, is marked by the presence of several so-called "soft spots," the fontanelles, where the bones of the skull are still imperfectly sutured together. Two are of particular importance. The *posterior* fontanelle normally closes at from one and one-half to two months of age; the *anterior* one usually at eighteen to twenty-four months. Defective brain development may cause premature closing, and rickets may retard the closing of the fontanelles. The following table of infant-adult ratios is a kind of rough scale by which to remember some of the descriptive features of infancy.

- Head of the infant : to head of adult : : 1:2
- Trunk of the infant : to trunk of adult : : 1:3
- Arms of infant arms of adult 1 : : 4
- Legs of infant legs of adult : : 1:5

However, in spite of his curious proportions, his wrinkled and often very red and maybe even hairy skin, his drawn-up arms and legs, the baby at birth is normally able to breathe for himself, cry for himself, make the beginnings of the sucking reaction, and perform all vital activities. He may yawn, sneeze, or hiccough very soon after birth.

Sensory and Motor Development

The matters with which we are most concerned here are those which have to do with the infant's mental life. They can be approached only through his sensory and motor reactions. Let us examine these in turn. The baby is not born blind or with his eyes closed. At birth he can see a few feet in front of him, but what he sees *means* nothing to him. Gradually he acquires sufficient control over his eyes to follow objects moving horizontally and, somewhat later, objects moving vertically.

Although individual differences no doubt exist among infants at birth in regard to hearing, the majority give little or no evidence of auditory sensitivity until sometime later. The middle ear is filled with mucus or with amniotic fluid and until these substances leave the ear, hearing is impossible. Aldrich devised a clever way of determining whether a young infant is deaf or whether he merely does not respond to sound stimulation in a way we can interpret. His method consisted of scratching the infant's foot at the same time that a bell was sounded near by. After sufficient repetitions of these simultaneous stimulations, the baby, if it were not deaf, became "conditioned" to the sound of the bell; that is, the withdrawal of the foot would occur when the bell was sounded even though the foot had not been scratched. This, of course, does not occur unless the infant is sensitive to the sound of the bell.

As to the infant's ability to respond to taste, authorities differ. Certain it is that *some* infants have shown definite responses to taste stimulation soon after birth. In fact, some investigators have even been able to elicit differentiated responses to salt, sweet, bitter, and sour in prematurely born children. The sense of touch probably functions more perfectly at birth than any other one of the sense modalities. Even premature infants are sensitive to pain stimuli. It has been suggested that marked insensitivity to pain might be used as a criterion of defectiveness. Touch sensitivity is peculiarly acute in the lips, tongue, and mouth. Extremes of heat and cold are potent stimuli; this is one reason for the caution always urged in regard to the temperature of the infant's bath water. Olfactory sensitivity is very difficult to test in infants. When they appear to be responding to smell, one cannot be sure but that they are reacting, rather, to taste, pain, or tactile stimulation.

Reflexes

In addition to the physiological activities necessary for maintaining life, at least two other matters in regard to the newborn are of interest to us. One is his reflex activities. These include gasping, coughing, choking, sneezing, swallowing, and many others. Let us consider a few others that are of peculiar concern because of the light they throw upon the development of the nervous system. One is the *grasping* or so-called *Darwinian reflex*. It is, of course, a matter of common observation that a very small baby will clasp its fingers around a stick or around an adult's finger and "hold on for dear life." Indeed, some babies, experimentally, have demonstrated their ability to support their own weight in this fashion for several seconds. The point of significance here, however, is not the length of time the baby can continue this grasp, nor yet the evolutionary significance that Darwin stressed. The matter which concerns us is that normally this reflex disappears as the nervous system develops. It is considerably weakened by the end of the first month and is usually gone by the end of the third or fourth month. Cases are on record, however, of defective children in whom it persisted much longer, since the nervous system in these children was not developing normally.

The *Babinski reflex* is an extension of the great toe and a fanning out of the other toes when the sole of the foot is stimulated. Most authorities agree that this reflex is due to certain immaturities of the nervous system. It is present at birth in most children and in cases where it does not appear in early infancy, it is thought that sufficient maturity may have been attained before birth so that the reflex has already disappeared. In time it gives way to the more mature *plantar reflex* in which the toes flex under when the sole of the foot is stimulated. (Some infants display the plantar reflex also.) The Babinski reflex usually disappears during the latter half of the first year—about the time that walking begins. Some authorities believe that, if the Babinski reflex persists until the second year, it is indicative of a defective nervous system. Certain it is that in adults who have central nervous system involvements, the Babinski reflex returns, and in such cases, its appearance is considered definitely diagnostic.

Another reflex, first described by Moro, is a kind of clasping reflex elicited by a tap on the abdomen or by shaking or moving the support upon which the infant lies. The *Moro reflex* likewise occurs because of cortical immaturity and as a rule is not evident after the first 3 or 4 months, persistence beyond that time being associated with other retardation. The characteristic movements include throwing the arms wide apart and then bringing them together again, bow fashion. At the same time the legs are going through similar arcs. There is no necessity, for purposes of this text, to argue through the research controversies as to the relation—if any—

between the Moro reflex and the so-called *startle response* characteristic of all humans from infancy, throughout life. Landis and Hunt, authorities in this field, feel that it is an error to identify the two.

While in the supine position the infant rarely holds his face forward. It is usually turned to one side. The arm on the same side of the body is usually extended out beyond the face, while the other arm is drawn up toward the chest or often nested at the back of the head. The extended arm, or rather the one that is extended most of the time, "is the dominant arm (and hand) as determined in feeding, play, and normative examination situations at 1 and 5 years of age," according to Gesell and Amatruda. However, it must not be understood that the infant assumes one position and maintains it constantly. When he does turn his head to the other side, by windmill-like movements he again extends the face arm and draws up the other arm to chest, shoulder, or occiput position.

Emotions in Infancy

The other matter of interest at this point is the primary emotions which a child brings into the world with him. As a result of his experimental work on infants, Watson claimed that they are capable of three unlearned emotional responses at birth. When support was withdrawn or loud noises were sounded, these infants responded, Watson says, with behavior indicating *fear*. Whenever the movements of the infant were hampered, he responded with *rage*; and whenever any of the erogenous or sex-sensitive areas of the body were stimulated, the infant responded with *love* or *sex* behavior.

Two types of experiment within recent years have led psychologists to question the infallibility of Watson's findings. Pratt, Nelson, and Sun found that infants do not always respond to the abovenamed stimuli in the ways that Watson's infants did. Sherman likewise did not get the responses found by Watson, but did get some of Watson's responses to stimuli other than those used by Watson. 'Furthermore, Sherman contends that we cannot tell from the infant's behavior what emotion he is experiencing. This was discovered by showing motion pictures of infants' behavior to medical and psychological students and to nurses. When the films where shown in proper sequence—that is, stimulus first and then the response of the infant—these adults agreed fairly well as to what emotion the infant was displaying. When, however, the film was cut and the sequence of stimuli and response was changed, there was little or no agreement among observers as to what emotion was being portrayed. Similarly, if the pictures showing the stimuli were omitted and only the infants' responses were shown, these adults were unable to say what emotion the infants were feeling. All of this indicates that it is unsafe to judge what emotion is being experienced by a child who cannot talk.

Sleep

As indicated above, a large part of the psychology of infancy rests upon physical matters. For this reason, it is necessary to consider the questions of sleep and of feeding. Psychiatrists tell us now that the security given to an infant by regularity of sleeping and of feeding plays a very significant role in the development of poise and serenity throughout childhood and adult life. There are probably no violations of child-training principles that more often give pangs to social workers and nurses than the violations which they witness in matters of sleep and feeding. Who has not seen young infants in the movies at night or being carried in arms to amusement parks or county fairs? In such cases, when the baby frets, he is likely to be given a few "sucks" on a lollipop or an ice cream cone!

Some interesting studies have recently been made upon the posture assumed by infant's in sleep. These researches need not detain us here. The matter which is all-important for our present purposes is that we be able to help mothers understand the importance of proper sleep for infants and help them institute regular and sufficient hours of sleep. It has been said that the child grows while he sleeps. At any rate, his very rapid growth makes necessary sufficient time for rebuilding and upbuilding. The, University of Minnesota Institute of Child Welfare gives the following as indicating, not the hours children should sleep, but the hours 1000 children in their own homes actually do sleep.

TABLE .
Hours of Sleep

Age	Shortest Sleepers (Lower 10%)		Average Child		Longest Sleepers (Upper 10%)	
	Hours	Minutes	Hours	Minutes	Hours	Minutes
1 mo. to 6 mo.	13	00	15	3	16	40
6 mo. to 1 yr.	12	12	14	9	15	40
1 yr. to 1 ½ yr.	11	50	13	23	14	33
1 ½ yr. to 2 yr.	11	47	13	6	14	00
2 yr. to 3 yr.	11	22	12	42	13	30
3 yr. to 4 yr.	10	53	12	7	12	59
4 yr. to 5 yr.	10	31	11	43	12	28
5 yr. to 6 yr.	10	14	11	19	11	56
6 yr. to 7 yr.	10	2	11	4	11	34
7 yr. to 8 yr.	9	53	10	58	11	29

A glance at Table below will show the wide range of differences between the longest and the shortest sleepers. However, a femw rather important considerations are somewhat obscured, perhaps, in this table. The sleep of an infant during the first month should undoubtedly be much greater than the sleep during the fifth month. Suffice it to say that the newborn child probably should sleep most of the time that he is not being fed or bathed.

The White House Conference Report shows that in 3,000 typical American homes infants under 6 months of age sleep about 16 ½ hours, whereas those from 6 months to a year sleep a little more than 15 hours out of 24. Of course, daytime sleep decreases in amount sooner than night sleep. Interestingly enough, in practically all studies that have been made on the length of sleeping time of young children, it has been shown that they actually sleep considerably less than is usually recommended. Naturally, a 6-months-old child needs, in addition to sleep, sensory experiences that he can get only when he is awake. The greater danger by far, however, lies on the side of too little rather than too much sleep. Perhaps for adults sleep "knits up the raveled sleeve of care," but for young children a large part of the function of sleep is to keep the sleeve from becoming raveled.

Infant Feeding

On the question of feeding, it is not in place here to go into detail as to amounts and formulae. Such discussion belongs to the field omf the physician and nutritionist. Anyone who desires to be familiar with approved practice on these points, however, will find much help in reading some of the references cited at the end of this chapter. It may be necessary to mention a few principles with which the professional worker should be familiar. Perhaps one of the most common-sense observations, but one which is commonly overlooked, is that, no matter how much milk or other liquid a baby is getting, he still needs *water*.

Another matter of importance pertains to the amount of food to be taken by children. There is not much danger that we shall inflict upon the *infant* more food than he needs. He sees to that by simply refusing to take more than he needs or wants. With children a little older, however, parents sometimes make a fetish of an adult-determined menu. Some such parents become obsessed with the idea that certain foods are good for children and insist that "the plate must be cleaned up." In the name of conscience, why should any adult know just how many spoonfuls of spinach or carrots are necessary at every meal in the course of a week? Exercise, sleep, and emotional disturbances cause normal variation in food requirements from one meal to another. This important matter will be considered again in connection with habit formation of children. The question of breast feeding is of great importance. It is undoubtedly good for the mother, in most cases, since it aids the uterus to return to its normal condition. Furthermore, food chemists tell us that ordinarily mother's milk is the best formula for a baby that can be found. For this reason, very carefully controlled systems of supplying human milk to children deprived of their own mother's milk operate through milk depots and mothers' milk registries.

Because of the emotional satisfaction to both mother and child, the protection of the baby's health through greater cleanliness and better nutrition, the ease of preparation and feeding, most mothers prefer to nurse their babies at the breast. However, a certain number of mothers do not want to nurse their babies. Some of these are those women still so immature that they hate to face parenthood and want to have as little to do with their infants as possible. Many such simply refuse to nurse their babies. In some cases, undoubtedly the obstetrician, sensing the mother's hostility and rebellion, feels that her attitude *and* her milk would be undesirable for the baby and recommend immediate weaning. Fries cites cases where cinema records indicate clearly that even the way such a mother holds her baby to the breast is indicative of her rejecting feeling toward the child.

Many hospitals are so convinced of the necessity of fondling and close physical contact while an infant is nursing that such is even prescribed on the order chart for those babies who must be fed by bottle. "This baby must be held in someone's arms while taking the bottle". Certainly this is a precaution that is not taken in most orphanages, asylums, and almshouses, and it is one of the reasons why institutionalization of infants is never recommended if there is any other possibility.

Ribble feels that very widespread physiological and psychological effects result from breast feeding and the mothering that should go with, it. She mentions the following as "favorable effects of unrestricted sucking": Deeper and more regular breathing (all of which stimulates flow of blood to the brain with attendant brain development); better sleep, digestion and elimination; earlier focusing of eyes and grasping of objects; earlier vocalization and articulate speech. Since Ribble reports no scientific control of the innumerable factors that bring about infant development, it is hard to say how much of the physiological and psychological superiority of her group of babies was due to "unrestricted sucking." However, there has been no question in the minds of pediatricians and psychologists for a number of years that the early nursing and feeding experiences of a child do have a profound effect upon the child's personality and his reactions to people and to life in general, as well as upon his health. Sherbon says: "With very, very few exceptions, every mother *can* nurse her baby. With almost no exception, every mother *should* nurse her baby."

In addition to breast feeding, physicians today recommend the introduction of supplementary foods, such as orange juice and certain vegetable purees, as early as the second or third month. This not only increases the supply of needed nutriments, but helps to prevent abrupt and emotionally devastating weaning from the breast. In this connection, we may stop long enough to mention an obsession that many modern parents have developed. For the last few years we have been told that we should not feed a baby every time he cries. Instead, the instructions say, we should accustom him to regular feeding periods with regular intervals between in which he should not be fed even if he does cry. Now, this program may be and probably is sound doctrine for babies that are well and babies that are receiving adequate nourishment from their food. One can but wonder, however, what happens physically and emotionally to those unfortunate babies that are allowed to cry hour on end before some grown-up discovers that *the child is actually hungry!* Regularity of time and of amount do not necessarily guarantee that a child is being *adequately* fed. Would that we could learn to temper scientific or professional advice with common sense!

Anderson says, in speaking of data supplied to the White House Conference, that two thirds of American infants are weaned by the age of 7 months and 93 per cent by the age of 10 months. Decision in those cases in which, for health reasons, breast feeding must be discontinued earlier than usual belongs, of course, to the physician. The question of weaning, however, introduces psychological as well as physiological factors of importance. Any food provides a pleasure experience to the child who is hungry. Furthermore, on account of the extreme sensitivity of the lips and mouth spoken of before, any feeding experience which stimulates these nerve endings is peculiarly satisfying to the infant. Both these factors are provided by the breast of the mother. Whether we interpret these pleasures as being sexual in nature, as the psychoanalytic school of thought does, depends, of course, upon the meaning we give to the words *sex* and *sexual*. Certainly when negative emotions are quieted and positive emotions are enhanced in the infant by breast feeding, the sum-total effect on the child is upbuilding and satisfying. These feelings may provide a primitive prototype of later bodily pleasures and gratifications, which on a broader scale may be called *physical*, *physiological*, or, if one prefers, *sexual*.

If the satisfaction of breast feeding is abruptly withdrawn, as happens in sudden weaning, no one will deny that temporarily, at least, there is considerable emotional disturbance for the child. Anyone who has seen the experiment tried will bear witness to the fact. Whether one wishes to go so far as to agree with Susan Isaacs that "the most serious disturbances in mental life are undoubtedly associated with severe deprivations in the suckling period" will depend upon the amount of proof one requires for the acceptance of a generalization. Perhaps no one will deny, either, that weaning, if postponed too long or accomplished too suddenly, may temporarily arouse hostile feelings toward the mother on the part of the child. It would seem somewhat unsafe, however, to go so far as some psychoanalysts have gone in saying that such an experience is the beginning of ambivalent (that is, contradictory emotional) or even hostile attitudes toward the mother.

One might just as well say that unpleasant ear-washings, administration of bitter medicine, or spankings foster hostile feelings toward parents. The fact of the matter is, as every social worker knows, that the child as a rule will tolerate an enormous amount of physical and emotional abuse at the hands of parents and still love the parents and prefer to "go back home with mother." This is not overlooking the fact, of course, that all normal individuals of whatever age probably have some ambivalent attitudes toward those they love most dearly.

The possible relationship between oral—that is, mouth—satisfactions and deprivations on the one hand and speech defects on the other hand, or between "weaning trauma" and such behavior disorders as kleptomania have been stressed by the psychoanalysts. If, in rare individual cases, such relationships do give a clue to therapeutic practices, we should welcome all such information. With the rarity of cited instances in which such relationships can be suspected, it seems, at present, unwise to *generalize* therefrom. For practical purposes we may perhaps with safety and without fear of much contradiction make the following statements. *First*, no pleasure is much greater to the young infant than those pleasures connected with sucking, biting, or other mouth and tongue activities. He is entitled to a reasonable amount of such satisfactions.

A deprivation at this point may result in a certain amount of frustration that produces fretfulness, loss of sleep, irritability, and widespread emotional disturbance. *Secondly,* from what we know about the principle of *conditioning* or connecting emotions with the source from which they arise, it is easy to see how the infant's pleasures very early in life are primarily associated with the physical satisfaction which the mother provides. This undoubtedly lays the foundation upon which later relationships with the mother will rest. It does not follow, of course, that every child who has to be weaned early will grow up hating his mother. In the *third* place, it would seem that, for the sake of wholesome emotional development, the range of "satisfiers" for the child should soon be extended beyond the mother. For this reason, we should question the wisdom of a mother's nursing her baby into the second or third year, or even later, as happens occasionally in unfortunate cases.

By exactly the same token, of course, we should question the wisdom of allowing a child the pleasure of sleeping with his mother. Such treatment results in fixation and emotional narrowing. In the *fourth* place, from what we know about the laws of habit formation, it is evident that the breaking of *any* habit is likely to be accompanied by a feeling of "being lost," being unsure of oneself, and of general inadequacy. For this reason, it is only fair to the child to make the weaning process as gradual and uneventful as possible. The introduction of supplementary foods mentioned above, given at first by a spoon held in the hand of an adult, water or fruit juice given by bottle, or any other extension of feeding satisfactions will make the removal of the breast in weaning less of a shock, both emotionally and physiologically, than would otherwise be true.

Toilet Processes

While considering some of the innate satisfactions, we may pause for a moment's consideration of evacuation from the body. It seems safe to say that the normal functioning of all organs and systems within the body should be, and as a rule is, accompanied by a sense of well-being and should normally not involve any pain. Toileting is perhaps no exception to this general statement, even though we may not wish to go so far as some who insist that *innately* there is great pleasure in evacuation and in getting various sense impressions from excreta. There would appear to be no reason why, if this were true in one field of elimination, it might not also be true in regard to perspiration or salivation. It is obvious also that normal elimination of the body waste-products will be intimately connected with bodily tone and health generally. It is doubtful whether we need go much farther than this. It seems like nothing but verbal analogy to say that a child who is constipated will be stubborn or selfish because, forsooth, *he will not give up*! This does not deny for a moment that, if a child's life is made miserable by an adult who insists upon too early or too meticulous toilet training, the child may become rebellious, irritable, ill, or *constipated.* Occasionally, a child may even deliberately refuse coöperation in toilet habits with one individual and not with another. Modern child training suggests that after about four months, let us say, it may be well to determine the child's natural time for bowel movements and, at that time, to hold him over a small vessel.

Likewise, if a child can learn to be more comfortable dry than wet, much has been accomplished. Just the minute, however, either adult or child becomes emotional over any item of toilet routine, just the moment that toilet comes to be associated unpleasantly in the child's mind with the adult, then training *per se* is getting out of bounds and would be better forgotten for the time being. We shall have more to say about such habit training in a subsequent chapter.

The White House figures show that, in American families, bowel control is established before bladder control, but that few children under one year of age have established either. The same study shows that, although girls establish control earlier than boys, go per cent of both boys. and girls have control by the end of the second year. Nurses and social workers will feel no surprise in learning from this report that both bladder and bowel control are established at later and later ages as we move from higher to lower socio-economic classes.

Growth

Perhaps the best way we have of knowing whether the proper physical environment is being provided for the baby is by watching his growth. The average child at birth weighs from 7 to 8 pounds and is around 20 inches in height, or should we say length? As a rule, children actually lose weight for a few days after birth for reasons which we need not take up. This loss, however, is usually regained by from 10 days to 2 weeks. As a fairly safe ruleof-thumb, we may say that the child should double his birth weight by 6 months and triple it by one year. If a given child deviates slightly from these figures, however, it may be that nothing abnormal whatever is signified. Too close observance of height-weight tables may become harmful. This is particularly true in the case of the nursing mother, who, in her anxiety, may weigh the baby two or three times a day. If she thinks he is not gaining as he should, she becomes disturbed, her milk changes, the baby is inadequately nourished and loses more weight; thus a vicious circle is established.

Another method of determining the amount of growth is by means of X-ray pictures of the bones. The bones of infants and young children contain a large amount of cartilage and fibrous matter, hence their softness and susceptibility to deformity. As growth proceeds, mineralization of the bones takes place. The hand and wrist provide excellent opportunity for X-ray examination of mineralization. Tables have been worked out with which given X-ray pictures may be compared in arriving at the "bone age" of a particular child. It must be kept in mind, however, that the phenomenon of "individual differences," within the range of normality, applies to bone development just as it does to all phases of neurological, physical, mental, emotional and social measurement. *Extremes* of bone development in either direction, however, can be easily identified by this technique.

Locomotion

The development of some form of locomotion in infancy is not only a fascinating function to watch, but also is of extreme importance in aiding proper growth. Usually by 8 months some form of getting from here to there has evolved. Commonly *crawling*, with the abdomen touching the floor or the bed, comes first; followed by *creeping*, in which the body is raised and is supported by the arms and knees. Relative strength of arm and leg muscles sometimes causes a baby to creep away from, rather than toward the desired object, much to the bewilderment of the baby. Needless to say, the introduction of locomotion brings about a great change; it not only increases the responsibility of the adult, but it also opens to the baby an increasing sphere of influence. One of the most detailed researches on how children learn to walk is to be found in the work of Shirley. Dr. Shirley studied 25 infants continuously over a period of 2 years. After the babies had progressed through their preliminary locomotor attempts and were old enough to begin the hazardous task of walking, Dr. Shirley devised a clever scheme for graphic rating. She used unglazed, white wrapping paper, 12 inches wide, which was stretched the length of the baby's own living-room floor.

The soles of his feet were then greased with olive oil and he was turned loose to "walk" along the paper path. As he did so, he left his olive-oil track behind him. In the laboratory, later, the paper was brushed with lamp black and other substances to make the records more or less permanent. "Assistants who did the detailed measuring of each record became so familiar with each baby's walking foibles that they usually guessed whose record they were measuring before they read the name on the paper." Great individual differences were noted, but, on the other hand, there was significant consistency throughout the developmental record of any one child.

Dr. Shirley found that standing alone did not occur in' most babies until they were able to walk alone. She concludes that, among the babies she studied, prediction could be made as to when the next developmental process would be manifest. For example, when stepping movements first appeared, it could be expected that the baby had reached one-fifth of his walking age; that is, if he were making stepping movements at 3 months, he would probably be walking at 15 months. Likewise, sitting well on an adult's lap would indicate that one-third of the walking age had been attained; standing with help or sitting alone would evidence one-half of the walking age; and creeping, two-thirds of the walking age.

All studies on walking agree that while it may appear as early as 7, 8, or 9 months or as late as 18 or 20 months, by far the commonest age is around 12 months. Obviously, walking may be delayed by illness, by a fright during an early attempt at standing or walking, by overweight, rickets, limit of floor space, slippery floors, improper shoes, hampering clothes, lack of toys or other inducement, or too much adult attention. Many babies probably could walk alone earlier if they only knew or thought they could. It is not unusual to see an infant, during the time of his first excursions under his own steam, put the tips of his fingers on the wall, hold onto his mother's skirt, or even, for that matter, to his own clothes, thinking thereby he will get support. At least, he does get moral support. Dr. Shirley makes an interesting observation of her experimental work. During the early stages of walking, and after some restrictions as to time and place had been imposed upon the young adventurers, Shirley's babies tended to become self-conscious. When they did so, they "reverted" to playing with their toes or their shoes. This regression to a lower level of habits on account of emotion is provocative of speculation in regard to some of the regressions seen in adult psychopaths.

Unfortunately, some children are retarded in walking because of a general retardation due to a defective nervous system. It is to be understood that, if a child appears normal in other developmental items and is slow *only* in walking, it is not fair to predict feeblemindedness. Although feeble-minded children, on the average, are slow in learning to walk, a perfectly normal child may also be slow for any one or more of the reasons mentioned above. In a table of items indicating abnormal or defective neuro-motor development, Gesell and Amatruda list the following concomitants of walking: failure to hold head erect after 12 weeks; failure to sit independently after 40 weeks; progression by arching the back while in supine position after 16 to 20 weeks; inability to walk after 18 months.

In this connection, it is interesting to notice also the relation of walking to general intellectual development in contrast to *talking* and general intellectual development. Obviously, talking is much more intellectual than walking, walking depending partly upon intelligence, but also largely upon gross motor ability and upon health. For this reason, feeble-minded children are likely not to be so retarded in walking as they are in talking. Conversely, exceptionally bright children are likely to be more accelerated in talking than in walking. Walking, as a rule, develops before talking except in the case of gifted children.

It sometimes happens that after a child has mastered a few of the first techniques in the art of walking be begins to talk. The speech may in such cases cause a kind of plateau in the learning curve for walking. Some parents report that after the child began to talk he seemed for a time almost to forget, or to lose interest in, walking. Conversely, if speech has begun first, it may be held in abeyance for a time with the advent of walking.

SPEECH

To give an adequate account of the development of talking, we should probably need to go back to a discussion of a baby's crying, which is one of his vocalizations. Little of that need detain us here except to say that medical authorities are tending now to the opinion that a certain amount of crying is *not* necessary for development, as some used to say. Doctors feel that crowing, gurgling, and other forms of vocal exercise serve the same purpose better. An interesting psychology of baby's crying, however, can be developed. For example, while all babies do not cry alike, yet an individual baby very soon develops one cry which for him is characteristic of hunger, another of pain, another of anger. Close observers soon learn to distinguish not only the different cries of one baby, but also the differences between the cries of different babies. One feature of a baby's crying is often misunderstood, and this is that as a rule the sicker a baby is, the less loudly and lustily does he cry. The loud wails of a baby may be distressing to hear, but ordinarily do not indicate so much danger for the baby as does the low, feeble, plaintive cry.

It has been the observation of the writer that babies who have spent their lives in institutions cry less than babies reared in private homes. No doubt they early learn that crying does not get them much. Whether such early inhibitions are in the interest of good mental hygiene is a debatable point. Dr. Shirley mentions the fluctuations in babblings and vocalizings as different motor skills develop. "While the reaching act was being perfected their vocal play was very much diminished." As a result of the interrelations observed between vocalizing and motor skills, Dr. Shirley concludes: A few babies who were slow at walking were great "talkers," to judge by quantity rather than quality of speech. . . . The substitute nature of speech response is very clearly illustrated by these observations. The baby who cannot act effectively takes it out in talking, it would seem, just as the adult does.

The happy vocalizing of a baby six months old sounds very different from that of a two-months-old. As the child progresses in his development, he adds more consonants to his repertoire. It is a profitable experience, and one which the students of the author always enjoy, to attempt to spell the babblings of infants. With a little analytical practice, one can work out a kind of key of his own for recording sounds, even though he may know nothing of the intricacies of the International Phonetic Alphabet. One will soon learn the differences between the reflex and random unemotional vowel sounds, like short e or short u sounds; the emotionalized vowel sounds uttered with much emphasis depending upon the emotional setting; the simple combination of vowel and consonant, such as ba (often quite explosive and salivary!) or da or ma; and finally the repetitive combinations like mumumumu or abababa. In a class demonstration the author once had an opportunity to examine two ninemonths-old children. The one child, when she finally became oriented to her strange surroundings, would give out occasional eh, uh, long e, eeeee, oooo, and uuuuuu sounds. The prediction was made at that time that this nine-months-old child would not be having articulate speech for many months to come. The other infant, on the other hand, was a highly social child who responded socially, verbally, and articulately very early in the demonstration.

One had the feeling that his speech contained emotionalized outpourings, a modicum of intellectual content, and a large measure of social relationship. After all, these constitute the core of language. This child babbled much of the, time, and one of his favorite expressions was aba daba dada. These six connected syllables were uttered with much elocution. The prediction was made that this child would be using a recognizable vocabulary within perhaps 2 months. We had an opportunity to check these predictions about 9 months later. The first child, then 18 months of age, was not talking at all; the second child had spoken several recognizable words when he was 11 months old and at 18 months "seems never to stop talking. He has a vocabulary of probably 25 or 30 understandable words."

Most children are saying from 1 to 3 or more words at one year of age. These words, of course, may be inaccurately pronounced, but they are consistently pronounced and applied. By the end of the second year, the average child has a speaking vocabulary of more than 270 words. It is to be understood that at all times the child understands more words than he actually uses. In a succeeding chapter, we shall have more to say about the reciprocal relation between a child's vocabulary and his thinking.

Teeth

Because of the close relationship between general bodily development and eruption of teeth, it is well for us to know in general something of what constitutes normality here. As in all fields of development, there are wide individual differences in the age at which babies cut their teeth. Some infants, in fact, may even have a tooth or two at birth, although this is rare. On the other hand, some babies may reach almost the first milestone without a tooth. This is unusual also and would seem to indicate the wisdom of a good medical check-up to see whether the baby's diet is adequate or whether some disease entity is operating. By far the commoner thing is for the two lower central incisors to come through at about six or eight months. These are followed a little later by the upper central incisors. The lateral incisors come next and then the first molars. The canines or "eye teeth" follow, and lastly come the second molars. As a rule, the lower teeth erupt before the upper ones. As indicated above, there may be considerable variation from one child to another, but as a rough rule-ofthumb one can say with some degree of accuracy that babies are likely to have about one tooth for every month past six months. At one year of age a baby will probably have about six teeth; at eighteen months, twelve; at two years, sixteen; and at two and one-half years, the entire milk set of 20 teeth is likely to be through. We must always bear in mind that the eruption of teeth is as normal as any other phase of growth and should not be accompanied by any great physical disturbances. When a child becomes violently ill or has a convulsion with every tooth he cuts, the difficulty should not be blamed upon the teeth and be passed over lightly. Medical advice should always be sought in such cases.

Proper diet, hard toast, or other such foods to chew upon, and cleanliness in the care of the first teeth will, in most cases, go far toward the formation of good second teeth. Some parents feel it advisable to take the child to the dentist during the second and third year, even though no corrective work needs to be done, in order to build up a confident attitude toward the dentist, his chair, and his instruments. Children's dentists nowadays understand much better than the dentists of a generation or two ago the necessity of dealing skillfully with the child's emotions. The White House Conference Report showed that over 20 per cent of the children two years old in urban homes had dental examination, as compared with something over 12 per cent in rural homes. Over 65 per cent of children two years old were found to have toothbrushes and about 55 per cent to brush their own teeth.

Stages of Development

In our discussion of walking, we quoted Shirley to show how one stage of locomotion can be used to predict the appearance of later stages. The same principle applies to other phases of development throughout the entire period of growth. For this reason, it is very important for anyone who is dealing with infants to have in mind a picture of what normal development is. The writer has been in the habit for a number of years of showing to her graduate classes in child psychology pictures of babies of different ages. The students are asked to examine the pictures carefully and to approximate the ages of the babies. The assignment usually produces much consternation and many students apologetically complain, "I never can tell how old a baby is!" Variations in estimates are extreme, sometimes being as great as 12 months on a one-month-old baby. It is obvious, of course, that one might display more skill in stating the age of a real baby in action than in estimating the age of pictured babies.

It is rather important, however, that we know something of what a one-month-old baby can do; a four-months-old baby; a six-monthsold; and so on. Otherwise we shall not know whether a given child is developing normally, is much retarded, or is considerably ahead of most babies of his age. In case the baby is retarded, we need to know whether the retardation is caused by any remediable condition and, if so, take steps to have treatment started. In cases of child-placing, adoption, and other social-work measures, we must know not only the present developmental stage of the child, but we must also be able to predict *somewhat* as to his future development. We shall have more to say later about so-called "baby tests," but at this time we have in mind developmental norms which can be roughly checked by *observation*.

Now, there are two principles that we must understand and keep in mind if we are to avoid error in these matters. The first of these is that any one developmental feature, such as walking or talking or teething, may be delayed for some specific reason which may not pertain to other development features at all. For this reason, one must never make a diagnosis of a young child's retardation on the basis of *one* criterion alone. We have previously mentioned several factors, any one of which may delay a child's walking. It might very well happen that in such a child teething and talking would develop normally. To summarize this principle, then, we may say that development of a child should be measured by a cross section of his abilities and never by one ability or one disability.

The second principle follows naturally if we have observed the first. That is to say, if we find that in *several* particulars a child in spite of good health is considerably behind normal developmental standards, there is serious reason for thinking that the child *will be* retarded. One has probably never seen a child, barring cases of serious illness, who cut his first tooth at 14 months, sat alone for the first time at 15 months, did not recognize his own name until 18 months, did not walk alone until two and one-half years, and did not talk until three and one-half years who ever "caught up" and "became normal."

Nature does not work that way. Because of the approximate consistency of rate of growth within an individual, it is exceedingly important to have a general idea of what a normal rate of growth is. For this reason, we shall give a few suggestive items of development at different age levels throughout the first two years of life. Obviously, health, social stimulation, and other environmental factors may produce considerable developmental variation among children even within the range of normality. Under anything like ordinary circumstances, however, the pattern is likely to be about as follows. The items in this table have been forced into *months* because outside a laboratory a child's age is more likely to be so designated. Scientific accuracy, however, prefers to give developmental norms in *weeks* of age during the very rapid development of the first year or so.

As one example of the difficulties involved, compare the nine-months-old baby who has been cared for in a private home and has had considerable individual atztention with the nine-monthsold who has spent all his life in an institution. The latter child may, perhaps, have been bathed, dressed, fed, cared for when sick, but otherwise left alone in his bed or pen. Now certainly vocalization, hand coördination, and social reactions may be different in these two children because of both nature *and* nurture. It is very difficult, of course, for clinicians to know exactly how much allowance to make in such cases for environmental deprivation. Or take the matter of two-yearolds. Some institutions for babies have an age limit at two years. When these babies are ready to leave the institution at age two, they almost invariably are talking either not at all or very little as compared with other two-year-olds who have been encouraged to talk in private family life. The institution children, be it noted, often suddenly break forth into relatively advanced speech after a short time in a family situation. They may have been ready—over-ready—and may merely have been awaiting the proper stimulus and copy for imitation. Test results on a two-year-old who has spent his life in an institution simply cannot be measured against a scale appropriate for a normally reared two-year-old. Test results are much more accurate and more usable when secured from babies from normal homes than from institution children or from children who have frequently been changed from one home to another.

One of the first ways in which intellectual life demonstrates itself is through acquisition of bodily control. For various reasons which we need not discuss in detail here, physical development and motor control are somewhat inadequate tests of so-called mental life. Tests made on infants, therefore, do not give us as accurate a basis for prediction of subsequent intellectual development as we should like. As shown by several studies, the correlations between test results on babies and test results on the same children when they are old enough for the use of standardized intelligence tests are not nearly so high as is desirable in statistical work. We shall have more to say about this matter in our discussion of intelligence tests as such. In that connection we shall also mention some of the tests for infants. By way of summary, for the present, we might say that Bayley and Shirley particularly stres the unevennes in development in the early stages of a child's life. This unevenness causes inconsistencies in test results from one test to another. This would appear to be true for the first year and a half, if not indeed for the first two or three years. Shirley says:

Inconsistencies in first-year development may be attributed to the great speed of development, to the catching-up of premature babies and the slowing down of postmature babies in developmental rate, and to the difficulties of motivating babies and of reducing unfavorable personality traits to a minimum. Finally, it is suggested that it is impossible for the baby to settle down to a consistent rate of development until a sufficient number of traits have emerged to serve as a foundation for future skills.

An experienced clinician who has had practice with babies will usually, however, be able to tell enough, within a certain range of error, to answer the questions of prospective adoptive parents. Needless to say, the judgment becomes increasingly accurate as the baby grows older and as he is observed 'more often by the psychologist. Usually the extremes of defectiveness and brilliance can be determined. That is to say, tests and observation periods will usually reveal the fact, if a baby is considerably retarded or if he is considerably advanced for his age. *Within* these two fields as well as within the field of average development, not a great deal of discrimination can as yet be made for predictive purposes.

Stimulation and Development

Infancy offers another question which may not give the client mother much concern but is of importance nevertheless, and that is the matter of the amount of stimulation which arouses the child to its own best efforts and the amount which tires, overstimulates, and wears out. The problem easily spreads out into the correlated question as to whether we can increase a child's mental capacity by providing sensory and motor opportunities. Interestingly enough, studies along this line have been made recently which leave us somewhat in doubt as to what the answer is. Dr. Myrtle McGraw took twin boys at the age of twenty days. She had them 7 or 8 hours a day, 5 days a week, until they were nearly 2 years old. One twin was cared for physically but otherwise was left entirely to his own devices except that he had 2 toys with which to amuse himself. At the same time, the other twin was given unlimited opportunity for practice in climbing, swimming, diving, getting on and off stools and incline planes, jumping, and roller skating. The skills acquired by the latter twin were most unusual for one of his age, to say the least. Dr. McGraw concludes, however, that in those activities necessary for normal development—such phylogenetic skills as reflexes, suspensiongrasp, creeping, posture, reaching reactions, and the like—practice had little effect.

That is to say, the untrained twin seemed to mature into or acquire *these skills* for himself without help. In the *accessory skills*, such as roller skating, practice and opportunity appeared to be absolutely essential. When the twins were 22 months old, the control twin was taken for a period of two and one-half months of intensive training. At the end of this time, he was still quite inferior to the originally practiced twin. He had in the meantime, Dr. McGraw thinks, developed certain attitudes and emotional traits which interfered with his learning the tricks that his skilled brother had already learned. One wonders how much of an inferiority complex was engendered in his own home, too, by comparison with his acrobatic brother. A later report on these two children appeared in 1939.

The other study, by Dennis, raises some interesting points of contrast with the McGraw study. Dr. Dennis took a pair of fraternal twins and placed them under environmental restriction for the first months of their lives. They were given no toys and were not allowed to attempt standing or sitting. Reaching, grasping, sitting alone, and standing with help were, therefore, retarded quite beyond the normal time for appearance. Each skill was easily established when opportunity was finally given to the children. Dr. Dennis concludes that the retardations could have been caused only by the restrictions on exercise. Curiously enough, while conditions were not quite the same, these are essentially the skills which Dr. McGraw concludes are not subject to stimulation from environment. A review of other experiments in this field may be found in reference 52.

Now, neither of these two studies must be confused with a more practical matter faced by mothers. The mother often asks: "Shall I let the baby stand on his feet? He tries to, and I can't keep him down. Isn't he too young?" We shall leave out of ronsideration children showing rickets or other illnesses. These cases must be directed by medical men. For the well child, on the other hand, there is probably little danger that the child himself will initiate more activity than his own body is ready to take care of adequately. Holt feels that a child should not be prevented from walking when he wants to do so, but also that he should not be continually pressed into the activity when he shows no inclination for it. He feels, further, that "nothing short of mechanical restraint" will keep a healthy child from standing or walking when he is strong enough to do so. Shirley says:

It is safe to say that the babies never spontaneously try anything that they are not perfectly competent to do. . . . The statement that a baby will not overtax his strength does not rule out the possibility of his being overstimulated to activity. The balance between optimum environmental opportunity on the one hand and nerve-wrecking overstimulation on the other hand constitutes one of the evidences of finesse in child-rearing.

One of the most conspicuous changes of the last few years in regard to the care of infants has been in connection with the matter of clothing. The amount and weight of clothing has decreased materially. Only such amounts as are actually needed for protection are recommended by pediatrists today. In addition to selecting clothing by the criterion of adequate protection, one should choose those clothes which require least handling of the baby, those which permit greatest freedom of movement for the baby, those which are most easily laundered, those which can be used over a period of considerable growth, and those most comfortable for the baby. Who does not remember the old-fashioned long dresses from which babies were "shortened" at about six months of age? Contrast with those styles the "telescoping" layettes in use now, in which all garments open down the front and fit one into another so that the baby can be laid right into the telescoped open garments, which can then be buttoned or tied without turning the baby over. We shall have more to say about clothes in connection with the care of preschool children in a later chapter.

One other point in regard to clothes may be mentioned at this time —the dressing of twins. Sometimes for the sake of convenience or economy, it seems wise for a time, at least, to dress twins alike. Probably no harm can come of that, providing the custom does not become a fetish. As a child grows, clothes not only *reflect* his personality but they actually do much to shape his personality. Clothes, then, should never be allowed to dwarf or overshadow individuality. That twins happen to be born at the same time may be hardship enough in many ways; they should not have to face the additional hardship of losing their personalities. When, and if, dressing twins alike results in making two personalities into one, it is bad in the extreme. .

Illness in Infancy

Although this is not the place to discuss in detail the illnesses of babies, it is well to call attention to a few facts with which social workers should be familiar. Normally a baby's skin is cool and moist. If it becomes dry and warm and if the baby shows any acceleration of temperature whatsoever, the doctor should be summoned. A baby's temperature is usually taken with a rectal thermometer rather than by the mouth. Mothers are sometimes greatly embarrassed by the fact that when they call the doctor the baby seems quite ill, whereas by the time the doctor arrives the baby appears normal. This is a very common occurrence and need cause no embarrassment. It should be remembered that babies and small children have had little experience, as a rule, with sickness and therefore have *little remembrance or anticipation* of pain. For this reason and for others, symptoms appear to chance very rapidly in young children. This is more, rather than less, reason why any marked symptom should be noted and medical advice sought immediately.

Sometimes watching a baby's movements will tell a close observer much as to the cause of the baby's suffering. A baby who draws his legs up is likely to be suffering from pains in the abdomen. If he holds any part of his body very still, it may be that the pain is in that art. If he turns his head to one side constantly or pulls at his car, he may be having earache which he cannot tell us about. Fever; unusual restlessness or unusual drowsiness; sudden and unusual vomiting; refusal to take food; diarrhea; rapid breathing; discharge from eyes, nose, or cars; hoarseness; coughing; rashes; or convulsions all indicate conditions that demand immediate medical attention.

Infant Placing

The social worker is constantly faced with problems of infant placing. Placing of babies is often a difficult matter. Many adults Who can understand older children sufficiently to provide them with good substitute home care feel utterly helpless and even afraid in the presence of a little baby. For this reason, unfortunately, it sometimes seems easier to find a substitute home for young babies in institutions than in private foster homes. In the latter part of the nineteenth century, it was discovered that of 366 motherless infants who were placed for institutional care on Randall's Island, N. Y., only 12 were still living a year later. In other words, there had been an infant mortality of 96.7 per cent. Further study showed that foundlings who were taken there under six months of age had a very small chance of surviving. Subsequent studies have tended to corroborate the suspicions aroused at that time; namely, that infants require a personal kind of individual care rather than mass care. Of course, emergencies oftentimes make temporary hospital care necessary, but for the ordinary welfare of babies the handling, fondling, and attention offered by a private home is infinitely preferable to institutional care. From the standpoint of mental hygiene, institutional placement may be just as bad for older children as for babies or, indeed, even worse. From the standpoint of the physical safeguards of infancy, the hazards of institutions are probably greater for the younger child.

The Infant and his Family

While the general question of family relationships will be considered in a later chapter, there are a few matters pertaining to infancy that may well be considered here. The entrance of a baby into a family is bound to make a great many differences in routine and to bring about many changes. Dr. Sherbon, refers to a study made on the amount of time required for the care of children under one year of age. The average daily time spent in the care of these babies was five hours and twenty minutes. Where all this care is provided by the mother alone, it is small wonder that she may find herself with little time left for other members of the family. All too frequently, in the case of first babies particularly, this sudden shift of interest on the part of the wife is something of a puzzle to the husband. Often it is hard for him to understand the actual physical weariness that attends the bathing, laundry work, bottle sterilizing, preparation of formulae, and other details. The wife, on the other hand, is equally surprised and disappointed that her husband seems none too enthusiastic over the gain of an ounce in weight or the details of formula preparation. Strained relations between husband and wife may result. The wife is too tired to attend to her own personal appearance.

The husband cannot be bothered with all the details of baby care; he knows nothing about it and may even be more or less afraid of it. In fact, many husbands really feel and show little affection for young babies. This does not necessarily mean that these same men may not make devoted fathers when their offspring have matured enough to be handled, played with, or showed off. From the standpoint of family mental hygiene, it is most important that the baby be made to take his proper place in the household regimen, neither demanding nor receiving too much attention. The mother, for her part, must not be selfish in her interest in the new baby, thereby neglecting other equally important family relationships. The husband, for his part, can often do much to relieve the wife of some of the extra duties imposed upon her by the coming of the baby and will, as a rule, develop thereby a tender affection for the baby. Otherwise, he may not experience this affection until the baby grows older.

6

The Behaviour of Infants

THE SIGNIFICANCE OF INFANCY

These two contradictory proverbs illustrate the diversity of opinions that have been expressed concerning the significance of early infancy. In the past, infancy often was held to be a transitional stage of small importance and of slight influence on the periods following it. According to this point of view, infancy was only a time when a certain maturation, preordained by heredity, took place, but when environmental influences had little or no effect. According to an extreme form of this theory, infancy has no influence upon development during childhood and adolescence is merely "a stage which is left as much behind as the rungs of a ladder after the summit is reached." Although entirely discarded by psychologists, this attitude is reflected in the conduct of many parents. They believe that the infant is too young to understand anything, and that how he is treated is therefore a matter of no consequence.

In sharp contrast to the former attitude, most authorities today regard infancy as the *formative period* when the foundations of personality are firmly and permanently laid. A mass of evidence now indicates the importance of infancy and suggests that mental as well as physical growth is a continuous process from the prenatal period to maturity.

Many authors have noted the significance of the increasing length of infancy as the lower and higher forms of the animal scale are compared. The longer period of immaturity characteristic of man enables him to secure better preparation to cope with his complex environment. In comparison with his capacities when mature, the human infant is indeed helpless. He is able to exist only because adults arrange the environment so that he can meet it effectively with his meager repertory of adaptive responses.

General Theories of Infant Behavior. Before proceeding to the detailed account of infant behavior, it is desirable to gain a preliminary orientation as to the nature of the reactions of the very young, and as to the nature of development. One outworn theory treats the child as if he were an *incomplete or miniature adult* who lacks certain functions such as speech, reproduction, locomotion and intelligent behavior, and has other functions only in an imperfect form. Development, from this point of view, is regarded as the acquisition of some fundamental adult functions and the perfecting of others. Unfortunately, the practical application of this attitude continues, although the theory is no longer tenable.

A second theory regards the young infant as primarily a *creature of reflexes*. His behavior embraces many simple reflexes, some more complex ones, the primary emotions, and possibly some other behavior patterns known as instincts. Development from infancy to adult life comes essentially from the modification and combination of these specific patterns of response. According to a third point of view, regarded as more useful today, the infant is neither a miniature adult nor a collection of specific reflexes. His behavior at first is more generalized, and development involves an increasing specificity of responses. As Irwin says, "Few definite sensory points are hooked up specifically with motor points as is called for by the reflex theory. The specificity demanded by the theory simply is not the rule in infant behavior." This point of view must be kept in mind throughout the discussion of the behavior of early infancy. Although it is often convenient to inventory the child's specific responses, these must be thought of as emerging from the original matrix of behavior-in-general.

Motor Behavior in Early Infancy

What does the baby normally do during earliest infancy? What sorts of reactions or responses does he make? What kinds of behavior may be elicited in experimentally controlled situations?

Behavior of the Newborn Infant. Until birth the child has been dependent upon his mother for respiration, nutrition, and elimination. These functions have been carried on through interchanges in the placental membranes. Beginning with birth, however, he must do these things for himself. One of the first signs of overt behavior is the birth cry, probably caused by the rapid passing of air over the vocal cords. Sometimes it has to be induced artificially by gently slapping or by dipping in warm or cold water. The birth cry is supposed to inflate the lungs and start off respiration. When the baby has some degree of hunger, sucking movements are readily induced by lightly touching his lips. Elimination of waste products begins within a few hours after birth. The three vegetative processes — eating, breathing, and elimination of waste products, together with sleeping, are necessary for his post-natal existence. Usually he begins them all from within a few seconds to a few hours after birth. He is now ready to carry forward his independent existence, if given the food and care which infancy requires.

The newborn child spends approximately eighty per cent of his time sleeping. The separate periods of sleep usually are very short, rarely exceeding three hours in length. Probably they are broken by hunger pangs or some other discomforting condition. Once the source of discomfort is removed, however, the infant drops off into another period of deep sleep. When awake he is incessantly active, wriggling and waving arms and legs, stretching, moving lips, hands, eyes and nose, in a random, uncoordinated manner. If he is asleep and becomes uncomfortable (cold, wet, hungry, or in pain), he awakens. After a few seconds he begins to cry intermittently. Soon, however, is likely to follow a period of continuous crying in which he brings every part of his body into action. He flexes and extends his arms, legs and toes; he is engaged in squirming, kicking, rolling his body and head, and crying rhythmically. All this activity is found in the normal, healthy infant during the first days of post-natal life.

The following activities have been observed during the first twenty minutes after birth: sneezing, yawning, the secretion of tears, sucking at the nipple, fixating on a light, putting the thumb in the mouth, jumping at loud sounds, grasping, crying with a box-shaped mouth, crying with the corners of the mouth pulled down, following a moving hand with the eyes, turning the head so as to get air when placed on the face, turning over when given a very slight advantage, and the cry of so-called anger. Not every infant, however, showed all of these activities during the first twenty minutes after birth.

Extent of Motor Activity during the First Two Weeks. Although the newborn infant sleeps most of the time, he is not quiescent during this period, but is very active. When infants are observed at home, clothing and covers often hamper their activity and prevent the observer from seeing all the movements actually made. When carefully observed under good experimental conditions, however, they are found to be very active, making in 15 to 18 hours from 500 to 3000 movements which observers could record, and from 10,000 to 45,000 which were recorded on the self-recording apparatus used. This was an average of 11 to 43 per minute, or about one every one or two seconds. During the first ten days after birth movements of head, body, arms, and legs occur, as well as those movements involved in the production of sounds.

During this time the infant turns the head to the left and right, draws it back, opens and closes the mouth, purses and licks the lips, closes and opens the eyes, winks, yawns, and tightens the eyelids when closed. He may move the body from lying on the back to lying on either side (usually a rapid movement), squirm or twist the trunk (usually slowly), stretch (with arms stretched over the head, legs extended, and trunk tensed), breathe rapidly, cry, shudder, gasp, jerk the body quickly, and arch the back. He moves his arms a great deal, flexes and extends them, slashes them about in various directions, throws them over his chest, and moves his hands and fingers. He moves his legs, feet, and toes, flexing, extending, kicking, jerking, rotating, rolling, or trembling. He makes many sounds which are referred to as crying, coughing, sneezing, smacking lips, sucking sounds, choking noises, hiccoughing, whimpering, sighing, audible breathing, throat sounds, vocalizing, and the hunger cry.

Head movements are a small proportion of the total motility of the, newborn, constituting approximately five per cent of his activity. Body movements and leg movements are each nearly 30 per cent, arm movements are 20 per cent, and sounds approximately 15 per cent of the child's responses.

Bryan observed ten infants who, when placed face down on a table, lifted the head off the table during the first twenty minutes after birth. Four of these pulled the knees forward under the body. One infant on the second day showed unusual muscular development. The knees were pulled up, the elbows pulled forward, and head raised until it was at right angles to the line of the spine, and then turned from side to side. After a few seconds the right arm was straightened so that the weight was shifted from the elbow to the right hand. Soon with a light push it rolled over to the left on its back. Blanton observed nine infants, ages two to fifteen days, who could hold up their heads from one to six seconds when held in an upright position on the examiner's lap with suitable body or back support. This, however, is quite unusual.

Much has been written about the character and meaning of the vocalizations of the newborn. Immanuel Kant, in pessimistic mood, referred to the birth cry as "a cry of wrath at the catastrophe of birth." Various observers have concluded that crying soon takes on definite meaning — within twenty-four hours, according to one writer, and somewhat later according to several others. When the infant is uncomfortable from wet clothing or from cold, is in pain, or is angry, his cries are said to show observable differentiating characteristics. Of this, however, we cannot be too sure, because investigation has shown that adults could judge the emotional accompaniment of the cry with very little success *when they did not know the stimuli* used to evoke the cry. The newborn infant's vocalizations usually are accompanied by some overt bodily activity, such as rolling the head, opening the mouth wide, jerking, twisting, bending the body and throwing it about, slashing the arms about, and kicking with the legs. Thus the human infant spends much of the first ten days of life after birth in ceaseless activity, much of it so rapid and difficult to observe that mechanical means are necessary in order that it may be recorded. Even when asleep the infant often is active a fifth of the time, even though no external stimuli are present, and when awake he is engaged in movement as much as two-fifths of the time.

1. *Early Specific Responses.* Feeding movements. During the first two postnatal weeks the infant is capable of making certain specific responses which we should now consider. Sucking movements have been observed at birth or even before complete delivery. (Preyer.) They are one of the earliest reactions of the newborn infant, occurring more frequently when the infant is hungry. They are most readily evoked by tactile stimulation of the lips, but

they may be elicited also by slight stroking or pressure upon the cheeks as well as above and below the lips. We would naturally expect the sucking response to such varied stimuli because this reaction involves the coordination of the muscles of the cheek, lips, and tongue, and the stimulation of any one of these parts might set off the total reaction. There is some disagreement in the results of investigations on this problem. In one study of sixty infants, feeding responses were elicited only by direct contact in the mouth or cheek region; but in another one the response was secured to an entirely different set of stimuli.

Pinching the large toe of seventeen moderately well-fed infants 164 times resulted in their resuming the sucking movements in all cases. Pulling the hair of the infants' heads for a total of 115 times and dropping three infants a distance of four inches a total of twenty times also led them to resume the sucking movements. The stimulus evoking sucking movements becomes more specific as the infant grows older. Swallowing usually follows sucking movements, but infants less than two weeks old have been found to discriminate between milk and air. When sucking milk they swallowed it; when sucking air they made no swallowing movements.

Thumb-sucking has been observed as soon as twenty minutes after birth. This response very commonly becomes a habit at a later age. Since thumb-sucking often follows from the infant's being hungry, proper nutrition and feeding schedules from earliest infancy should help prevent some cases of it. Furthermore, it would seem advantageous to allow the infant ample opportunity for gross-muscle activities. Suitable clothing, bed, and covers give him more range for moving about.

2. ***Foot and leg movements.*** When the sole of an infant's foot is stroked lightly along the median line from toes to heel, we often observe an extension or spreading of the toes, known as the *plantar reaction*. Certain features of this reaction were studied by Babinski who advanced the theory that the extension of the toes in adults is a pathological condition due to an injury to primary motor centers of the brain. The presence of the reaction in infants was ascribed to the immaturity of these same tracts. As a result of his work on this reaction, certain features of it came to be known as the Babinski reflex. The extension of the great toe upon plantar stimulation is known as the positive Babinski. It may or may not be accompanied by a spreading or flexion of the others.

   At the present time its appearance is not regarded as indicative of the maturation of nerve tracts. Many infants do not give the positive Babinski reaction upon plantar stimulation. Other specific movements also are elicited by plantar stimulation as well as the extension and flexion of toes. In a study of the reactions of 96 infants, one application of the stimulus resulted in flexion of the toes (negative Babinski) in 57.3 per cent of the cases, and in extension of the great toe (positive Babinski) in 42.7 per cent of the cases. To the infants who showed the positive response, five additional, stimulations were then applied within thirty seconds, and "the summation of subliminal stimuli" resulted in a flexion response in 89.6 per cent of those cases which first gave the positive Babinski. Flexion was not followed by extension in any case in this experiment.

   In another study of 100 infants during the first ten days of post-natal life, the Babinski reaction was not elicited in any case on the first day. Before applying the stimulus the infant's leg was placed across the palm of the experimenter's hand, the thumb and forefinger clasping the leg lightly just below the knee to prevent the infant from jerking his leg away, as from tickle. Some of those showing the Babinski reflex early were retested on the eleventh and twelfth days. By this time the reaction appeared immediately upon the infant's leg being taken in the hand, before the sole of the foot had even been touched. This raises the question whether the reaction can be elicited by stimulations of other areas than the plantar, or whether it was conditioned to other stimulations. The *knee-jerk* or *patellar reflex* occurs upon appropriate stimulation in nearly all newborn infants.

3. ***Grasping.*** If a small rod or a person's finger is brought into contact with the newborn infant's hand he is likely to grasp it tightly. This reaction is very common and has been observed during delivery and immediately thereafter. Sometimes immediately after birth the infant, having grasped the rod or finger, continues to hold on when the examiner raises it and supports his weight for as long as a second. Usually the infant is not able to support his own weight at birth in this manner, although he may hold tightly enough to lift his shoulders, or his head and shoulders. Of course, we cannot conclude that an infant does not have this ability because he fails to support shoulders, head, or entire body at some particular time. Conditions within the infant seem to affect the results, as in one observation when a crying baby responded readily, whereas a baby that was quiet responded only with difficulty. A hungry child might hold on, whereas he would let go when not hungry. A sound stimulus seemed to have a reinforcing effect. After the fourth month the grasping reflex tends to drop out and become organized into a voluntary grasping response.

4. ***Locomotion during the first two weeks.*** A few evidences of locomotion have been observed during the first two weeks of post-natal life. Many infants when supported at the arm-pits will make walking movement. Their whole body, however, will be flabby. The legs will flex and turn under it if weight is put upon them. Unusual cases have been reported. In one, the infant while held in the warm bath immediately after birth to set up respiration (but before breathing was well established), "suddenly began a treading motion with its feet which was perfectly rhythmic and regularly alternating at the rate of 80 per minute," except that the left foot lost 10 beats in one minute whereas the right foot lost none. Another baby, nine days old, in being handled, was brought near a table and its feet touched it. Immediately it stiffened and bore its full weight on its feet. It even balanced itself for an instant on its feet with arms outspread and its toes "dug in" in characteristic fashion to the table.

One infant on the fifth day showed unusual muscular development and coordination in creeping a few inches. Another, on the eighth day, crept forward six inches to a wall twice in one minute, the second time with its head in the air. Another infant, when placed prone and given something to push against with the feet, moved across a table (18 inches) twice on the seventh day and once each day thereafter until the tenth when it was removed from the hospital and no further observations were possible. A sixth infant showed this ability on the ninth and tenth days. All of these cases are unusual. As we shall see later, crawling, standing with help, holding head erect, and similar coordinated motor phenomena ordinarily are not found until sometime later.

5. *Vomiting.* The coordination of muscles involved in this reaction is usually present at birth, and the activity may be seen very shortly thereafter.

Coordination of Arms During Early Infancy. A very simple test may be used to ascertain if an infant can coordinate his arm movements. The examiner presses on the child's chin with the, finger and then observes the nature of the arm and hand reactions thereby induced. Coordinated movement is present when both of his hands touch the examiner's finger at the chin in a pushing manner. When this simple test is tried with infants a few hours after birth very diffuse reactions of the hands are made. The infant's hands are thrown about in an irregular manner, occasionally striking the examiner's finger, but purely by chance. Development is rapid, but the child is not likely to make a coordinated movement until after he is 21 hours of age. In one study, no child before the age of twelve days made a well-coordinated movement in less than four trials.

Reactions to Sensory Stimulations

Reactions to Light. If a light of suitable strength is flashed in the eyes of a normal infant immediately after birth his eyes seem to have a fixed stare. If this is done again in about three hours, the pupils of his eyes may contract slightly but very slowly. If we repeat this at intervals of a few hours, we will find that the speed and amount of contraction increase so that by the time he is 30 hours old the reaction is prompt and adequate in amount. After the age of thirty hours the reaction seems to be well established in all cases. The increase in the effectiveness of this reaction during the earliest hours of infancy may be seen roughly from Figure below. During the first day or two, prolonged stimulation often is followed by turning the head from side to side or by drawing it back away from the source of light.

Coordination of the eyes. The development of the coordination of the eyes occurs in early infancy. Sometimes the newborn infant can move each eye independently of the other, one turning in one direction at the same time that the other turns in another direction. This lack of coordination does not last long. Very soon he coordinates the movements of the eyes in fixating a light stimulus, sometimes before the sixth hour after birth. Coordination improves very rapidly, and is likely to be almost perfect in a day an half.

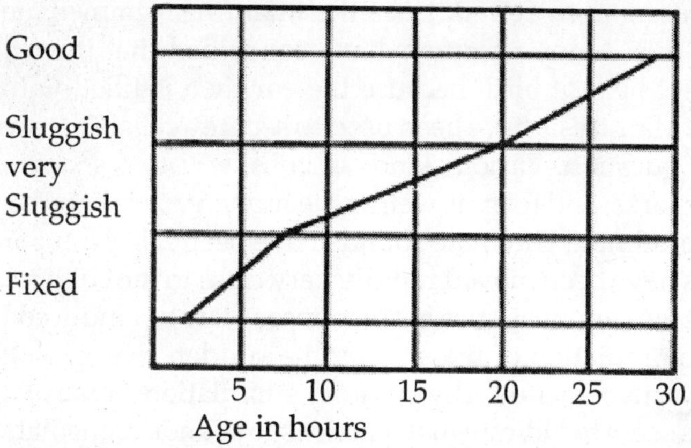

FIG. *Adequacy of Reaction of the Pupil to Light, Infants from Birth to the Age of 30 hours*

Optic nystagmus in early infancy. When an adult looks at a moving object his eyes slowly follow it or move in the direction in which it is moving. Then they make a very rapid backward movement, opposite to the direction in which the object moving. This is known as *optic nystagmus*. Infants at a very early age show optic nystagmus upon the first presentation of the moving stimulus. One displayed this response at 11 ½ hours after birth, another at 1 ¼ hours after birth, and another, a child born one month prematurely, at 11 ¾ hours of age. From this it appears probable that the neural mechanisms underlying nystagmus are ready to function at birth.

Ocular pursuit of a moving object. The ability to follow a light moved horizontally develops before ability to follow one moved vertically, while the reaction of following a light moved in a circle develops still later. Slowly moving objects can be followed at an earlier age than rapidly moving ones. Unsuccessful pursuit eye-movements may be present a few minutes after birth. By the third or fourth week some infants respond successfully, but all infants are not likely to do so until sometime after the sixth week.

Reactions to Sound. Does the infant hear immediately after birth? Many observers have concluded that the child does not hear at birth because the ear then is filled with a liquid. Many tests have been used to secure a reliable answer to this question. Various kinds of bells, whistles, snappers, tuning forks, and toys, as well as the human voice, have been used as stimuli. Often the sounds have been fairly loud and objects have been moved rapidly very close to the child's ear so that we cannot be sure his responses were not induced by tactile stimulation of the skin by the sudden change in the air currents rather than by auditory stimulation. Some of the studies seem to indicate that reactions to sounds immediately after birth were unusual; that children two to six days old reacted to sounds such as the rattling of paper; that during the first ten days infants did not respond to the light ringing of a small hand bell; that some did respond to a loud ringing of a hand bell swung close to the ear but not touching it; and that high shrill tones aroused more active responses than did lower ones. Other studies indicate that the amount of activity following auditory stimulation increased from the first to the tenth day.

More recently better techniques have been used which control the intensity, duration, and pitch of the stimuli. Apparently the newborn infant does respond to sounds. Greater intensities seem to bring greater responses. When stimuli lasting one, three, five, and fifteen seconds were used, the longer the stimulus the greater the percentage of response. When the sound stimuli were continued six minutes their greatest effect appeared after two to four minutes and lasted until the end of the six minutes. Sounds at various pitches (128, 256, 1024, 4096 cycles) elicited more than 75 per cent of responses. Variations in pitch within the foregoing limits do not seem to show any consistent differences in response. Infants' responses to sound seem to depend in part upon their condition at the time. Those awake and inactive are likely to make the greatest responses, those crying respond the least, and those silent and active or asleep make an intermediate intensity of response.

A few cases have been reported in which movements of the fetus in response to a loud sound have been observed as early as a month before birth, but we cannot be sure whether the infants responded to the auditory elements of the sound stimulations or to mechanical vibration. Certain changes in the breathing and in the pulsations of the fontanelle have been observed in infants subjected to auditory stimulations on the first day.

Sensitivity to Taste Stimulations. As early as the second day infants show clear-cut differential reactions to salt solutions. On the first day after birth many infants make some kind of a response to a great variety of taste stimulations, citric acid, quinine, sugar, salt, and water having stimulating value in this descending order.

Responses to Olfactory Stimuli. The child at birth seems to have a poorly developed sense of smell. Infants under two days old reacted to 49 per cent of the olfactory stimuli used by one investigator, ammonia being, the most effective. They have also failed to differentiate different kinds of milk during the first ten days after birth. Apparently smell develops more slowly in the newborn than do some of the other senses. Reactions to Temperature. Infants seem to respond to temperature on the day of birth. If the stimuli are considerably above or below body temperature, the reactions are stronger.

Reactions to Pain Stimulation. The infant at birth or a few hours thereafter shows sensitivity such stimulations as pricking with a needle. In investigating this response, a constant amount of pressure of the needle is applied to the cheeks, the anterior surface of the thigh, and the lateral surface of the calf of the leg. If one stimulation brings no response, additional ones are applied, but never more than ten. The face is sensitive to pain at an earlier age than is the leg and also requires fewer repetitions of the stimulus at any time during the first two days. It seems significant that pain reactions not only appear earlier in the anterior end of the body but also develop more rapidly than those in the posterior ends. After forty hours of age the infants in one study responded to the pain stimulus upon its first application to the face; after the age of seventy-five hours they responded upon the first application of the pain stimulus to the calf of the leg. The correlations between age in hours and the number of applications of the stimulus necessary to elicit a response were -.87 for the legs and -.70 for the face.

Reactions to Tactile Stimulations. The skin on all parts of the body is sensitive to touch at birth. If certain areas, such as the heel, are stroked lightly, the member is jerked away as if from tickle. An infant born without a cerebrum made overt reactions to pain, pressure, contact, and cold, but not to light, smell, taste, and warmth. This observation gives some indication of the relative parts played by higher brain centers and lower spinal centers under the action of various kinds of sensory stimulation.

Some Other Reactions of Infancy

Sleep. The amount of sleep during each twenty-four hours decreases from birth until the end of the first year. According to one study, 69 infants in Vienna slept nineteen hours the first month, but only twelve hours the twelfth month. Studies in America, however, reveal that children two years old sleep more than twelve and one-half hours on the average. Children three years old sleep from eleven to twelve and one-half hours, and children four years old sleep from nearly eleven to approximately twelve hours. The length of single sleeping periods increases during the first year, the longest periods of unbroken sleep often being less than four hours from birth until the age of one month. By the third month, however, a baby often sleeps without waking for six hours, and by the seventh month or later he may sleep continuously nine or ten hours.

Smiling and Laughing. We forego all reference to the romantic literature which purports to show the causes and meaning of the baby's laughter and smiles. Psychologists are interested in the age at which smiles and laughter first appear, the stimuli for such responses, and the differences between the smiles of early infancy and those at later ages. Experimental work indicates that the infant usually can be stimulated to smile as early as the eighth week, and to laugh as early as the twelfth week. Observers, however, have reported occasional instances of smiling as early as the first, third, fifth, sixth, or fifteenth day, and laughter, on the fifth or nineteenth day. An infant four days old smiled while feeding, another, seven days old, smiled at the end of bottle feeding. Another infant, thirteen days old, smiled at a bright light; while still another case, twenty-eight days old, is reported to have smiled while feeding. Infants one, two, four, and six days old have been observed to smile slightly to a tickling touch under the chin when awake and comfortable.

Early smiling (without specific stimulation) is usually ascribed to a state of euphoria or general well-being. On the whole, spontaneous smiles are rare during earliest infancy. The number of laughing responses may not increase very much from the fifth to the twelfth month (Washburn) but the number of smiling responses may do so. The following characteristic differences have been observed in the smiling responses from the twelfth to the fifty-second week:

Twelve Weeks

- Twitching of lips and other facial muscles preceding smiling.

- Round, open mouth.
- Protrusion of chin (incidence and degree decreasing up to 40 weeks).
- Vocalizations monosyllabic — "ah" (decreasing up to 40 weeks).
- Hands are moved up and down over center of body and come to rest in the mouth region.
- Knees are drawn up toward the abdomen, with rolling of body.
- Mobilized attention with reduction of bodily activity precedes smiling (decreasing up to 44 weeks).

Thirty-two Weeks

- Retraction displaces "opening" of the mouth with consequently greater bulging and raising of cheeks.
- Horizontally elliptical mouth most typical.
- Tongue protrusion at its height.
- Exposure of gums begins.
- Eyes often half-closed rather than narrowed slightly.
- Chin drawn in to neck.
- Vocalization — prolonged "ah." Varied jargon-like sounds.

Fifty-two Weeks

- Greater effect of "control" in the above forms of behavior; less bodily activity.
- More individualization in subjects' smiles.
- Teeth almost invariably seen.
- Double naso-labial fold first seen.

Emotional Reactions in Infancy. In addition to the milder forms of response so far considered, it is possible to elicit from even quite young infants muscular responses of much greater intensity, accompanied by marked visceral reactions, that are universally designated as *emotional*. When subjected to certain forms of stimulation, the infant will start, catch his breath, clutch his hands, pucker his lips, scream, cry, and sometimes kick and struggle. The inner components of this response usually include changes in heart beat, in blood pressure, and in the action of the digestive system.

This very intense, and often annoying, form of behavior has been the subject of a great amount of research with infants and children. At present there is no perfect agreement among psychologists on the number and kinds of emotions shown by children, or on any list of stimuli that will dependably arouse this mode of response in all youngsters. In general, it is agreed that the emotional behavior of young infants is diffused and non-specific, since definite patterns of "fear," "rage," etc., cannot be distinguished clearly. The stimuli for emotion seem to be characterized by intensity, suddenness, and unaccustomedness.

A blunder that must be avoided in all child psychology, and especially in relation to emotional responses, is that of assuming that infant behavior has the same meaning for the infant as similar behavior has for the adult. Adults are quite prone to read into an infant's tantrum the significance that this reaction would have for an older person. Such interpretations of infant emotion have little value. In the first place, it is shown later that even experienced adults are unskillful in detecting the stimuli that have caused certain observed infantile reactions. They cannot, therefore, judge or discriminate the various forms of infant emotions. A second objection is to the practice of ascribing introspectively designated emotions to infants. It is impossible to know just how the infant feels, and to interpret his mental state in adult terms is unreliable. Because of the great theoretical and practical importance of emotion in childhood, two chapters are devoted to this topic later. A more detailed discussion may be deferred to these sections.

Diffuse and Specific Reactions During Early Infancy

Probably the most significant result of recent experimental studies of the behavior of very young infants is the accumulating mass of evidence showing the extent of diffuse movements or responses under various specific sorts of stimulations. Reference has already been made to this approach, and some specific data may now be presented.

Diffuse Movements Under Specific Sensory Stimulation. If specific sensory stimuli are applied to infants during the first two weeks of postnatal life, their reactions are not confined to the particular organ or segment to which the stimulus presumably has been applied. Responses of the particular segment do occur, but also movements or reactions involving more distant parts of the body. Thus responses to light during the first two weeks after birth include not only contraction and dilation of the pupils and other responses as described in a preceding section, but also movements of other parts of the body, such as head, trunk, arms, and legs.

Two-thirds of the responses to light are likely to involve movements of the eyes, which is to be expected; but one-third of them involve movements of bodily segments not directly related to the stimulus. By the end of two weeks the amount of general bodily activity resulting from stimulation by light is very much reduced. When stimulated by a loud sound during the first two or three weeks of postnatal life, infants are likely to make a variety of responses. In one study nearly one-third of these were arm and leg movements; one-third were eye movements; one-fourth were general bodily movements; and a small percentage consisted of facial and head movements. Reactions to sound seemed to be no more specific for this type of stimulus than for others, since 36 per cent of the responses were of the head region and 64 per cent were of other parts of the body. Similarly, responses to taste and temperature stimuli during this early period show a wide variety of segmental responses, rather than being limited to specific reactions of the particular part of the body stimulated.

The Significance of Mass Activity. From the experimental results that have just been presented, it appears that specific reflexes to definite stimuli are not the final elementary units from which all of the other more complex behavior of the human being is compounded. It is now clear that infant behavior of the diffuse or mass sort is an earlier type, from which more specific modes of responses gradually become differentiated.

This discovery is sometimes known as the *organismic hypothesis*. It is ably presented by Irwin, as follows: The organismic hypothesis on the structural side assumes that the organism differentiates into cells, tissues, organs, and structures, all the time maintaining its integrity. The various zoological sciences afford a large and convincing body of evidence for the hypothesis. Turning to the behavior side of the problem, patterns differentiate from a primitive general matrix of behavior called mass activity. Mass activity is at its maximum during the first fetal months, and during uterine existence the differentiation of activity into patterns is under way. After birth the processes of differentiation proceed with increasing degrees of specificity, definiteness, and preciseness of pattern until they attain the degree of maturity which we recognize in the adaptive behavior of the organism. However, the fact should be emphasized that experimental evidence for an organismic view from studies on human behavior is only beginning to accumulate.

Another interesting confirmation of the precedence of diffuse over specific response comes from the studies of the conditioned reaction. Pavlov concludes, "The study of conditioned reflexes has shown, however, that a conditioned reflex appears at first in a generalized form, that is, that excitation irradiates from its point of initiation to embrace also cells belonging to other receptor elements beyond the boundary of the area of the cortex primarily connected with the stimulated receptor."

Newborn infants show, therefore, (1) an amount of mass activity or general diffuse movements which seem to be caused by impulses irradiating throughout the body. During the period of early infancy, these give way to (2) an increasing number of specific and adaptive responses emerging from the former mass activity. This process of differentiation is a continuation of the line of development begun before birth and extensively described in the two preceding chapters. The maturation of inherited structures and the influences of environmental stimulation both contribute to the process by which the newborn infant becomes the child.

7

The Preschool Child

One might very well ask why recent interest has focused so largely on the preschool child. To answer that question definitively, to state all the contributing factors, or to date the exact beginnings of this interest is just as impossible as to undertake the same task for the Industrial Revolution, the Civil War, or Communism. One can, however, mention a few factors which played a part in the segregation of preschool children for study and research. We cannot stop long on the unpleasant theological ideas of Comenius (1592-1670) who believed that childhood is innately depraved. He elaborated doctrines for the training of very young children by their parents. The theories of John Locke (1632-1704), Pestalozzi (1734-1805), Rousseau (1712-1778), Oberlin (1740-1826), and Froebel (1782-1852) are of interest to students of education and sociology. Space does not permit an examination of these theories at this point even though the philosophy of education for early childhood has largely developed from this theoretical background that they supplied. Another contributor was showman P. T. Barnum, who, in 1842, had the first Baby Show. This may have provided the idea which, in later years, developed into WellBaby Clinics.

Robert Owen, a pioneer in European thinking, is of particular interest in the United States. During the Industrial

Revolution, he, as a cotton-mill owner in Scotland, became concerned over the welfare of industrial workers. In addition to underpaid adult laborers, there were hundreds of small children who worked as much as 12 hours a day in factories. Other very young children were left at home alone while older members of the family were employed. In 1816, Owen opened an infant school for these children. Later he came to America and bought out the entire Rappite Village of Harmony, Indiana. He wished to try a social experiment, one feature of which was a nursery school, which he opened about 1826. More than 100 children were enrolled. Such a procedure is quite different from that of the best nursery schools of today, which usually limit their enrollment to 20 or fewer. This experiment left no lineal descendants in either the social or the educational world.

More recent social phenomena have had more direct and intimate connection with the current interest in the early years of life. Perhaps one of the most influential of these factors was the realization of the necessity for improving health conditions. Early experiences during World War I in European countries, and later in America, showed that a large part of the draft population was handicapped by physical conditions that could have been prevented or corrected had attention been given to them in childhood. During the early 1920's, many studies were therefore made of the health of those who were then of preschool age. Results were distressing in the extreme. Details of the findings may be read in reference 77 at the end of this chapter. Health measures were instituted throughout the country, and baby clinics were opened in many places. These health centers offered educational and counseling service for parents.

At about the same time—indeed, even before—another factor had arisen which called to our attention the necessity of providing health and educational facilities for young children. Both in the United States and abroad, mothers were leaving home to work in industry. Day nurseries had been operating in this country since the time of the Civil War, when they were opened for the children of women needed in some of the auxiliary war services. The day nurseries were largely fashioned after the French *crèche*, which has no doubt served also as the model for the more recent Russian *crèche*.

Day nurseries developed rapidly in our country, some good and some bad. At any rate, their intention was to provide physical shelter, at least, for the children of working mothers. The social fallacy of separating young children from their mothers was largely overlooked. Mangold says: When Rabbi Hirsch at the White House Conference of 1909 declared that the public should pay needy mothers so that they could care for their own children in their own homes, the sophisticated child welfare workers of the country glanced furtively at each other and smiled superciliously.

However, two years later the first state mothers' pension law was passed by Illinois. At about the same time, other forces were joining in an effort to improve educational, social, and psychological environments of children. In 1921, the Commonwealth Fund in New York instituted a five-year study and demonstration for the prevention of delinquency.

This program included the services of the New York School of Social Work, the National Committee for Mental Hygiene, the National Committee of Visiting Teachers, and the Joint Committee (made up of executive heads of all the participating agencies). Visiting teachers and child-guidance clinics for five years conducted demonstrations in many neighborhoods throughout the country. Most of these communities took on local responsibility for continuing the services after the demonstration period was over. Obviously, this program in all of its branches rendered a great service to the fields of preschool and parent education.

In understanding the rise of the preschool emphasis, we should also recall that in the last decade of the nineteenth and the first and second decades of the twentieth century educational doctrines took on a new philosoph. The influence of John Dewey as well as the earlier work of G. Stanley Hall was in the direction of regarding the child, even the little child, as a self-motivating, inwardly dominated, and powerfully active *individual*. The twentieth century, in educational literature, is often referred to as the *Century of the Child*. The vocabulary of this period includes such terms as the child-centered school, the project method, pre-parental training, self-activity, progressive education, and mental hygiene. The child had begun to come into his own and to bring his little brother and sister with him! Not only that, he had begun to bring his parents to school.

Two more recent developments in the care of young children must be mentioned. During the 1930's, migrant workers, particularly in the fruit-raising areas of the West, attracted the attention of the public. These families were lured from one district to another as fruit and other agricultural crops were to be harvested. Usually the entire family moved, taking most of the family belongings with them. Residence in any one locality was likely to be of relatively short duration. The children were either not in school at all or else were moved every few weeks from one school to another. Care and schooling for these children, while their parents were away working, was arranged for in many places—sometimes by local citizens, sometimes by the migrants themselves, sometimes by the employers, and in some cases by the government. Reports from districts where such care was provided indicate that efficiency differed from one locality to another. However, in all cases some organized care was probably better than no care.

After the entry of the United States into World War II, the problem of child care was again brought into the limelight. In large numbers of cases, both parents worked in defense plants, often on different shifts. In other cases, the father was in military service and the mother was employed. Lurid magazine articles about the neglect of children under these conditions told of children locked in automobiles for safekeeping or roaming the streets with the door key tied around their necks. Many of these children were never reached by any of the educational, social, and governmental facilities set up to remedy such conditions. In many districts around army camps and defense plants, day-care centers were opened where children could be cared for while their parents were away from home. Such breakdown of family life and home care for children is, of course, one of the strong arguments against war and constitutes a very potent reason for an enduring peace.

Kindergarten and Nursery School

Because it is sometimes difficult to appreciate the history and program of contemporary events, it may be well to consider for a time our present kindergarten and nursery school. Kindergartens, unlike day nurseries, have always been *educational* in aim, even thougt many of them were of private or philanthropic origin. The influence of Froebel and of Montessori is well known. Suffice it to say that the first kindergarten in the United States for English-speaking children was opened about 1860, although there had been some German-American kindergartens prior to that time.

We need not stop at this point to go into the question of kindergarten doctrines and philosophy. However, it must be admitted that in this country for many years kindergartens were very highly routinized and regimented. The principles of Froebel probably went Froebel one better in the hands of some rigid kindergartners. Within the present century, however, kindergartens in many places have taken a right-about-face and now operate largely on a self-activity program. Needless to say, this change of procedure and philosophy has not come about without much discussion, debate, and figurative bloodshed.

Most cities now include kindergartens as an integral part of the public school system. However, even in such cities, kindergartens do not operate in *all* the public schools.

Furthermore, it must be remembered that the benefits of both kindergarten and nursery school education are limited almost entirely to children living in cities or towns. Perhaps one can console himself somewhat by saying that such education is more needed in urban centers. Julia Wade Abbott once said, "The public school kindergartner was the first visiting teacher." Certain it is that the kindergarten has been a veritable godsend to the foreign child and his mother in our crowded cities.

The now famous Fisher Act of 1918 in England provided, among other educational facilities, for nursery schools throughout the whole of England "to lay the foundations of health, habit, and responsive personality." The nursery school movement developed rapidly both in England and in the United States. While originally the nursery schools were not opened as philanthropic ventures, as were many of the early infant schools and kindergartens, and all the day nurseries, yet during the economic depression in the third decade of the century, many nursery schools were opened in the United States with federal funds. In some instances, the philanthropy consisted largely in providing a training program and subsequent employment for nursery school teachers.

Nursery schools tend to enroll children from about two to four years of age. The average nursery school is likely to have a majority of its children around three to three and one-half years old. The commonest age range in kindergartens is four to six years. There are differences other than age range between the typical kindergarten and the typical nursery school. The kindergarten program may be said to be somewhat more formal and slightly more *educational* than that of the nursery school. It usually includes rhythm, play, and construction—partly, at least, with materials requiring smaller and finer coördinations than nursery school equipment. In general, the educational aim of the *progressive kindergarten* of today is not essentially different from that of the nursery school except for those differences imposed by the dissimilar age range.

The kindergarten program usually provides for only half-day sessions. In many cities where facilities are limited, the five-year-olds attend a morning session and the four-year-olds, an afternoon session. Many nursery schools provide an all-day program. This means that health, rest, and eating are as much a part of the nursery school plan as are the play activities, rhythm, or art work. The child is examined by a nurse or physician as soon as he arrives in the morning. If he shows no evidence of communicable disease, he is allowed to go to the play yard. During the first part of the morning, the give-andtake of play activities is watched over and directed, when necessary, by one teacher or assistant for every six to eight or ten children. In the middle of the morning, the child helps himself to his codliver oil, fruit juice, or whatever is provided for him at that time. Following this, he may have a rest period or, in some nursery schools, a time of very quiet play or music until the midday meal. At this meal, the child is taught to help serve himself. Feeding problems have a way of disappearing after a child has been in a nursery school group with a mild-mannered and professionally trained nursery school teacher. After the noon meal, all children retire to individual sleeping cots or floor blankets to sleep. Here again, it is gratifying to notice how easily proper habits can be instilled into children by a person trained in such matters. Usually parents come for their children toward the middle of the afternoon.

One often hears the question raised as to the wisdom of "school" for children as young as eighteen months, two, or even three years. Certainly, compulsory education laws should not be pushed down into this age area. Where little children have opportunities for social contacts with other children in their own home or neighborhood; where parents are well equipped to undertake the emotional, social, and physical rearing of young children; where ample space and time are provided for safe outdoor play; where the child is gradually weaning himself from his parents; or where a nursery school is so far distant that traveling to and from it involves physical strain—there perhaps no great harm will come from the omission of nursery school training. On the other hand, it can be safely said that, at the hands of a skillful nursery school teacher, mental hygiene of little children can be better directed than is the case in the average home. As an example of the opportunities provided by a nursery school, one might mention the large sheets of paper, paintpots, easels, or oilcloth-covered tables where little children can finger-paint or brush-paint to their hearts' content without there being any necessity for caution or nagging. It is wellnigh impossible for the average home to provide for such wholesome, but adult-disturbing painting experiments, or for other similar creative activities.

The example of other children who eat well or sleep well, or who are "learning to take turns" also provides a powerful stimulus toward right conduct. Self-help is encouraged in nursery schools more than is usual in the average home. One cannot overlook the fact that entrance into nursery school, like all great adventures in life, demands *some* adjustment. Mothers occasionally report that the first days in nursery school are highly stimulating and make for excitability. This is probably true in relatively few cases and does not persist long.

Another question rises in the mind of one who watches little children for their first few days or weeks in a nursery school. Individual differences are very marked in respect to children's willingness to leave mother and enter into this new world. Some children protest not at all, some for only a day or so, some for much longer time. Except in the rare case, the child does learn to accept the separation after a time. Nursery school authorities have been prone to argue that if a child finally does allow his mother to leave without his protesting too much, such a child has "learned" to do without his mother for a time, at least. It would appear that the matter is not quite so simple as that. In the old days, for example, many children finally did learn to read after some fashion who, we now believe, did not have "reading readiness" and who would much better not have been exposed to reading for several months, when they would have made much more satisfactory progress with less emotional expenditure. The thought then occurs to us that perhaps some children are not yet "ready" to learn to do without mother and might learn this skill more readily a little later. Certainly there is accumulating evidence that separation from the nursing process in infancy is fraught with emotional and personality hazards for the child who is not matured sufficiently to accept such a situation. By the same token, separation from mother at age two or three must be under such conditions, at least, that fear wanes rather than increases and emotional security becomes stronger and not weaker.

One other possibility must be questioned. Is a child ever thrown into turmoil by a conflict between home and nursery school procedure? This is more than a theoretical possibility. A skillful nursery school teacher often senses such situations and has to resort to very subtle methods of parent education. Perhaps one of the chief advantages of nursery schools is the training they provide for parents. Most nursery schools accept children for enrollment only with the understanding that the parents will keep certain records, will attend conferences and consultation periods concerning their child, and perhaps attend group meetings of parents.

Many nursery schools are equipped with a "one-way vision screen." These screens are made of specially treated finely meshed wire or, in some recent experiments, black cellophane, or specially treated glass. They are an excellent adjunct for parent education. The parent who sits back of this screen can see his or her child in action without the child's knowing that he is being observed. Many a parent has thus seen his child in relation to, and in comparison with, other children as he could never do otherwise. The writer distinctly remembers the case of little John. John's parents had exploited him in the city newspapers for months by the time he was two years of age. It was claimed that he could read two or three hundred words and that he surely must be a genius. A psychologist was inveigled into attempting to administer an intelligence test to the child, much against her own better judgment.

All efforts to take the child into the examining room without his parents resulted in tears and temper tantrums. Once in the examining room, the parents continued their stream of admonitions and prohibitions to the child. The usual form-boards, pegboards, color sorting, and other "preschool tests" were attempted. John could do none of them. In fact, there was nothing that was tried, appropriate for his age, that he could do. All the while, he was demanding constant attention from both parents. After half an hour of witnessing failure by their "genius" son, the parents insisted that he be allowed to give a demonstration of his "reading." Sure enough, he could read off some two hundred or more separate words from flash cards held by his parents. It was evident that he did not know the meaning of some of the words which he recognized on sight, but he "read" them, nevertheless. The parents were finally persuaded—for a short time, at least—that what their child needed was social training rather than training in reading. He was accordingly enrolled in a nearby nursery school. The one-way vision screen enabled the parents to watch John in his contacts with other children. Perhaps one should say his *absence of contacts* because, whereas all the other children participated in small-group activities, John could not be prevailed upon to do anything with anyone else. When other children carried their own food to the table, he could not or would not carry his. When other children, with help, learned to "unfold the blanket," then to "turn it down," and to "tuck the corners under," in making their own beds, John was helpless. The sight through the one-way vision screen day after day was not pleasant to the parents.

The realization of their son's social incompetence, his wretched mental hygiene, his helplessness in eating, dressing, and toileting were brought into bold relief. All the while, they were insisting that the nursery school should allow John to go on with his reading. Incidentally, the mental hygiene of the *parents* was so bad that the unpleasant discoveries about their child were too much for them. In popular parlance, they "could not take it," and they withdrew John from the school. Recent items in the newspapers have brought this case up to date. John is now performing, at about age 12 or 14, on the concert stage and has attracted considerable favorable notice from the critics. It is certainly to be hoped that the parents are not merely fostering another achievement for their own gratification. It is evident, of course, that the child has certain abilities in large measure. It is perhaps also evident that neglect of social, emotional, and other mental-hygiene principles in the case of brilliant children has tended to give gifted children, as a class, an undeservedly bad name. The real all-around "education" that children receive in well-staffed nursery schools and kindergartens is one of the best safeguards for good mental hygiene in childhood.

Preschool Attendance and Later Development

One often hears the question raised as to whether kindergarten-or, more recently, nursery school—does anything more for a child than to keep him happily employed for the time being or to develop certain skills appropriate for his age. Kindergarten and elementaryschool teachers have been interested in this question for many years. They have wondered, for example, whether children with kindergarten education progress any more rapidly through the elementary schools than do non-kindergarten-trained children. There are difficulties in the way of getting a reliable answer to this question. For example, are children who are sent to kindergarten selected from a different social and intellectual stratum than children who are not sent to kindergarten? As public nursery schools and kindergartens become more common, it will be easier to eliminate this statistical knot. Only two of the numerous studies of this question will be mentioned here, but from their bibliographies, one can discover citations of many others.

Goetch compared the progress in Grades I through VI of 968 kindergarten-trained children with that of 968 non-kindergartentrained children. He reports that much public-school time was saved for the former group, since they entered Grade I younger and progressed through the grades more rapidly. At the end of Grade VI, Goetch's kindergarten group was, on the average, more than four months younger than the non-kindergarten group. Their general scholastic average, as well as their social ratings, was higher. One wonders about these findings when it is discovered that the *intelligence test ratings* of the kindergarten-trained group were *also* higher. Goetch, however, does say that the kindergarten-trained children made higher achievement scores than the non-kindergarten-trained children *of the same mental age*.

MacLatchy's study of more than 2,300 kindergarten-trained children compared with over 2,500 non-kindergarten-trained children shows that the former group received higher ratings on industry, initiative, and oral language. They also did better on an intelligence test. Their achievement in reading was much superior to that of the children who had not gone to kindergarten. Other research studies have, for the most part, been in agreement with the findings here mentioned. Claims are also made for the superiority of kindergartentrained children in respect to social maturity.

Studies on nursery-school-trained children, including their later school progress, are appearing in various publications. As yet, there is need for more investigation in this field. Some of our first nursery school children are now well along in the grades. Studies will be made of these children, no doubt with a view to determining the effect of previous nursery school training. Jersild and Fite have already reported that at the beginning of the year in kindergarten those children who had had nursery school experience the previous year tended to have more social contacts with other children than the kindergarten children who had not previously attended nursery school. This advantage in favor of the nursery-school-trained children tended to disappear before the kindergarten year was over, however.

Two other research questions have received considerable attention within recent years. One is the question as to whether attendance at nursery school raises the child's intelligence quotient. Page, as well as various authors in the 1940 Yearbook of the National Society for the Study of Education, concludes that nursery school attendance does not raise the intelligence quotient. Another matter interest is the possibility of emotional training and therapy through the nursery school. Those who have watched individual children in good nursery schools can attest to the fact that temper tantrums often become less frequent, sharing comes to be more frequent and more enjoyable, and self-help more proficient. No one knows as yet, perhaps, what the final verdict will be as to the possibility of reducing mental disease and emotional maladjustment through the facilities of the nursery school and kindergarten. Some of these schools are working in close contact with child guidance centers with a view to obtaining as much therapy as possible. Day-byday diary records of the individual child's behavior are being used in progressive schools and are telling their story about the child's development. Those interested in reading further on the therapeutic value of early education may be interested in reading Baruch, Benjamin, Bowley, Chittenden, Gerard, Headley and Foster, Lerner and Murphy, Lippman, Read and Conrad, Thompson, and Washburn.

There is a practical question in regard to placing a very bright child in kindergarten at the age normal for such placement. The writer has known several very superior children who spent about a year it. kindergarten and had at the end of that time mastered all the techniques. They had also matured socially and emotionally to the point that kindergarten was obviously no longer the place for them. They were still too young to be admitted to the first grade. In several such cases, the child actually had to be kept home from school for a year or so. This break in school life is rather disconcerting to a bright child and presents a real problem. Obviously, it is a little hard to anticipate, in advance of his being admitted, that the child will "outgrow" kindergarten. Of course, where it is possible to enter the child in a progressive school having both kindergarten and first grade, the difficulty is minimized, since grade lines in such schools can easily be cut across. Otherwise, the best thing may be to keep the child at home until it is more nearly time for entrance into the elementary school, before allowing him to go to kindergarten. In the meantime, of course, provision must be made for plenty of play with other children and for constructive activities of many kinds.

The "Illusion of the Definite Period"

The point has been stressed continuously throughout this book that the personality and even the habits of an individual do not have sharply differentiated time intervals. Therefore, the discussion of the formation of such habits as toilet, washing and dressing, eating, sleeping, and the like is reserved for the next chapter. Does such a discussion logically belong to a consideration of the preschool period any more than to any other period in life? Even though habit training in such matters *begins* in the early years, does it not require supervision throughout the entire period of childhood and adolescence? The answer to the latter question is certainly an affirmative one. Psychology has taught us to question the absolute fixity and permanence of anything that we regard as a "habit" in a child. If this were not true, the task of child-rearing would be much easier in many respects—and much harder in others.

Obviously, many other topics might be considered while one is thinking about the preschool period. The mental hygienists speak of this age as the "golden age of mental hygiene," and it is certain that most of the nervous disorders and unhappinesses of later life have their beginnings in early childhood. Many habits and attitudes, for good or ill, are established so early in life that adults forget their source and origin. There is always danger, however, in the "illusion of the definite period." For this reason, it may be better to stop the discussion of the preschool child as such.

The period of life once called the "neglected age of childhood" now threatens to usurp the center of the stage and to push the later periods of childhood into oblivion. In fact, as one looks over current psychological literature, one wonders what has become of the old-fashioned *school-age child*. There are plenty of references to him as he functions in school with his reading, subtraction, long division, or the social sciences. One can find plenty of research about him as an academic learner. Other phases of the life of the six- to twelve- or fourteenyear-old, however, appear to be sadly neglected so far as scientific research is concerned. One wishes the books and periodicals could give us more help with the ten-year-old who does not want to go to school; the twelve-year-old who thinks everything in his chum's home is right and everything in his own home is wrong; the child with musical ability who will not practice; the child who *appears* to be lazy; the child who is selfish and thoughtless in his home; the child who always seems to prefer playmates from a social class other than that to which his family belongs; the child whom nobody likes. All these are living human beings about whom not enough is being written or done. In the meantime, the preschool child goes merrily on in the focus of many a laboratory microscope, so to speak, and furnishes material for endless research projects, master's theses, and innumerable articles and books.

Negativism and Temper Tantrums

Unkind as it may seem to say so, negativism and temper tantrums do seem to be peculiarly characteristic of the preschool-age child. For this reason, they will be considered at this point, whereas some other behaviors and habits that belong equally to older children will be discussed in a subsequent chapter. Negativistic behavior has been the subject of much research. The negativistic child is unwilling to do what is asked of him. In fact, at times he deliberately does the opposite. Some families make the mistake of trying to meet such situations by giving directions for the contrary of what they really want to have done. A certain amount of negativism in young children is not only to be expected, but is probably wholesome rather than otherwise. As a child's environment widens through the development of walking, talking, running, and playing, it is inevitable that he will, for his own protection, face the necessity of restriction and curbing from adults. It would be a spineless child, indeed, who never showed resentment at such thwartings. The fact must never be overlooked, however, that *much* adult thwarting of children is entirely unnecessary and unjustifiable. When one finds that he has a negativistic child on his hands, it is well to see whether he may not also have an adult-dominated and nagged child on his hands. Part of education, at any age level, however, is to learn the most socialized ways to meet thwartings and dispose of resentment. We must arrange matters so the child learns that, by and large, he attains more self-satisfaction by acceptable behavior than otherwise.

Temper tantrums are extreme forms of negativism. They may include anything in the repertoire of kicking, screaming, stamping feet, throwing things, breaking or scratching furniture, hitting, throwing one's self on the ground, holding the breath, or banging the head on the wall or floor. In analyzing the inception of such a behavior disorder, one must always keep in mind possible physical predisposing factors, such as itching skin conditions, malnutrition, and insufficient sleep. By far the most cases seem to occur in children in whom there are other behavior problems also. These may include fears, feeding problems, thumb-sucking, nail-biting, night terrors, or any of the gamut of personality disorders. Kanner says, however, that in his experience temper tantrums are rarely if ever found in patients showing hypochondriacal symptoms.

Where there are any physical disorders present, they should obviously be eliminated as the first step in treatment. Much more frequently, however, as Sherbon points out, the difficulty involves the fact that we are dealing with a case where "both parent and child are suffering from 'adrenin intoxication.'" Parents of tempertantrum children are likely to be overprotective, overindulgent, and highly excitable individuals themselves. Rest cures, sedatives, removal from school are never indicated for tantrums *per se*. A survey of the emotional atmosphere in the family regimen is of prime importance. If calmness in meeting the tantrum, coupled with wholesome ignoring of the episode both at the time and afterward, cannot be induced into those responsible for the care of the child, then he may have to be removed from the home. Kanner says, "Display of indifference is a punishment much severer and much more effective than any other disciplinary measure." Only in the case of severe heart involvements is there danger that a child will jeopardize his health in a temper tantrum.

In this connection the breath-holding spells common to infancy and early childhood should be mentioned. Anyone with much experience has seen children hold their breath during crying spells until they became cyanotic or maybe fell unconscious. It has been noted in some of the medical writings that breath-holding frequently has its inception either just before or just after an attack of whooping cough. Breath-holders are also likely to show other evidences of disturbed mental hygiene. Authorities differ as to whether breath-holding *ever* has serious physical outcomes. Holt and McIntosh say:

Although there are instances on record in which such attacks have terminated fatally, respiration not being renewed, the condition is ordinarily a benign one and need occasion no concern. It must be carefully differentiated from tetany, with which it was long confused.

Kanner, on the other hand, says: "The spells involve no danger of any kind. No child has ever died or been injured in a breathholding spell." Holt and McIntosh permit the old-fashioned remedy of dashing cold water in the face of the breath-holder. All authorities agree, however, that the treatment *par excellence* for breathholding or head-banging is the establishment of more stability in the child, the removal of emotional disturbances in the family situation, and, as a rule, wholesome ignoring of the episode.

Perhaps one other word need be said about negativism in young children. We have already referred to the fact of the discrepancy between the little child's expanding environment and his abimlity to manipulate this environment with safety to himself or others. For this reason, extreme aggression and negativism are very common in feeble-minded preschool children. Their somatic development calls for vigorous use of arms and legs, but doors won't open, chairs fall over, blocks won't stay on top of each other, and so it goes. The writer has seen many feeble-minded preschool children who were destructive to the point of being almost manic in their behavior.

The same situation but with a different etiology is to be found in the deaf preschool child who has never heard well enough to learn speech. At around three or four years of age the deaf child, if he has normal intelligence, becomes dimly conscious that there are things going on around him in which he cannot participate. The families of such children often comment on the fact that when the family are around the table the deaf child often becomes extremely aggressive in behavior and may throw his food on the floor and show other signs of conflict. A friend of the writer in charge of a residential school for deaf children often says: "Please come to visit our little children any time at all except the first week of school in September. It's like a madhouse then." After these children have been given some control over their environment through the development of communication and the understanding of the language of other people, one large reason for negativism disappears.

8

The Child's Emotions

LIFELESSNESS OF TEXTBOOK DISCUSSION OF EMOTIONS

There is perhaps no topic in psychology that has accumulated more theory and has effected less change in behavior than *emotions*. The writer has been amazed again and again in conducting advanced classes in psychology to find that many students trained in the orthodox elementary courses do not recognize any *personal* acquaintance with emotions whatsoever. In fact, one is led to wonder whether their courses, their textbooks, and their laboratory assignments have not taken all the *flesh and blood* elements out of emotions. Sometimes these students are not sure whether one is conscious of emotions or not. They are at a loss when asked whether they know they are sad when they are, or whether they have to be told by someone else when they are joyful, or anxious, or angry. Textbooks have given detailed descriptions of facial appearance during violent emotion, and endless discussion has concerned itself with attempts to list and classify emotions. Such discussion of emotion, however, has done little to help individuals with their own emotional problems.

OUR IGNORANCE IN HANDLING CHILDREN'S EMOTIONS

Many teachers, parents, and others trained from the older didactic textbooks may know much of the theoretical and experimental material on emotions and yet go about arousing negative emotions in the children whom they meet. A very popular textbook in child psychology devotes *six and one-half* pages to a discussion of *anger* in children. Of this space, *twelve lines* have to do with prevention, consequences, and treatment! The same author discusses children's fears throughout six and one-half pages, of which only one and one-half pages are concerned with prevention and treatment. Textbooks and laboratory courses have not taught us yet how to rear children so that by the time they reach adult life they can produce and enjoy upbuilding emotions and can eschew negative and debilitating ones. Many adults either still do not know how to avoid embarrassing children or else they deliberately do so. They either do not know how to find out a child's sore spots and step gently thereupon, or else they really enjoy opening the wounds and putting salt on them. A teacher once said to the writer: "I suppose children do bring their own worries to school with them just as we teachers do.

Individual Differences in Emotions

Emerson has said that we boil at different degrees. This is a poetic way of expressing *individual differences* in emotions. It is at this point that we encounter one of the two most important classes of individual differences—*intellectual and emotional* differences. Individual diiferences in height, weight, musical ability, physical endurance, rate of tapping, speed of reading, accuracy in mathematical calculation, or speed of typing are as nothing, in social and psychological significance; compared with individual differences in intelligence and in emotional reactions. The matter of intelligence we shall discuss in another chapter, but individual differences in emotions are pertinent at this point. The range of individual differences in such matters as the stimuli that arouse anger, hate, love, joy, fear, embarrassment, or mirth; the speed with which different individuals react to these stimuli; the extent and kind of reaction we make to them, makes each individual in the world unique from every other individual. These individual differences in emotionality constitute a large part of what we call *personality*.

It is because of these individual differences that human behavior appears to be unpredictable and to follow no laws such as seem to operate in the physical world. It is also for this reason that the answers given by psychologists and others in the social sciences must at times seem vague and uncertain. "If I just pay no attention to Johnny when he sulks, will he come out of it sooner?" is a perfectly justifiable question and one that a psychologist might possibly be expected to answer. In reality, however, the psychologist would say in answer, "I cannot tell you without knowing why Johnny is sulking, with whom he sulks, how long this behavior has been going on, what methods have already been tried and with what results." In other words, one sulking child with a certain set of emotional patterns, physical constitution, and life experiences would react to the *neglect treatment* quite satisfactorily and be helped by it.

Another child of different temperament and outlook would retreat more within himself and feel more and more rejected under the same treatment. For this reason, prescriptions and panaceas for human behavior are neither possible nor wise. Emotional differences are very evident from one child to another, even within one family. For example, Blatz and his associates studied the social development of the Dionne quintuplets from the twelfth to the thirtysixth month. They say: ". . . these five children already manifest quantitative and qualitative social and personality differences of a more or less stable nature." The data include the number of social contacts directed *towards* each child by each of the other four; the number of contacts *initiated* by each child; the number of *responses* made by each child to every other child; the number of times each child *watched* each of the other four; and so on. The analysis of these and other data leads the authors to say:

Thus, it is Annette's high frequency of initiated to contacts that undoubtedly attracts to herself the watching attention of the other four, which in turn must stimulate Annette to further aggressive social behavior in order to satisfy the developed need for an audience. . . . Annette and Marie have *fewer* contacts directed towards them than they direct towards others. Cecile and Yvonne have *more* directed towards them than they direct towards others, and Emilie is in the centre position. . . . Annette provides the most initiated to contacts and Marie the least. What beautiful examples of individual differences in early childhood! With both heredity and environment so nearly identical for the five children, what a puzzle for the geneticists and environmentalists to solve!

Autonomic Nervous System

We might at greater length discuss other of the technical and academic matters relative to emotions and emotional life. Our present purpose will best be served, however, if we omit hairsplitting distinctions. We shall attempt to get more nearly into the life of the child by arbitrarily saying that we shall include in our discussion of emotions all such words as excitement, distress, joy, delight, fear, anger, jealousy, aggression, hostility, affection, disgust, shame, guilt, elation, anxiety, apprehension, inferiority, and thrill.

We must be familiar with some matters of research, however, if we are to understand the child's emotions. One of these is the role of the nervous system in emotional life and the effect of emotions upon bodily health. For a more thorough understanding of these matters, the reader is referred to Cannon's classical study. In addition to the *central nervous system* (spinal cord, brain and its appendages) and the peripheral nervous system (afferent nerves leading to the central nervous system and efferent nerves leading from the central nervous system out to the muscles and glands), there is the *autonomic nervous system*. The latter is an efferent system of nerves, ganglia, and plexus which innervates the smooth muscles of the internal organs and the glands of the body. As its name indicates, it is (largely) independent of the central nervous system.

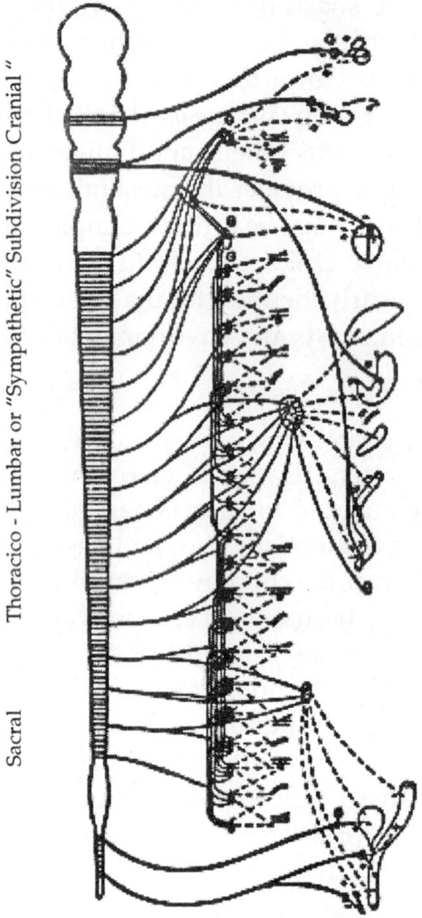

__FIG.__—Diagram of the more important distributions of the autonomic nervous system. The preganglionic fibers are in solid lines; the postganglionic in dash-lines. The nerves of the cranial and sacral divisions are distinguished from those of the thoracico-lumbar or "sympathetic" division by broader lines. A + mark indicates an augmenting effect on the activity of the organ; a - mark, a depressive or inhibitory effect.

Since the autonomic system has so much to do with emotions, we must consider its three parts somewhat more in detail. The uppermost division is called the *cranial* division. It lies near the head and the upper part of the spinal cord. Its fibers reach out to the tear glands, pupils of the eyes, artery of the salivary gland, hair follicles, sweat glands, and visceral organs, including heart, stomach, and intestines. The lower division is called the *sacral* division because it emerges from the spinal cord in the region of the sacrum. Its fibers innervate the colon, bladder, rectum, and the artery of the external genitalia. It can be seen that by one or the other of these two divisions, the cranial or sacral, practically all the internal organs are reached, the cranial innervating those in the head and the upper parts of the trunk, and the sacral, those of the lower trunk. While the body is doing its ordinary work-a-day activities, each of these divisions is sending out impulses to its respective field.

During mild emotional states, such as joy, pleasure, contentment, elation, or satisfaction, the cranial and sacral divisions are also busily at work regulating normal heart action, respiration, salivation, digestion, and the like. Incidentally, it will be noted that the description of this activity sounds like a fairly adequate description of "good health" and a possible prescription for "long life." For these reasons, some have proposed that all the aforementioned upbuilding emotions be called *positive emotions*.

The middle division of the autonomic nervous system behaves quite differently. It is a very wide-spreading set of nerve fibers and ganglia leaving, and lying adjacent to, the thoracicolumbar region of the spinal cord. It is therefore known as the *thoracicolumbar division* of the autonomic nervous system, and also as the *sympathetic division*. Its numerous fibers extend to all the organs which (as we have already said) are also activated by either the cranial or the sacral division. The circumstances in which the thoracicolumbar division acts, however, are very different.

Suppose, for example, that an individual were sitting at a flower-decked table chatting pleasantly with his family and enjoying good food and kindly social relationships. One need not be versed in psychology to envisage what takes place in the salivary glands, heart, lungs, and stomach under these circumstances. Suppose an emergency, such as a fire or an acute illness of one of the family group, arises. Roughly speaking, the cranial and sacral divisions slip out of gear. At least, for the most part, their control over the internal organs stops, and the work is largely taken over by the thoracicolumbar division. The effect of this interchange is to get the body ready for the "emergency." Speed, endurance, strength, and brute force are needed now. In consequence, the flow of saliva and the digestion of food may stop. The heart and lungs, on the other hand, increase their activity.

Cannon has further contended that the adrenal gland is stimulated into activity by the thoracicolumbar division (and only under these conditions of strong emotion) and then releases its store of adrenalin into the blood stream; this in turn, he says, causes the liver to pour out its store of glycogen or blood sugar. The blood sugar makes possible rapid combustion of food for muscle activity. Thus, the whole picture has changed from one of mild activity to one of great activity. All this expenditure of energy is brought about, of course, at the expense of great strain on muscles and vital organs. Furthermore, since there is such great catabolism going on, there is more strain thrown upon the organs of excretion. Cannon therefore speaks of the "emergency theory of emotions," meaning thereby that strong emotions and the thoracicolumbar division of the autonomic nervous system prepare the body for the strains and stresses that emergencies thrust upon us. It is easy to see why the effects of the emotion do not immediately disappear when the emergency has been faced and handled, for even the chemical composition of the blood is changed during violent emotion. The effects upon heart, stomach, and other organs may be felt for hours afterward. The picture of the activity of the sympathetic division is one of debilitation; hence some have called the emotions that accompany the emergencies of fear, panic, anger, hate, and the like, *negative emotions*.

The role of adrenalin (or epinephrine) in emotions or in pain has been challenged by Rogoff. He does not question the role of the sympathetic nervous system, but he claims that the results attributed by Cannon to adrenalin have been found "in animals that have been deprived of their adrenals or whose epinephrine secretion has been suppressed." Furthermore, Rogoff says that epinephrine is released from the adrenals under ordinary conditions constantly, and not just under emotional reactions, and that the conditions which under the "emergency theory" increase this flow "do not detectably modify this rate of secretion." Rogoff goes on to say that the autogenous continuance of adrenal secretion, which, according to Cannon, accounts for the persistence of the emotional state, cannot be demonstrated, but that, on the contrary, evidence has been obtained indicating that there is no such autogenous continuance.

The role of the nervous system in emotional life has not been challenged. The hypothalamus, which is a part of the interbrain, is now known to be the brain center for the autonomic system, although the cortex plays a part also, as witness the fact that *thinking about* an emotional stimulus may make one become emotionalized. Although this account of the activities of the autonomic nervous system is only a shorthand description, so to speak, it nevertheless shows us that a child who is allowed to grow up having constant fits of anger and rage, or suffering debilitating fears all the time, will have his thoracicolumbar system "in gear" far too frequently. Such a child will suffer not only from the standpoint of social acceptance and mental hygiene, but also from the standpoint of physical health.

Conditioning of Emotions

In connection with a study of emotions, mention must be made of the process of conditioning. It will be recalled that Pavlov was able to cause the dog's mouth to water by ringing a bell (after the bell had previously been rung in connection with the presentation of food). Such connections or conditionings also take place in the human being.

Many of the likes and dislikes that children display, and even their fears, are built up in much the same way. The child under wholesome home conditions comes to associate fondness not only with the members of his family, but with their appearance and their behavior. For just such reasons, most of us still like food prepared in the way we learned to like it in our own homes as children. On the other hand, suppose a child is frightened by a stranger who happens to be carrying a black satchel. If the fright has been sufficiently intense, he may, for some time thereafter, be afraid not only of all strangers but of all black bags and satchels. Some children who have experienced pain or fright in an office after having ridden on an elevator come to fear all elevators. Similarly, a child may connect emotions with words. Many times in clinical practice, the writer has met parents who apologize for omitting the title "Doctor" in address. They often say, "My child has been frightened by doctors so often that I thought it was best in bringing him to you just to speak of going to see *Miss*. . ." Incidentally, modern pediatricians and children's dentists make it a serious part of their professional technique to avoid, insofar as possible, the building up of fears on the part of their patients.

The fact that one builds up new connections in his nervous system by *conditioning* (it now appears that the Russian word might better have been translated originally as "connecting") or by *connecting* either new stimuli to old responses or new responses to old stimuli is very apparent. Two points, however, must be mentioned in this connection. In the first place, there is ample experimental evidence that all human learning cannot be explained by, conditioning, and that there are gaps and discrepancies between animal conditioning and human conditioning at certain points. In the second place, from the practical point of view as regards emotions, a caution must be introduced. One often reads case histories of individuals whose whole emotional life was colored, or conditioned, by one strong emotional experience. The existence of such cases cannot be denied. However, it must be remembered that human personality *normally* has a kind of integrity that gives it a great amount of resistance. The normal child is perhaps not likely to be thrown into a lifetime phobia of dogs through one frightening experience with a dog. By the same token, a child, as a rule, does not become afraid of a parent who punishes him severely once. Whenever we see a child with abnormal fears or other emotions, it is probably because of *multiple causation*. For example, the child who is not loved is likely to be more fearful and therefore to respond more violently to a fear stimulus. The child who is hungry becomes the more easily angry. The child who is tired is more emotional generally. The extreme life-long emotional behavior found in an individual who had one "conditioning experience" is probably an evidence of a nervous system that was highly unstable and overreactive to begin with.

Psychogalvanic Reflex

A challenging laboratory study of emotions has to do with the *galvanic skin reflex*. This reflex, or perhaps more correctly "response," is the resistance of the skin under varying kinds of stimulation. It is recorded and measured by electric currents. The electric response of the skin is an indication of the activity of internal organs or viscera. Jones has experimented with the galvanic skin reflexes of infants. He was interested in determining thus the relationship between the infant's outward behavior (crying, for example) and his internal or visceral behavior during emotion. Interestingly enough; Jones found that, in general, there was an inverse relation between the amount of visceral reaction and the amount of outward activity. This would seem to mean that the more the infant cried, the less disturbance went on in his visceral organs, and, conversely, that the more crying was repressed, the greater was the visceral activity.

This is a finding of such significance that it is curious that more research has not been done in the field. Light might thus be thrown on the age-old question as to whether giving expression to our emotions increases or decreases them. Just when and to what extent should we attempt to stop crying in children? How and when should we try to prevent fighting in anger? Should we encourage children not to "cry it out" or "fight it out" or even, for that matter, "swear it out"? G. Stanley Hall used to say that undoubtedly swearing had saved many a man's soul, meaning thereby that swearing was probably less dangerous or offensive than some of the things man might do (or think) if he were obliged to restrain all unsocial behavior.

The question is of extreme importance. On the one hand, we know that "crying it out," if encouraged, may become a habit and may become stronger through repetition. Indeed, crying, hysterical personalities are no doubt produced, or at least fostered, by just such programs. On the other hand, how about those individuals in whom feelings have been bottled up for a considerable time with no outward expression? Matters get worse as their feelings become cumulative. Giving vent to the feelings in such cases does seem to clear the atmosphere and to diminish the feeling and emotion. Suppose a child is frightened on a dark night. Does he become more or less frightened by running? The reader who had the good fortune to see a war film called Journey for Margaret (based upon actual records of English children removed from their homes and evacuated to rural districts for protection against air raids) will remember the peculiar behavior of the child who thought she must not cry. When she was given assurance that it would be all right to cry, and to cry as hard as she wished, her behavior began to be much more normal. Some psychiatrists responsible for the care of psychoneurotic soldiers are now raising the question as to whether the early training of these soldiers may have stressed too severely the inhibition of emotion and the desirability of "acting like a little man."

The question as to what happens to our emotions when we give expression to them is complicated in the extreme. There is one school of thought which believes that problem children should be allowed to express their emotions in order to get rid of them. This is much like the old theory of *catharsis*. The child, for example, who feels aggression or hostility must, according to this belief, be allowed to "work out" his aggression, thereby getting rid of it. Much current psychotherapy works along these lines. The child who wants to break windows or destroy furniture is allowed to do so without restraint and without being made to feel guilty. This technique has had beneficial results with many children.

Now the question arises as to *why* such handling of children has therapeutic values, when it does, and whether it always would. There seems to be no scientific justification for believing that aggression or hostility or any other emotion exists as an entity having measurable amounts; nor can we scientifically believe that the expression of such emotions drains off or uses up any of such amount, thereby leaving less to trouble the individual later. In the second place, we cannot overlook one of the accepted laws of learning, to the effect that one of the factors by which a reaction is strengthened is by making the reaction; the oftener, the stronger.

What reason is there, therefore, for thinking that the child will stop doing the thing he is allowed to do? This policy would seem to run counter to all that we know about learning and habit formation. The answer probably lies, not in "getting rid of" the feelings, but rather in what satisfaction (or annoyance) the child gets out of the activity. If hitting or breaking or striking gets him attention, victory, feelings of superiority, or the like, he will in all probability continue the performance and *strengthen* the aggressive habit instead of getting rid of it. If, on the other hand, his undesirable behavior attracts no attention, brings him no prestige, does not get him into the limelight, or brings him a feeling of futility or pain, he will in all probability desist—not because he has gotten rid of his hostility, but because he decides that such behavior gets him nothing. This is called in psychological language "the law of effect," in other words, behavior that brings one satisfaction is likely to be repeated, and behavior that has either no results or annoying results will not be repeated.

It would appear that there is no one answer to the question as to whether giving expression to the emotions increases or decreases their intensity at the moment. The answer is probably "yes" under some circumstances and "no" under others. Perhaps the following criteria may help in formulating an answer. Let us look first at those cases where it appears that giving expression to the emotion diminishes the emotion at that time. Every social worker and counselor has had clients come for consultation so overcome with grief that choking back a betrayal of emotion was very difficult. It may have been so difficult that the sufferer's whole *attention* had to be devoted to speaking at only those times when he could trust his voice. Sometimes under such circumstances, we may have suggested that perhaps it would be easier for the client if he were to make no effort to control his feelings for a while since it "must be very difficult to talk without crying." Such reassurance that his behavior is not considered childish may release the flood gates. Thereafter, the client's attention is given freely to the interview and is not distracted by trying to choke back tears. In all such cases, where giving vent to expression thereby *releases the attention to the problem* rather than confining it to the voice, the mouth, or the eyes, certainly composure is more quickly reached and the emotion itself is more quickly dissipated. Perhaps there are other emotional episodes where giving expression to the feelings. provides a new point of attack, facilitates solution of the problem, and eventually lessens the emotion. When this is true, there is certainly no harm in giving expression to the emotions.

Let us look at the converse of the picture. There are probably circumstances in which giving overt expression to the emotion may be bad for social or psychological reasons, regardless of whether it increases or decreases the amount of the emotion itself. The blind fury with which some children fight when angry may illustrate the point. The exchange of blows may not even bring a solution to the problem that originally set off the anger. Nothing happens except that blows are exchanged and hurts are inflicted. The attention is not confined to restraint, as in the previous example, but is rather diffused and concentrated on nothing, perhaps not even on the skill required to end the fight. Usually in such cases the emotion is strengthened. The behavior is blind, and the results may be also. Psychologically, then, the emotion may be intensified. From the social point of view, one always wants to raise the question as to whether giving expression to the stronger and particularly the negative emotions may not interfere with the formation of higher and more socially acceptable habits of response. If a child were always allowed to fight when angry, he would certainly be delayed in learning the techniques of argument, debate, and finally of consultation and conference.

To avoid misunderstanding at this point, let us notice that growth in matters of emotional control in no wise means the *suppression* of all emotion. The kind of emotional control that makes for ultimate mental hygiene necessitates *expression* as well as *suppression*. In the matter of laughter, for example, we desire, not that children refrain from laughing, but that they laugh about the right situations at appropriate times. Likewise, many a child would have developed into a more emotionally balanced adult if he had been encouraged to express affection. Education is not complete until a child is taught both to acknowledge his mistakes and to express his gratitude. Joy, thankfulness, love, and humor should be stimulated through appropriate expression.

CHILDREN'S WISHES

In connection with the situations that put emotional coloring into the lives of children, consideration should be given to an investigation by Jersild, Markey, and Jersild. Four hundred children, including 25 boys and 25 girls at each age level from 5 through 12 years, were interviewed. One of the questions asked of the children was: "If you had a wish and your wish could come true, what would you wish?""If you had another wish?""If you had another wish?" Almost fifty per cent of the replies indicated a wish for some specific material object or possession. This type of wish was more common among younger children, among boys, and among less intelligent children. Interestingly enough, the wishes for specific material objects and possessions occurred almost twice as frequently among the children from public schools as among the children from private schools.

Do we sufficiently realize how great may be the desire for some particular object, especially among poorer children whose possessions are not too numerous anyway? It would appear that herein lies a factor of great importance in explaining the behavior of some children. The appeal of some material object—a ring maybe, a bicycle, or a knife —may furnish such a driving impulse that theft results. Most adults can remember, no doubt, a youthful desire for some coveted possession, so strong as to interfere with sleep. Some of us can remember carrying a treasured object to bed with us and putting it under our pillow. It was so precious we wanted it with us all the time. Perhaps, if we had been among the younger or among the less intelligent, our desire, if ungratified, might have led *us* into delinquency. A good deal of our virtue may not have required much moral fiber. It may be accounted for perhaps by the fact that our parents appreciated our longings and attempted to satisfy them whenever possible. In the group of children referred to, the other wishes (something over fifty per cent) were distributed among wishes having to do with family relationships (have a baby, have a sibling, retain parents, be married, have friends, make visits, and so forth), personal self-aggrandizement, general benefits for society, amusements, and specific benefits for parents.

The trends shown by the answer to Jersild, Markey, and Jersild's question "What would you do if you had a million dollars?" are much the same as those just enumerated. It should be noted, however, that by far the most common answer to this question was "bank it," "spend it," or "keep it"—seeming to show no particular plan for the immediate spending of the money. A large percentage of the children also indicated that they would use their million dollars for a charity or benevolence of some kind. In conversation later, however, the hypothetical amount was reduced to 25 cents; then ". . . . it did not seem to occur to children who had made eloquent provisions for the poor when possessed of a mythical million dollars that they might begin work on a small scale with a small sum." Although asking a child about what he wishes for is not a particularly subtle technique, nevertheless it does sometimes reveal desires of great intensity about which we should know if we are trying to help the child. Pressey and Robinson tell of an adolescent Negro girl who expressed as her strongest wishes a "gold front tooth and a sweater."

Children's Fears

Fear is such a paralyzing experience that it seems strange we know so little about methods of preventing it. The life of most readers of this book is beset at some point or other by fears that produce discomfort, inefficiency, and perhaps at times even illogical behavior. Many intelligent adults do not realize the devastating effects that fear produces in their own lives. This is largely true perhaps because they do not understand that many, if not most, of our fears are not fears of objects but fears of social situations, of human relationships, and of our own weaknesses, real or imagined.

A few years ago, in a graduate class in psychology, the writer asked each student to think of some prominent person whom he greatly admired—the President, a great scientist, a writer, or an actor, for example. The students were then asked to tell what they would do and how they would feel if they were told that on the same day they were to be given an opportunity to meet and visit with the celebrity. Various emotions were registered on the faces of the students at this request. The first one called upon looked somewhat embarrassed and finally said falteringly: "Oh, I think I should actually run away. Of course, I never could talk to *him*! I should be so frightened I would not have a thing to say—not even about the weather." The second student called upon said: "I should *enjoy* such an opportunity immensely. There are so many things that I would like to ask him and talk with him about." The remainder of this group of adults divided about equally on these two positions: about half were eager and willing to meet another human being in spite of his prominence; the other half were *afraid* to do so. If we nclude such social fears as these, the list of things of which human beings—adults and children—are *afraid* would be much longer than any such list that has ever been published. If by study we can learn anything about how to prevent such paralyzing experiences as the one just cited, a consideration of the fears of children is certainly appropriate.

In passing, it must be noted, however, that a *little* fear is not an altogether unpleasant experience for a child. In small enough amounts, fear is an essential element of "thrill" and affords a part of the enjoyment of climbing, walking on stilts, swinging, riding on a roller coaster, watching wild west pictures, or reading mystery stories. Beyond that critical point, however, fear becomes paralyzing in its effects.

In the work of Jersild just referred to, the same children were asked about the things of which they were afraid. The outstanding feature of the results was the "apparently irrational character of children's fears." More than one-fifth of the first-named fears of these five-through-twelve-year-old children were fears of the occult, the supernatural, mystery, skeletons, corpses, and death. When checked against the children's own reports of "the worst thing that ever happened to you," no connection was found between things the children feared and the things they had real occasion to fear. Fears of animals and of the dark also loomed large in the children's reports of their fears.

These verbalized fears of children are certainly important. On the other hand, equally important, if not more so, are the fears that children carry around but are either unwilling or unable to verbalize. The fear of punishment, of the death of parents, of being different from other people, of being inferior to other children in sports or in school, the fears induced by competition, or even the fear of blushing, may be devastating to a child without any adult's ever really knowing that the child is having the experience. Many an interesting tale can be told of such individual fears that dominated the life of an individual child but that never came to light until years later. A child known to the writer grew up under fairly comfortable economic circumstances. However, at about age eight, she heard the expression "sold out by the sheriff" applied to friends of the family. When she asked the meaning of the words, it was explained to her. From that moment, for a period of several years, she never heard "hard times" or "difficulty of collecting bills" discussed without imagining that her own family was in imminent danger of being "sold out by the sheriff." She would actually hurry home from school to see whether the household goods might be sitting on—the curbstone ready to be carted away. Now, her parents could have given the child a reasonable degree of assurance that such a calamity was not likely to overtake the family *had they known* that she was harboring such a fear. She, however, supposing that the parents were as fearful as she was about the family's economic security, thought there was no use worrying everyone by talking about it. It is difficult to imagine the variety of ways in which this child's conduct was modified during this time by the pall that was hanging over her. It is likewise impossible to know the extent to which her ideas of money and of economic security may have been more or less permanently influenced. It hurts to picture the agony through which many children have lived in recent times where the danger of being evicted was not only a possibility but an actuality!

How much more intelligently we could help a child with difficulties of school adjustment if we knew that the reason the child was not getting along was that he was *afraid* of some of the speed drills so common nowadays in number work and reading. Much has been written on the value of competition as a spur to effort. Only half of that story is usually told, however. A large number of children, far from being motivated to greater productivity by competition, are on the contrary thereby made to shrink up within themselves and to lose what skills they do possess. How often a child in school may fail to give the answer that he really does know because he is *afraid* that it will be wrong, or that he will blush while he is reciting, or that someone will laugh at him! Failure and a black mark are infinitely to be preferred to such agony!

So much of children's conduct would be explicable if we were only more adroit in reading their minds (which, by the way, they are likely to think we *can* do). A small girl in a minor illness one time annoyed everyone who was attempting to care for her by her constant activity in bed. She would not lie still; she kept moving her feet continually. Her behavior was so exaggerated that no one knew what to do about the situation. Finally, it became known that at one time the child had asked an aunt how one knows when a person is really dead. Facetiously the aunt had replied, "Oh, when they stop wiggling." The child, being literal-minded, as children are likely to be, had concluded then that the way to keep from dying was to make sure that she continued "to wiggle," and this she faithfully tried to do!

Fear is instilled into children probably more often than we realize by their religious training. Of course, this danger depends greatly upon the type of religious training that the child receives. Certainly the thought of a personal devil, a hell in which one may burn for sins that he *unwittingly* has committed, a God who has an all-seeing eye particularly intent on seeing misdeeds, or the likelihood of sudden death without repentance, may be very terrifying to a child.

There is very little in the literature on children's ideas of death. The fear of death, unlike some fears, is not one that can be prevented by our preventing a child's contact with it. Sooner or later, a child meets death situations, whether it be the death of a pet, a grandparent, a playmate, or a member of his immediate family. Perhaps we can spare the child the experience of seeing highly emotionalized adults at funerals, or of witnessing interments at a cemetery, or of looking upon dead bodies that are prepared for burial. However, we cannot protect a child from the fact of death. For that reason, the death of a bird or an animal along the roadside may be an easy approach to a subject that must inevitably arise. One of the difficulties that parents experience in helping children to meet death situations is that the parents do not know what they themselves really believe about death and the hereafter. One hesitates to reassure a child on these matters, if he does not feel confident himself. Many parents, however, do not hesitate, regardless of their other beliefs, to assure a child that the deceased person is not suffering and will not suffer. We can also stress the undyingness of memories and of influence. The once rather common fear among children of being buried alive can, with reasonable assurance, be dismissed nowadays by a slight reference to improved medical attention and, if necessary, a reference to improved embalming methods.

Some parents ask for help on the question of their children's fear of kidnaping. Unfortunately, this fear is not so groundless as some children's fears. It is rather in a class with the fear of being run over or the fear of becoming ill. For all such possibilities, we must try as best we can to help the child to develop intelligent *caution* without the terrors of fear. In regard to kidnaping, for example, there are certain simple precautions in which we can unemotionally instruct our children-never to go along with a stranger without the knowledge of parents; never to accept gifts from strangers; always to be able to give one's own name, address, and telephone number; always to ask for information or help from policemen or uniformed officials. All of this must be done with a minimum of emotion, however, and with a care lest we develop fear of all strangers and a loss of confidence in human beings generally.

In an earlier chapter we spoke of the theory of the "birth trauma." Physical damage, of course, often results from prolonged or difficult delivery. Some psychiatrists feel that there is also *psychic* birth trauma that occurs in some infants. The question seems to be: "Do individuals suffer emotionally later because of the vicissitudes of birth?" In addition to the discussion of previous pages, we might add here one bit of experimental data on this point. In Holmes' study of the fears of young children, a comparison was made of the fears of preschool children who had had difficult births and those of children who were not reported to have had difficult births. So far as susceptibility to fear was concerned, no difference was found between the two groups. Evidence of disturbed emotionality produced by *psychic* birth trauma seems to be lacking.

All who have had wide experience with children have encountered some children who, in spite of our best efforts, go from one fear to another. A case comes to mind of a child seen by the writer a few years ago. The mother reported a sequence of fears that had terrorized the child almost to the point of panic and mania. First he had been afraid of bells and would cover his ears, hide, or even run away from home when nearby church bells or school bells rang. After a time, without anyone's knowing how or why, this fear passed away. It was succeeded by a fear of becoming bald. Where this fear originated the mother was unable to tell. It so gripped the child that he would painfully and tearfully ask his mother if he would "*ever go* bald." After reasoned explanations and attempts at unemotional handling, the mother felt herself driven finally to assure the child that he would *never become bald*. One can imagine the feelings of an intelligent mother who felt herself being forced into giving such an unwarranted assurance.

This fear also passed away, only to be succeeded by a fear of appendicitis. The origin of this fear was obvious enough, since the father had been taken ill in the night and had been removed to the hospital for an operation. The extent and depth of the fear, however, was so all-absorbing as to be pathological in the extreme. In all probability, most of this child's fears did not so much represent fear of the avowed cause as they did a generally unstable nervous and emotional condition within the child. Evidence of this is that some of the child's delights were just as abnormal in intensity and scope as his fears. At one time, for example, he became interested in streets and street names. Not only did he talk about streets and street names to the point of annoying those around him, but he also inflicted great physical strain and hardship upon himself by walking miles without food through remote and unknown parts of the city, looking for new street names. What essential insecurity prompts his manias, no amount of examination has as yet revealed. The point is that, although in such cases we should, of course, strive to remove fears as they arise, we must not be surprised if our task has to be repeated for a continuous succession of fears. Although we are studying the child to discover the source of his essential lack of emotional security, we should in the meantime strive to give him as much emotional security in his home relationships and in his own evaluation of himself and his abilities as we can.

We shall pass with a word the question of *phobias*. They are relatively uncommon in childhood. A phobia is an exaggerated and unusually pathological fear and dread of some specific object or situation, such as animals, high places, enclosed places, and so forth. An ordinary and decreasing fear of animals is not, of course, a phobia. When, however, the fear of dogs is so intense that one's life activities have to be planned so as to avoid all contacts with dogs, and when an encounter with a dog produces nervousness almost to the point of illness, we are justified in speaking of a phobia. The origin of the phobia is usually obscure, and the sufferer will probably require psychiatric treatment if he is to be helped.

We shall now discuss the prevention and cure of fears in children. Much more on the side of prevention *can* be done than usually is done. Many parents do not understand that the logic of a child's fear and the reality of it are two different things. The fear may be groundless from an adult point of view, but remain a devastating reality to the child, nevertheless. Laughing at a child's fear would be helpful only to the occasional child with a stoicism that may ultimately be more of a detriment than an asset. Most children get over fears more quickly and develop a more wholesome attitude toward life if their fears are given considerate recognition by adults. Since *suddenness* and *unexpectedness* seem to be potent fear-producing situations, a little cleverness on the part of adults will help much in preparing a child for the unusual. Sometimes a preliminary explanation or a little preliminary practice, together with a word of reassurance, will go far toward preventing the building up of a fear in the first place. Imitation of the behavior of a reasonably assured and composed adult in whom the child has confidence is also a powerful help in establishing poise in the child. In general, it may be said that if we can build up in a child good health, increasing skills, emotional security, free access to a parent or parent substitute with whom he can talk and in whom he feels confidence, we have done the major part of the task of preventing disabling fears. There may still arise an occasional fear in such a child, but, after all, a child who is safeguarded in this way can come through an occasional fear without suffering too greatly thereby. Furthermore, as soon as a child learns that it is possible to receive help in handling his fears, he has a powerful weapon of self-protection. Such a child has less occasion to fear *fear*. He can look back upon previous fears as "water gone under the bridge," so to speak. The unfortunate child, however, whose fears have been ridiculed or who may even have been punished for his fears, meets each new fear-provoking situation beaten before he starts.

So much for prevention. Suppose, however, prevention has been neglected, as is the case with so many children with whom social workers and psychologists have to deal. Suppose the fear is already there. We shall speak a little later of devices for finding hidden or unverbalized fears. But how about the fears that are evident? The question is sometimes raised as to whether we should allow a child to talk about a fear or a fearful experience. The answer to that question is certainly an affirmative to the point that the child learns he *can* discuss his troubles with an understanding adult; to the point that he feels he has a resource to which he can turn when he needs help; and to the point that by allowing him to talk we may, at certain places, be able to introduce a little explanation that may correct misunderstandings on his part. Let him talk about it? Not to the point that he loves to talk about it in order to appear different from other people, or in order to secure attention.

A willingness to *admit* a fear is a good way of making it one's *own* problem with which one must deal mostly himself. Children become rather adept sometimes in devising methods of helping themselves overcome their fears. A child, for example, once said to his mother, "I believe if I could have a cord on my electric light so I could lie in bed and turn on the light myself for just a minute when I get scared, it would help me get over this silliness."

In the case of both social and physical fears, we shall be of aid to the child if we can help him develop specific skills in the fields of his weakness. A mother helped her adolescent son who became increasingly fearful as the day for his first dance approached. Many an adult can personalize this agony! What did they talk about at dances? What did they do after each dance was over, and so on, and so on? (One can picture the mother-son relationship when the boy was able to ask these questions of his mother.) The mother realized that the attitudes and enjoyments or fears resulting from this first big social affair would go far toward determining the boy's social skills and social adjustments for the rest of his life. She realized that she must help him develop his own skills. She also realized that self-consciousness must not be allowed to wreck the scene. She suggested to him that the thing for him to do was to keep on his mind all the time during the eventful evening whether *Margaret* was comfortable and whether *Margaret* was having a good time. Now, obviously, this is not a specific that would work with all boys, or that all boys would need. It worked in this case, however, for the mother knew her boy, knew his feelings toward Margaret, and understood all the other subtleties that would enter into the situation. The point is that the boy went to the dance fairly confident that he knew what to do, with something to think about other than himself, and bounding youth took care of the rest.

A little help in developing physical skills in skating or dancing or playing games will help to make physical fears disappear. A little help in building up skill at some of the hard points on long division, or fractions, or reading will be of inestimable value in preventing academic fears. Fortunately, particularly with younger children, nature helps too, inasmuch as some fears seem to disappear more or less of themselves, especially as the child learns more skills in various fields.

In addition, we must not lose sight of the fact that learning in the field of emotions and emotional control conforms to the same laws of learning that apply to arithmetic or spelling. Fears tend at least to fade, if not to disappear entirely, through *disuse* just as the multiplication tables get weak if the child does not practice them. There is much to be said, therefore, for not exposing a child to dogs while he is in an acute stage of fear of dogs. *Knowledge of one's own success*, we are told in the psychology of school subjects, is a great incentive to learning, and it is probably no more true in any field than in the field of learning emotional control. If the child is helped a little at first in meeting his fear situations, he can take courage from his success and will feel motivated to go on trying.

Negative adaptation, or becoming *used* to a situation, may be used in building up emotional control, but *with care*. For one thing, there is no point in trying to build up negative adaptation to *all* fear-producing situations. We are not interested in getting a child negatively adapted to being teased about freckles by a thoughtless adult, for example. We should rather *prevent* such situations. However, those situations which are inevitable, such as thunderstorms, must be rid of their terror for the child if he is going to live comfortably. They must be accepted and must be gotten used to. Negative adaptation, of course, requires repetition of the situation. It can perhaps be tried with safety in cases where the fear is not too intense, where each repetition clearly demonstrates the uselessness of the fear, and where each repetition can be accompanied by more reassurance and security (the law of effect). To attempt negative adaptation by throwing a child already fearful of the water into the water is certainly not to be countenanced. Neither would it be wise to force a child who is afraid of the dark to go into the cellar alone. These methods would fail to bring about negative adaptation. They would, instead, intensify the fear, and at the same time would break the thread of reassuring contact with the adult who ought to appear in the role of helper.

Just a word may be said about breaking down fears through a process of conditioning—better *reconditioning*—after the fear has already been conditioned into the child. If the fear-producing situation can be changed in such a way that the child associates it with *satisfaction rather than with fear*, we have accomplished a desirable reconditioning. One mother changed fear of lightning into enjoyment for her small son. When a storm came, the mother would take the boy on her lap. (This in itself made *all* things seem more nearly right.) Then she encouraged her son to count aloud with her to see how far they could count between a peal of thunder and a flash of lightning. It is difficult to ascribe proper amounts of the therapeutic value of this procedure to the composure of the mother, to her willingness to help the child, to her presence, to his having something to do (counting), to his observation that nothing much really happened because of the lightning, to increasing maturity, or to a number of other possible contributing factors.

Another mother helped her daughter overcome a fear of the dark by a process of conditioning. The child would complain of the dark after being put to bed. The mother said: "Yes, I know it is dark and black. I like it though. The dark is *soft*. It is like black velvet." She then brought out her black velvet evening dress which the child always loved to see her wear. Together they would sit for a few minutes in the dark while the child ran her fingers over the soft black dress. A few such reassuring experiences entirely changed the little girl's feeling about the dark.

ANGER IN CHILDREN

We shall not discuss at length the question of anger in children. Reference should be made to Florence Goodenough's study for a detailed account of anger. In passing, however, we should note that, although all anger is not necessarily evil, *too much* of it has a depleting effect upon the individual physically, and an ostracizing effect upon him socially. The fine point would seem to be to learn the things about which we should feel angry and to learn constructive ways of using anger. Individual differences in the ease of arousal and intensity of anger are very great. The writer remembers her own surprise when she discovered that "seeing red" was not a figure of speech but was, for some persons, an actuality. If we do not experience the sensation ourselves, it is difficult for us to understand it in others.

As was emphasized in the discussion of fear, the strongest bulwarks in handling anger also are good health, emotional security and reassurance, prevention, and self skills. The angry child is a struggling child, a child struggling with a problem. There is something he cannot do or something in which he is being thwarted. A child who characteristically is angry and petulant is either a sick child or a child who is being constantly hampered, interfered with, or thwarted.

With little children, the hampering often arises out of their own physical ineptitudes. In this connection it is interesting to notice that the quarrels of children in anger during the first four or five years of life are almost entirely physical and non-verbal in nature. A child has matured considerably when he begins to quarrel by the use of language rather than by the use of legs, arms, or teeth. Adults can help by discovering what a child's particular "sore spots" are, and by protecting these from injury so far as possible. Most of us are thoughtless about embarrassing children by dragging out the skeleton from the child's emotional closet. "My, how you are growing!" may seem harmless to us, but may be so hurtful to the child with the long arms and legs that he could happily slay the thoughtless person who has so little regard for his feelings.

Anxiety, Guilt, and Jealousy

Anxiety, conflict, and *guilt* are negative emotions that not only make a child uncomfortable but also hinder his building up selfconfidence in meeting the world. They are somewhat hard to classify and seem to partake largely of some of the other emotions we have discussed. *Jealousy* likewise is devastating in the extreme. It is possibly a combination of fear, anger, and a feeling of incompetence. The jealous child is likely to be emotional in many other respects also. Much of what has been said about prevention and treatment of other emotions applies here with equal force. Jealousy has so many devious and indirect ways of manifesting itself that it is not always recognized for what it really is.

Anxiety has much resemblance to fear, but it is not likely to be attached to particular objects or situations, as is fear. Nothing perhaps is more debilitating to an individual's well being than feelings of anxiety. The specific handling of anxieties is too involved to consider here, except to say that, in general, the best antidote is the development of feelings of security in affectional relations, of skills, and of feelings of self-confidence.

Guilt is a negative feeling that modern religion and modern psychology do not strive to cultivate, as was formerly done. A child may be literally weighed down with a sense of guilt. Guilt, as such, may be altogether paralyzing. Confession of his behavior often helps. We want a child, of course, to develop discrimination about his own conduct and to be dissatisfied with conduct that does not meet his own requirements. When he does fail in this particular, however, we wish him to be sorry but to have the confidence and the ability to be able to do better the next time.

Evidences of Other Emotions

Although there seems to be justification for some discussion of fear, anger, jealousy, and other specific emotions, it must not be forgotten that there are many evidences of emotional disturbance to which we cannot assign a particular name. Take the matter of nail-biting, for example. Nail-biting is an evidence of emotional disturbance. Viets has shown that the nail-biting children whom she studied tended to come from homes where there was emotional instability, drunkenness, overprotection, jealousy, or other devastating factors. The nail-biting child, as a rule, presents a different picture from the thumb-sucking child. The latter is likely to be more placid; the former, more restless and active. This is scarcely the place to discuss the psychoanalytic theories of the origin of such oral habits as nail-biting or thumb-sucking. The point is that treatment should begin with and should proceed from health and emotional security as points of reference before we think about any external methods of restraint. The psychology of encouragement helps after the child has actually made the problem his own and is trying to help himself. A manicure set has helped many a child who is trying to break the habit of nail-biting.

The "Nervous" Child

The *nervous* child is a kind of *John Doe* besieged by any one of a number of emotional disturbances. The category includes children whose nervous activity originates in such diverse factors as fatigue; health factors such as diseased tonsils, eye strain, carious teeth, heart trouble, chorea, and other diseases; embarrassment; emotional burdens; or perhaps even actual psychoses. The treatment for the *nervous* child obviously depends upon the etiology of his nervousness. For this reason it might be better if we gave up the use of the term. If its use is justified at all, it might be for the occasional child who comes from a stock whose nervous systems are highly irritable, a child who tends to over-react to all stimulation.

Unfortunately, there are some children whose nervousness is so extreme that the outlook is quite bad. In other words, there are some children who are actually psychotic, or at any rate prepsychotic. Such children require the care of specialists in nervous and mental disease.

The teacher, nurse, or social worker who meets children with extremely bizarre behavior or marked retreat from reality will, of course, refer such children to a child guidance center, a psychiatrist, or a psychologist who has had experience in this field. Such cases illustrate one of the instances of the necessity for knowing when a problem is beyond our ability to solve and when it thereby becomes the problem of a specially trained person.

Suicide in Children

An extreme of emotional imbalance is represented by the suicide or would-be suicide. Several studies of suicidal children have been published. There is a question whether some of the children who have killed themselves have actually been suicidal in intent, if by suicide we mean deliberate or intentional self-destruction. A two-year-old child who fell out of a second-story window and was killed has been described as a "suicide." The case resulted in death, but was it intentional self-destruction? A thorough understanding of the mental processes of a two-year-old would not permit our ascribing an adequate knowledge of the dangers of height or, for that matter, of death to a two-year-old mind.

Emotional Tests

Within recent years there has been much research in the matter of *emotional tests*. The line between *personality tests, tests of emotionality*, and so-called *psychoneurotic* inventories is not clearly defined. Ascendance and submission, introversion and extraversion, suggestibility, annoyance, and persistence have all been investigated by the use of adjustment score cards, developmental age tests, interest and attitude tests, behavior rating schedules, and numerous other devices. Many of these tests are "paper-and-pencil" tests. Some are so planned that they may be used either with an individual child or with a group of children. Often there is a series of questions that the child is asked to answer. The answers are then scored and checked against supposedly *normal* or *typical* answers. Obviously, the larger the number of *atypical answers* the child gives, the more he is unlike, in these particulars, the children upon whom the test was standardized originally. This technique presupposes, of course, that the child understands the meaning of the questions, is in rapport with the examiner, and answers the questions as truthfully as he is able to do. There has been much misunderstanding about the use and interpretation of the results of such emotional tests. Obviously, the score that a child makes on such a test is not in any sense comparable to an intelligence quotient. It is not a fixed entity.

The fact is that the better the test, the more the child's performance on it will differ from one time to another, since his actual emotionality will vary from one time to another. Furthermore, the size of the child's score may actually not be so important as the *types* of questions to which he gives atypical answers. For example, suppose a child did not make a large number of atypical answers but those that he did make all indicated fears about his body, or his health, or his physical prowess. Obviously here is an *area* in which the child needs help. The test would seem to justify itself in such a case, regardless of the validity or reliability of the total score. The clinical psychologist is likely to feel that such tests display their greatest value as *interview aids* rather than as testing or measuring devices. Very frequently the chief usefulness of such tests comes from some one particular question or group of questions that reveal a field of emotional difficulty. The way may thus be opened for therapeusis, the need for which would not otherwise have been apparent. However, it must be understood that none of these devices is diagnostic all of the time.

Other Diagnostic Aids

There are several methods that can be used by experts for unveiling and curing emotional difficulties in children. We shall mention these techniques, not because the readers of this book should use them, but rather that they may be familiar with newer movements in therapeutic work with children. So-called *play analysis*, to cite only a few references) is a psychiatric technique in which the child comes to the psychiatrist at regular times; is allowed to choose his own play materials; and, within reasonable limits, to do as he wishes with them. The nature of his play and his comments as he plays are all carefully noted. It is often found that the hostilities and fears which a child experiences in real life he acts out also in play, even though he may not have been able to verbalize them. This method would appear to have in it much of value, with one proviso. As the analysis continues, the psychiatrist sometimes puts in a word of interpretation to the child as to *why* he is playing as he is. Obviously, this interpretation depends upon the psychiatrist's own particular "school" of psychiatry. Here would seem to be the critical point. Knowing as we do the high degree of suggestibility in children, it is easy to see that an interpretation might, by dint of sufficient repetition, be accepted by the child, verbally at least, even though it had not originally been an actuality.

It is scarcely possible yet to evaluate the cures claimed by the play analysts. Play analysis usually requires many hours of play interview extending over a long period of time. How much improvement might have come about, because of other factors, in the same length of time, it is usually impossible to say. As a matter of fact, teachers and parents have for years been observing children's play and learning much about children's feelings and emotions thereby. The *group worker*, trained in modern schools of social work, learns the value of interpreting the behavior of individuals as they participate in group activities. Social workers and clinicians can probably go much further than they have gone in providing somewhat controlled play situations in which to observe child behavior.

Dolls which may represent different members of the child's family or others with whom he has frequent contacts, automobiles, paints, blocks, pictures, scissors, sand, plasticine, and many other objects can easily be kept in one's office. The child's reactions to these objects, even without psychiatric interpretation, may be very illuminating. His conversation as he plays, the toys which he prefers and those which he avoids will likely reveal to us more than he realizes himself. It would appear that interpretation to the child of what *we* think he is feeling as he plays is not necessary for either diagnosis or for therapeusis. Diagnostic play activities will probably be used more by social workers and other clinicians as time goes on.

Drawing, art work, construction with plastic materials, and finger painting may give children an excellent opportunity to work out their aggressions harmlessly. Much that would otherwise be inexplicable in their behavior is sometimes thus revealed. At Bellevue Hospital in New York City, interesting work has been done in the children's ward by the use of puppets. The puppet plays are so written as to illustrate common emotional situations in which children find themselves. It is much easier for the child to see the right and the wrong of a situation when the actor is a puppet, rather than himself. The children in the audience often call out vigorously to the puppet characters, telling them what to do and what not to do. Much conversation goes on between the children and the puppeteer. Discussion in the ward follows: the children evaluate the characters change the plays, write new ones, or help make the puppets. The impersonality of the whole situation makes it easier for the child to face the situations with which he himself may be struggling. Valuable therapeutic results are being accomplished.

Of course, the "own story" and other personal documents method of getting a child's account of his feelings and actions is one commonly used in clinics and courts. References 29 and 104 might be read in this connection. The analysis of children's dreams is another device used by some clinicians.

The so-called "association test" aims to reveal the connection of ideas that the child has in his mind. He is given a stimulus word and is asked to respond with the first word that comes to his mind. Unusual associations may indicate unusual experiences that the child has had. If the stimulus word were "afraid," for example, and the child should immediately reply "thunderstorm," there could be little doubt as to what he was thinking. Kent and Rosanoff have a list of a hundred stimulus words to each of which the subject is asked to respond with the first word that comes to his mind. Emotional reactions are indicated when the response is very slow in coming, when it is unusually fast in coming, when no response whatever is given, when the stimulus word is repeated, or when strange and apparently irrelevant responses are given. An adaptation of the Kent-Rosanoff norms for children has been arranged by Woodrow and Lowell and many other applications to work with children have been made.

Projective Techniques

In 1939, Frank wrote a paper that he called "Projective Methods for the Study of Personality". Frank stressed the point that much of our study of personality had hitherto been made by the use of media that were highly suggestive of the impact of culture and that what we must have was culture-free media into which the individual being studied could "project" his own personal. modes of reaction. Some such projective techniques had, as a matter of fact, been used before that time, but they had never been so designated. In 1945, Sargent reviewed the literature on projective techniques for the study of emotionality and personality. Her review cites 274 references. Obviously, the field is quite too extensive, controversial, and technical to be critically evaluated in such a text as this. Only fairly brief reference can be made to some of the methodologies. It should be borne in mind that some of the projective techniques are both diagnostic and therapeutic. The references already mentioned will give some familiarity with various play techniques, the mosaic tests, picture tests, psychodrama, art techniques, drama and puppets, the world test, frustration tests, and others. Among picture tests perhaps the best known and best standardized is the Thematic Apperception test. The Szondi test is also a picture test for eliciting personal projective reactions developed at the Menninger Clinic.

The Rorschach Ink-Blot test is one of the oldest and best means of getting under the surface and into the real personality make-up. Standardized ink-blots are printed on cards and the subject is asked to tell what they look like and what he sees in them. Great differences are found in the reactions of highly emotionalized, apathetic, deranged, and normal individuals. The administration and scoring of the test require a great amount of technical training. The. literature on the Rorschach test is voluminous, Sargent citing 41 references in her review alone. The tautophone, or verbal summator, is a device in the auditory field for doing essentially what the ink-blot and picture tests do in the visual field. Low vowel sounds are produced on a machine and resemble speech without being speech. The subject is asked to tell what the voice is saying, and he is left free to inject his own meanings and thoughts into the sounds.

Another device much used at present is moving pictures of children in certain situations in which they presumably are acting emotionally. Some of these films show children doing finger painting, reacting to supposed frustration, or acting aggressively with balloons. There may be danger, at this point, that we fall into an error that earlier psychologists made. The moving picture of a child in a situation where an adult has presented certain stimuli which the adult imagines will call forth certain emotional responses is no guarantee whatever that the child actually *feels* those emotions.

We have been discussing highly technical methods that can be used best by professionally trained specialists to discover deep-lying emotions in children. Does that mean, then, that the social worker, the teacher, the nurse, the school counselor, or the visiting teacher can never hope to discover any of the matters that may be troubling a child? Fortunately, there are methods that can be used which may be very revealing. Common sense would dictate that one of the first things to do in trying to understand a child is to watch him and to *allow him to talk*. Even these two apparently simple techniques require more real understanding of child psychology and more finesse than is apparent on the surface. Observation and listening by a skillful child worker will often give real information. Much of what children *write* either spontaneously or on assigned topics reveals a great deal of their own feelings.

There are also *questions* that have been used skillfully by many workers. One hesitates to print a list of such questions lest someone get the idea that all one has to do is to take a pencil and paper and proceed to corral the child, make a frontal attack, and, like a talking machine, "ask the questions." Obviously, there are times when some of the questions are not appropriate at all. In any case, they are probably more effective when used conversationally and maybe not all at the same interview. Sometimes a few questions will give us enough material with which to work for some time. Sometimes we may suspect that the child is not ready to talk about certain things and that therefore we had better omit certain questions entirely for the time being. Perhaps the safest precautions for all who deal with human emotions are good *sense* and *empathy*, or the ability to feel oneself into another person's situation. These two criteria would seem to make the following imperative:

(1) Don't forget that the child may be decidedly uncomfortable. Make the situation as easy for him as possible.
(2) Be kindly, but objective—not effusive.
(3) Don't talk too much yourself. Get the child to talk.
(4) Don't "talk down" to the child.
(5) Don't ask questions until rapport has been established.
(6) Don't try to get too much the first time.
(7) Don't follow any outline or interviewing device woodenly.
(8) Don't take notes obviously.
(9) Don't show shock at anything the child tells you.
(10) Don't try to handle problems that require expert handling in a particular field.
(11) Don't betray confidences except where by doing so you may actually be giving help or protection.

Emotional Maturity

We hear much nowadays about *emotional maturity*. Emotional maturity would seem to be a desideratum that is more easily discussed than defined. Those of us who are directly or indirectly responsible for the eventual attainment of emotional maturity in children should give serious thought to the matter. Although our ideas of emotional maturity will differ as our philosophies of life differ, perhaps there are some points that we might agree have been achieved by the individual who has emotional maturity: (1) the maximum selfhonesty in regard to one's own emotions; (2) growth, with age, in a selection of the things that arouse one's emotions; (3) constructive and productive behavior in emotional situations or crises; (4) such control that the balance between positive and negative emotions and feelings is in favor of the former, even in spite of environment; (5) an understanding of, and respect for, the emotions of others.

9

The Psychological Scientific Study of the Child

The aim of psychological science is the same as that of any other science—the development of predictive accuracy in antecedent-consequent relationships. In child psychology the aim is to develop predictive accuracy about child behavior and experience—that is, to establish the lawful relationships among the phenomena which can be observed. To chronicle the facts of child development is not enough; laws or principles must be discovered which will explain and give order to the facts.

It is obvious that this goal cannot be achieved by a mere accumulation of information. A thousand isolated facts about childhood contribute little to our understanding of child behavior. Only the placing of facts in larger perspective enables us to perceive the lawfulness of behavior and thus to understand it. By interrelating established facts, *principles* or *laws* of behavior are derived, and it is these laws or principles which identify a mature (or maturing) science. Our scientific task is to account for the multitude of particulars that make up the behavior and experience of the child with as few general laws as possible.

The chief test of the validity of a scientific law is whether it enables one to predict future events with reasonable accuracy. Such prediction makes possible the elimination of those influences which interfere with development—that is, which make for unhealthy and unhappy children—and to arrange for conditions which facilitate optimum growth. Lest it appear that "optimum growth" is regarded as some mystical, omnipresent factor which is the same for all children and all cultures, a reminder is in order here that it is difficult, if not impossible, to divorce science from the world of values. That is, behavior which is considered "healthy" by one group at a given time in history (for example, an authoritarian attitude among the children of Nazi Germany) might be regarded as grossly abnormal by another group or by the same group at a different time. Yet "control of behavior" implies that it might be possible in one or two short generations to manipulate conditions so that virtually everybody in a given social group behaved or thought in a certain way and that this pattern of behavior or thinking in turn precluded the development of different patterns. Conceivably, such arbitrary manipulation of conditions (environmental and perhaps genetic) might eventually make such scientific puppetry possible. A system, however, of checks and balances operates in this as in most aspects of social life, so that it is not likely in a diversified, democratic society.

The above description may seem to imply that scientific prediction (and thus control) is an all-or-none affair. This, however, is not the case; predictions are not statements of certainty but of probability. The degree of accuracy of prediction will depend upon, first, how many relevant variables (that is, conditions which can vary and thus influence results) affecting the behavior in question are known, and, second, how much control can be exerted over the relevant variables.

Occasionally, a formulation of a scientific law will be made before all the relevant variables are known and prediction made only in terms of those which are recognized.

The unidentified variables will always contribute a certain amount of error to the predictions made. For example, Boyle's calculations on the predicted relationship between pressure and volume of gases held only for experiments performed at a constant temperature. One source of predictive error remained until Charles, some hundred years later, worked out the precise relations of temperature to pressure and volume. With the recognition of this newly discovered variable, prediction became significantly more precise.

To choose an illustration from the field of child psychology, we might cite work in mental testing. Although never formulated as a law in the sense of Boyle's law, a principle which several workers in psychology have proposed is that the relationship between mental age and chronological age of a child is a constant. However, prediction for an individual child in terms of this presumably constant relationship (the intelligence quotient or IQ) can often be in error ten or more units. This error in prediction might be due to some weakness in the measuring instrument itself (just as predictions about the behavior of gases erred in part because of inadequate techniques for measuring pressure), but it might also indicate that other variables remained uncontrolled and lowered accuracy of prediction. Such variables have indeed been discovered and include such things as socio-economic status, health of the child at the time of examination, the amount of stress evoked by examination procedures, and so on.

Accuracy of prediction does not have to be perfect for predictions to be of value; actually, predictions may be valuable if they are barely better than chance. The closer predictions approach (but never reach) certainty, the more valuable they are. To defend this position concerning probability as differentiated from certainty, it is necessary only to remind the reader that in testing a certain hypothesis, not *all* humans can be studied. Generalizations are, of necessity, made on the basis of partial evidence even if there are no other limitations. All that can be done is to make inferences having a certain degree of probability. All branches of science share in this limitation. It may be that more established sciences, such as astronomy, have attained a higher degree of probability in their laws. Nevertheless, although it is highly probable that the sun will rise tomorrow, it is not absolutely certain!

Scientific advance may be interpreted, with some justice, as an increase in the ability to predict correctly. If there is a respectable degree of accuracy of prediction, the ability to control behavior comes into being. Thus, to take an oversimplified example, assume that it is known that environmental conditions A, B, and C produce in children effect Z. This knowledge makes it possible to take the further step of arranging for a given child to be exposed to an environment conducive to development of these conditions, which in turn leads to the desired effect. This would occur, of course, only if there were not too many unknown variables, such as D, E, and F, also related to effect Z.

There is also what might be called negative prediction and control. As a matter of fact, at the present limited level of knowledge, many of the more valuable contributions of child psychology arise from such negative or avoidance control. In such instances, we are not concerned with arranging a given effect to come about, but in preventing certain adverse effects from appearing. Thus, if L, M, and N produce effect Y, where Y represents a warped or some socially undesirable personality trait, conditions L, M, and N can be changed or eliminated so that this effect will *not* take place. Many selection procedures, such as those used in determining suitability of a child for entrance into public school or for readiness to read, are illustrative. Thus, if we know a child is not ready to read because certain predictive devices point to this lack of readiness, the frustrating experience of failure in this activity may be avoided by delaying reading.

In arriving at these laws, instead of dealing with the behavioral items or facts as they stand, sometimes constructs are used. Constructs, in the sense used here, are inferred attributes of the child's behavior. They are not immediate observables, but rather are ways of furthering understanding of certain observables. Behavior tendencies, such as aggression or dependence, are of this nature. No one has ever seen "aggressive tendencies." However real they may be to the experiencing person, they are abstractions, the existence of which the observer infers from behavior. The child behaves in such and such a fashion; the observer infers aggression and relates it to other experiences that may be subsumed under the same construct.

With this introduction we are now in a position to further refine the meaning of science. Although "science has become a common household term, it is not an easy word to define. In a recent attempt to formulate a definition, Conant has written: "As a first approximation, we may say that science emerges from the other progressive activities of man to the extent that new concepts arise from experiments and observations, and the new concepts in turn lead to further experiment and observations". It will be noted that this definition highlights the methods—experiment and observation—by means of which new concepts emerge. Of course, the terms "experiment" and "observation" connote various things to different people, for, to be sure, not all activities described as experiments warrant being termed "scientific." Also much observation is subjective and biased and not worthy of being designated as scientific activity. Only observations made and experiments conducted under carefully controlled conditions will permit reliable conclusions to be drawn from the data. Naive acceptance of presumed "facts" without concern for how the facts were obtained is inimical to science.

The Methods of Study

Many different classifications of the scientific method may be found in the literature, but all of these can be recognized as offering to the investigator the opportunity to select one of two major procedures. Briefly, he may intervene with nature, and thus perform an experiment, or he may observe differences in nature as they are found, and thus use the differential method. Each of these will be considered in turn.

The Experimental Method

An experiment is a particular way of making observations. It differs from the differential method in that it affords the experimenter a greater degree of control over the variables involved in the situation. Those variables over which he has control are called *independent* variables. These he manipulates or changes as he sees fit, within the limits of his problem as he has defined it. As he varies the independent variable (or variables), he observes the changes occurring in some other variable (or variables) to see whether they are related to the changes introduced. These other variables in which the effects of the changes are observed are called *dependent* variables (that is, they are dependent upon certain other conditions). The investigator is seeking information on the concomitant variation between the independent and dependent variable. It is clear that this discussion of "identification" and "control" introduces the factor of prearrangement, and hence a laboratory situation is usually (but not always) the setting in which an experiment is performed. In summary, the task of the experimenter is to study the relationship or concomitant variation between independent and dependent variables.

As Woodworth indicates, an experimenter makes an event happen at a certain time and place and thus is alerted to make accurate observations by knowing when and where to make them. Also, he can systematically vary the independent variable through predetermined stages while noting the concomitant variations in the dependent variable. The factor of control, in the sense that the independent variable is varied in a specific and known manner, also makes possible the repetition of the experiment either by the original or by another investigator.

Not too many years ago it was considered essential that the experimenter hold constant all variables that might be independent variables (that is, "affect" the results) except one. Certain factors that might have affected the dependent variable are not allowed to vary during the course of the experiment, that is, are held constant. Here another meaning of control is introduced. If they had not been controlled *in the sense that they were kept constant*, they might have affected the measures under consideration, thus obscuring the effect of the independent variable under study. Of course, in another study they might themselves have been systematically studied or even, with a different experimental design, been included in the study under consideration. One independent variable studied at a time was at one time considered an essential rule. Now that certain advances in statistics, particularly analysis of variance, have been made, it is possible to handle several independent variables in a particular study at the same time. It is, moreover, also possible to observe more than one dependent variable in the same experiment.

When "control" of factors as a restraint of other variables is spoken of, it is important to emphasize that the control is not complete. Indeed, if complete control were possible, only one observation for each degree of change in the independent variable would be necessary. Since we do not always have exact control of variation of the independent variable, various degrees of stimulation are possible. We may vary the intensity, pitch, and timbre of an auditory stimulus through predetermined steps exactly controlled by the experimenter. This is likewise true in other sensory fields and for some other areas of child study. However, for many important problems, we simply do not know enough about the independent variable to vary it through finely graded steps. Thus, we study whether the presence or absence of a certain factor has any effect at all and leave for later research the study of gradation of effect. There are certain different experimental procedures which might be identified briefly. Thus, one common research design calls for using the same subjects once under normal conditions and then again with one condition (the independent variable) changed. In this, the *method of difference*, a subject is his own control since he is studied under both conditions.

If practice effects are involved, as in studies of children's learning, it is not possible to use the same children under both conditions. If doing the task itself makes the child different because he has now learned something new or how to do something better because he went through the first session, he is no longer the same person as he was at the beginning of the session. In order to circumvent this blurring of results, the *control group* technique is used. In its simplest form, two groups are used. Children of the total sample are assigned to the two groups in such a manner as to make them as alike as possible. For example, suppose that in a study of reading ability one wishes to control (equalize) for the effect on the results of individual differences in intelligence. With scores on an intelligence test available, the top child may be placed in the experimental group, the next highest in the control group, the third highest in the experimental group, and so on, alternating between the groups. Thus, both the average intellectual level and the variability of the two groups are equalized.

The problem of placement becomes more complicated when other matching variables, such as sex, age, socio-economic status, and so on, must also be considered, but basically the way of equating is the same. In general, the intent is to make the experimental and control groups as similar as possible in the independent variables *not* under consideration; it may nonetheless cause concomitant variation in the dependent variable being studied. The choice of matching the groups on certain variables depends upon whether it is known or suspected that there is a concomitant variation with the dependent variable. For instance, as Anderson observes, in studying motor skills with all except very young children, it is not necessary to control intelligence or socio-economic factors, because concomitant variation with motor ability is known to be very low. On the other hand, in studying language, which is positively related to (concomitantly varies with) these factors, both must be controlled.

Now that this necessity of equation of the groups has been indicated, it is possible to elaborate on the nature of the control group study. Two equated groups of subjects are used, differing only in that one group, the experimental, has the independent variable introduced (or has a greater or lesser magnitude, and so forth), while the second or control group does not. In the simplest form of this technique, both groups receive a prior test to establish equality; following this one undergoes the experimental procedure, while the other does not. Both then take a final test. The difference in this final test-results between the experimental group and the control group is considered the result of the experience undergone by the experimental group which the control group did not receive and is the measure of the effect of the experimental (that is, independent) variable.

An experiment is "manmade" in the sense that the investigator arranges the conditions. Thus, rigid control of conditions is possible. Since another person can do likewise, replication of the conditions under which a given experiment was performed is possible. Since science depends upon *verified* knowledge, and verification is relatively more exact with the experimental method, it is, in most instances, the method of choice. There are certain circumstances, however, in which arrangement of conditions by the experimenter is not feasible and he must seek a different method of verifying a hypothesis.

THE DIFFERENTIAL METHOD

In the experimental method, the distinguishing operation was the introduction or the manipulation by the investigator of some specific stimulating condition, the independent variable. But there are some problems in which this intervention on the part of the investigator is impossible or impractical. Indeed, there are sciences in which experiment is impossible, so far as major problems are concerned. This is the case with astronomy and geology. The space and time dimensions of these sciences do not permit manipulation. An astronomer cannot vary the orbit of a star to see its effect; nor can the geologist introduce an ice age to observe the resultant changes. These sciences, as well as certain problem areas in other sciences, depend in the main upon the differential method. This consists of the scientist studying differences found in certain conditions without purposive manipulation (other than selection of phenomena to be studied). A star already varying in its orbit is studied; evidence of the effect of ice ages is examined in relation to other events occurring at the same time.

Many psychological problems likewise do not permit experimental manipulation. Sometimes to do so would be too costly in time, money, or effort. Sometimes an attempt to study a problem experimentally would mean ethical or moral violation of the personal rights of others. An illustration would be the attempt to make the independent variable of an experiment the development of an experimental psychosis in a child; so, too, would be the placement of heretofore emotionally stable children in a family environment designed to produce emotional trauma. Moreover, respect for living things prevents workers in all sciences from inflicting unnecessary pain in the course of their experiments. Child psychologists are further limited in their use of the experimental method because of their desire to avoid interfering in any way with the best development of the child's personality.

This precaution is followed even when harmful effects are but remotely suspected. For instance, a question, which is of considerable relevance for the field of child development and regarding which contradictory data have appeared in the literature, is whether insufficient oxygen (anoxia) at birth causes lasting damage to the child. The surest, most efficient technique of answering this question would be to subject large numbers of new-born infants to varying degrees of anoxia and to follow their subsequent development. However, so long as there is even the faintest suspicion that such a procedure might cause lasting damage to the children, such a method is not likely to be employed. Instead, the differential method, capitalizing upon cases of anoxia that occur despite the best obstetrical care, must be relied upon to answer the question.

For some problems, life as it is lived, and thus the differential method, offers greater promise than does an experiment. Studies of normal development, for example, are central to child psychology. Since we are interested in the *normal* changes concomitant with age, we do not attempt to alter the course of development precisely because it is the normal child we are trying to study. Sometimes the differential method is employed by necessity, but for certain problems it is the method of choice. In using the differential method, the investigator finds a situation rather than arranges for it. The children are behaving in ways that are natural to them. The children are already "intelligent," "mentally retarded," or "disturbed" when the differential method is applied. Instead of setting up a situation and inducing the subjects to do something, they are already being, or doing, or experiencing what is to be investigated.

In psychology, the differential method employs individual differences among persons as the independent variable. Subjects are chosen according to a criterion, and the measurements themselves form the variable. Thus, the researcher does not manipulate the independent variable and, consequently, he has less control of it. However, concomitant variation, the use of control groups, and other characteristics of the experimental method are still possible.

Many studies using a correlation technique fall in the class of differential methods. Indeed, somewhat loosely, the term "correlational studies" (or "statistical studies") is used to describe what are called here instances of the differential method. Studies of intelligence, aptitude, and personality mostly take people as they are and are studied against some predetermined criterion. Let us consider for a moment the use of the control group in research by the differential method. Suppose the problem is the relation of aggression in children to parental attitudes. By a means irrelevant to the issue at hand, 50 aggressive children are isolated. (Note they are already "aggressive," not made so by the research worker.) Let us further suppose that in 42 of the homes from which these aggressive children come, parental rejection of these children takes place. It would be tempting to conclude that parental rejection brings about aggressiveness. Actually, the study is inconclusive without a control group. We must isolate a control group of nonaggressive children to find out what proportion of parental rejection is present in this group as well. Then, and only then, can we speak with any degree of assurance about the meaning of the results. The differential method is the basis for both the longitudinal and cross-sectional approaches to development.

The longitudinal and cross-sectional approaches. In investigating many problems in child psychology, interest focuses upon the course of development. It is enough to say at this point that for both practical and theoretical purposes knowing the rate and manner of change of psychological processes is central to an understanding of child behavior. Since knowledge is wanted about the normal course of development, the attempts to alter its course, which an experiment would do, make the differential method the more appropriate. There are two ways in which development may be studied differentially-the longitudinal and cross-sectional approaches.

In the longitudinal approach, the *same* children are studied at *different* ages. The same children may be studied when they are seven, when they are eight, and again when they are nine years old. In the cross-sectional approach, *different* children are studied at *different* ages. Thus, seven-, eight-, and nine-year-old children may be studied all at the same time. This latter approach is obviously both more economical of time and easier to arrange for, since a given child may be seen only once, with no necessity to wait to retest while time passes. Moreover, drawing new samples for various age levels introduces a check on the data found at other levels. Thus, if there is some bias in a given age sample, it might be more readily detected by the cross-sectional approach than if one sample were studied at several ages.

Despite this possible weakness, the longitudinal approach is generally to be preferred in developmental research. Cross sections give only approximations instead of the more accurate representations of the developmental process which the longitudinal approach affords. A study by the cross-sectional approach of 13-year-old girls would place together many girls past puberty with others who would not reach that developmental stage for some time. The longitudinal approach allows the study of individual as well as group development and an appraisal of the interrelations among developmental processes.

Use of the longitudinal approach, however, does require more care in selecting the sample and introduces the additional problem of keeping track of the original group for later study. Since only one sample is used, an "all eggs in one basket" approach, as it were, is unavoidable. Moreover, the corrective influence of other samples inherent in the cross-sectional approach is not present. Likewise, one may by choice bias the sample, for the sake of keeping track of the subjects for later study, by selecting a group which for some reason is judged to be geographically more stable and thus easier to locate at a later date. Thus, a community with known low mobility for its members may be used. But this introduces in itself a bias which will influence the findings. Moreover, individuals may be lost through death, or illness may make cooperation impossible, or individuals may show a changed attitude about cooperating. These very situations which make cases unavailable may actually have a bearing upon development which, of course, cannot be reflected in the results at the later ages.

In fact, these difficulties have caused some investigators (for example 3), to advocate discarding data on incomplete cases. This, however, reduces the size of the sample, and in order to be so cavalier about discarding data, one has to start with a group considerably larger than that reported in the final results. Another complication of longitudinal research is that, during the course of the study, improvements in technique are made, but in order to make comparisons from one age level to another, continuity of measurement is desirable. The longitudinal method is the only way of accurately measuring *individual* growth curves. At first glance it might appear that we could use a series of averages obtained from cross-sectional samples for this purpose. Actual comparison between norms developed in this way with individual curves shows that individual variability is blotted out, thus giving a distorted picture. For example, in a study of physical growth patterns, late maturing girls and early maturing girls showed different growth curves which were not apparent when age cross-sectional samples were used.

Variations of the longitudinal approach, each with its specific values and weaknesses, include the baby biography previously examined in historical perspective and certain aspects of the case history to be discussed later. Both baby biography and case study have in common certain limitations—a paucity of cases, a probably nonrepresentative selection, and the possibility of bias on the part of the observer. Furthermore, lack of control of other variables operating, although not necessarily inherent in either technique, operates to reduce their scientific usefulness.

The most systematic and thoroughgoing use of the longitudinal approach requires extensive facilities and continuity of personnel. Hence, it is not surprising that the child welfare stations, described earlier in connection with modern trends in the history of child psychology, take the lead in such studies. Investigators working in isolation from their colleagues seldom have the time, money, or patience to use this approach profitably. Cross-sectional studies do have value and are open to them. Not only do both the longitudinal and crosssectional approaches give us information on the developmental process of childhood, but they also supply material to be used as norms with which the performance of other children can later be compared. A scale thus becomes available for the evaluation of other children. Height and weight charts, intelligence tests, motor development scales, reading tests, and vocabulary tests are simple illustrations. The child's present performance may be compared with children at his own, higher, and lower levels, thus accurately placing him—provided the groups on which the norms were based are representative of the population from which they have been drawn.

The Techniques of Study

Basic to all scientific research, psychological or otherwise, is observation—the noting of events as they occur. Both the experimental and differential method rely ultimately upon observation. Something is done to the child by the experimenter (experimental method) or by nature (differential method), and observations of the results are made. But our senses are faulty and limited, and our wishes as to the outcome can possibly distort our observations. We cannot see everything that is going on. A magician, for example, capitalizes on our limitations in this respect. Moreover, we are set to see certain things, so we see to a certain extent what we expect to see. Thus, one purpose of research techniques and devices is to increase the accuracy of our observations. A handmaiden of accurate observation is immediate and accurate recording. If what is observed is not recorded properly, then a source of error just as serious as inaccurate observation has been introduced. The necessity of immediate recording comes about from the well-known phenomenon of faulty and distorted memory to which all of us are subject.

Observation is an experience of the observer. In a sense, then, all observation remains subjective because it depends upon the organism of the observer. We attempt to make it as objective as possible by arranging conditions of observation so that the human element can be minimized (although never eliminated). Devices and procedures increasing objectivity are attempts to reach the goal of minimal dependence upon subjective impression. It follows that all such devices have varying degrees of objectivity-subjectivity. It is impossible, therefore, to speak as though differences among techniques are qualitative; rather they represent quantitative differences along the objectivity-subjectivity continuum. In many research situations, but especially in clinical settings, the investigator is not merely passively recording observations but actively interacts with his subject. Thus, he becomes, in Sullivan's apt phrase, a "participant observer." This may lend subtlety to the situation, but it also makes it more complex. In effect, the investigator, because he is part of the research situation, becomes a variable in the research which may affect the results. Thus, it is necessary to study the investigator to see to it that his very participation does not cause him to make errors in his evaluation of the situation. Feelings of like or dislike may color his evaluations. Sometimes we must have observers watching the observers!

Many of the techniques discussed in this and later chapters-chronoscopes, tests, motion pictures, and so on—are means of making observations more correct and their recording less subject to error. Just as lenses are ground to enhance vision, the devices and procedures employed in psychological research are means of making more exact and more acute the observational processes of the investigator. And just as a voice recorder is used to capture historic events, the techniques to be discussed include those which help to make sure that what is observed is recorded accurately.

Once the method of study has been chosen, a problem facing the research investigator is the selection of the appropriate technique. That is to say, he must now decide within the limits set by his method of study what he is going to use to study the child. Will he observe through a one-way screen the child as he plays and rate his behavior on certain preselected characteristics? Will he record the child's response to intelligence test items and then score the test? Or will he have him learn to thread a maze and record time and errors? These and many other techniques may be used depending, of course, upon the problem to be solved. In fact, in many studies, several techniques are likely to be used.

The investigator's choice of study techniques will be dictated by certain considerations. Most important of all, he attempts to use a technique that is directly related to his problem. There must be as high a degree of congruence as he can arrange between his hypothesis and how he goes about studying it. If his hypothesis calls for an investigation of the differences between girls and boys in reading ability, he uses a test of reading, not a test of intelligence, to establish these differences. But the crucial point is more subtle. He wants to use a test of reading that, on the basis of earlier studies or his own experience with the test, he is confident actually measures reading. Hence, he wants a *valid* test, or one which measures what it is supposed to measure. Although validity is customarily treated as a topic to be discussed when tests are concerned, it enters into consideration in the selection of all techniques.

It is merely that in a test its validity is not as self-evident or overt as it is with many other techniques. In learning studies, for example, one arranges for the child to be faced with a new problem, and if after practice trials the child commits fewer errors and takes less time, one can then say that learning has taken place; or he asks a child to tell which of two lights is the brighter, and he can then say that he has studied visual brightness discrimination. But in both these instances there must be some direct, unequivocal connection between that which he says he is studying and that which he actually is studying. The investigator describes the operations by which his results are obtained. Similarly, marks on a weight scale may be used directly to measure weight. But if weight is used indirectly as a measure of nutrition, then it is up to the investigator to demonstrate that there is a necessary connection. The relation between the indicator and that which it indicates must be determined. If it measures what it purports to measure, it is valid. If it is a valid measure of what he wants to investigate, the instrument is suitable for his purposes.

Objective Techniques

Objective techniques depend upon the subject's behavior as noted by the observer-investigator. The child does something either spontaneously in a free situation, such as a playroom, or on request, as when he reads from a book, pushes a button when he sees a light, learns a problem, or lifts a weight. Characteristics of his physiological processes such as blood pressure may also be investigated. In objective techniques, then, the observer looks at the subject and reports on his observations.

Subjective Techniques

Subjective techniques make use of what the subject has to say about himself to an observer. They consist of an account of his experiences, points of view, traits, aims, needs, or interests. These statements are taken by the investigator for what they are-disclosures by the subject about himself. Thus, the subject looks at himself and reports to the observer.

Subjective techniques are based upon what the individual can reveal and what he chooses to reveal about himself. Some things he does not know and other things he does not choose to tell. In other words, in varying degree, subjective techniques are weakened by selection on the part of the person concerned. Often subjective techniques depend upon the subject's interpretation of the meaning of the material at hand without his being given much of a guide or source of reference as to how to interpret the material. The autobiography, for example, has the disadvantages associated with its adult useselection, conscious and unconscious, of what the informant should tell—plus the additional disadvantage of language and other developmental limitations of the child. Subjective techniques nevertheless possess value. It is undoubtedly important to know what a person thinks about himself. An unfounded belief, even if masquerading as a fact, is still a valuable datum for psychology. In addition, there are certain problems for which subjective techniques are particularly appropriate. With children the questionnaire and the interview are the most widely used of subjective techniques.

Projective Techniques

Projective techniques are not concerned with consciously held opinions of the subject nor with his overt behavior but with imaginative responses which aim to uncover indirectly whatever personality variables are under investigation. The subject reveals something about himself to the observer by the way he organizes the material presented to him—the way he projects meaning into neutral or ambiguous material. According to Rosenzweig, this is tantamount to having both the subject and the observer "look the other way" at some neutral object that is capable of permitting the subject's personality dynamics to be "projected" out where they can be observed.

Projective procedures use techniques which permit the individual to reveal aspects of his personality by the organization of stimulus material into which he projects the meaning it has for him. Since idiomatic responses are sought, no external criterion of what is right or what is wrong is used. Since the testing situation is arranged in such a fashion that the child does not know what is expected of him, he reveals by his spontaneous way of handling the stimulus materials some of the ways he organizes his view of the world. In the source of structuring the relatively unstructured material, the child reveals his structuring principles which are, it is hypothesized, the principles of his personality. It is evident that the projective approaches put a heavy burden upon the interpreter. The clinician or researcher, since he is dealing with relatively unstructured material, must be alert lest he read his own projections into the material.

This subjective element in interpretation of projective material has justifiably been a source of criticism. Only through the awareness of this danger, the use of norms, the investigation of validity and reliability, and careful cross-checking can this criticism partially be met. Projective instruments such as the Rorschach Ink Blots, play techniques, drawings, and the spontaneous telling of stories to pictures all have in common the fact that they all are relatively unstructured and yet provide a standardized stimulus situation. They are stimuli which readily allow the child to impose upon them his own meaning and organization, private and idiosyncratic though they may be. The stimuli are to some degree unclear or equivocal, allowing the child to interpret or structure them himself. The same principle applies to the instructions given to the child. For all of these techniques in essence the instructions reduce to, "Do with or interpret the material as you want to."

Thematic apperception technique. The Thematic Apperception Technique (TAT) is another widely used projective device. It consists of pictures somewhat similar to illustrations for magazine stories. Some pictures are suitable for children, some for adults, and some for both. The boy or girl is told that he is to be shown some pictures and that a story is to be made up for each one. In telling his story he is to imagine what led up to the event shown in the picture, to relate what is happening in the picture, and what the outcome will be. Any questions asked by him are answered noncommittally, with the nature of the situation and kind of story left entirely to the child. The fundamental assumption concerning projection with the TAT is that the child identifies himself with a central figure in the story. The way the figure is described, the problem faced, and how it is handled are considered to be reflections of the child's own feelings and attitudes.

But how are these stories interpreted? There are various methods of anlaysis and norms toward which to turn. All methods of interpretation have in common the process of careful reading and inspection and assimilation of the stories by the interpreter. The first task is often considered to be the identification of the character in the story with whom the child has identified. Then an analysis is made of what happens to this central character. Is he seen as happy, defeated, rejected, or how? What are his needs? Victory at all costs, to be protected, to escape from the situation untouched by it, and the like? What are the environmental forces with which he must contend? Is it the family hampering him at every turn, is it an impersonal obstacle which blocks him in his efforts to reach his goal? What is the outcome? Is he successful in reaching his goal or does he suffer frustration and defeat? Special emphasis is placed upon recurrence of themes from one story to another—father-son conflict, feelings of guilt, hostility, etc.

These recurrent trends are interpreted as revealing characteristic ways of responding to situations. Comparison with norms showing the recurrence of a given theme in comparable subjects is important, with more significance being attached to appearance of themes where normatively they are infrequent. This is in keeping with the assumption that if something is "pressing" at the child, he will use even unlikely materials on which to project this conflict. Telling gloomy stories about pictures generally interpreted in a more pleasant way would be a case in point. There are many nuances to the scoring and interpretation of TAT protocols which need not be discussed, but are presented in the extensive literature which has appeared, for example. After this somewhat lengthy discussion of the techniques, it is appropriate to remind the reader that the discussion was placed in a setting where the ones that are available to the research investigator could be suitably chosen for his particular study. Once he has made his choice he then proceeds to apply the technique or techniques to his already selected subjects.

The Clinical Approach

The clinical approach is an application of the scientific findings within a clearly recognized value system, namely, helping individuals. The clinical approach may be used for scientific research, but not all instances of its application have this aim. Rather, it is used most extensively to help individuals with their difficulties. It is in this sense that the approach will first be examined, leaving aside for the moment the scientific application which arises during the course of working with patients or clients.

The disciplines of psychiatry, clinical psychology, and social work have developed information that is useful in understanding and helping children. Some of the other settings in which a clinical approach is applied in work with children will be referred to in later chapters. It is enough to say at this point that they include special school agencies and classes, courts, hospitals, and homes for the delinquent, feeble-minded, and physically handicapped. Clinical workers include not only those from the major specialty groups already mentioned, but also a host of other workers, such as pediatricians, nurses, remedial teachers, speech and reading specialists, dentists, parole officers, social workers, and psychiatric aides.

The clinical approach refers to the evaluation of children in the course of their diagnosis and treatment. Originally confined to medical practice, the meaning of the clinical approach has been extended to include practice by nonmedical personnel. The essential spirit, however, is preserved. Whether it be a speech specialist, a clinical psychologist, or a school guidance expert, the task involved is to understand the difficulties of the patient or student in terms of the causes of his problem, how he reacted to them, and what can be done about them in order to correct the condition. A person comes to the clinician because he is troubled. As Klein says of the clinician, "How well he understands and ministers to his patient is the yardstick of his success". Those from whom the patient seeks help have in common an aim, the alleviation of his difficulties, and an approach, the clinical. This aim and this approach hold whether psychiatrists, pediatricians, clinical psychologists, or educational remedial specialists are called upon for this help. The clinician views the person as a *patient,* not as a *subject*. In this sentence is the essence of the clinical approach in differentiating it from use as a scientific method in studying children.

The clinician, in the course of diagnosis and treatment, uses knowledge obtained from the experimental and differential methods. In his approach he draws upon all that he knows based upon scientific research and applies it in connection with the needs of the specific patient. He also draws upon his personal-social heritage of insight into human nature and upon his personal clinical experience. Since the patient is a patient, he needs help *now*. The clinician cannot pause, as does the scientist, and depend only upon scientifically verified knowledge. Therefore, imperfectly validated diagnostic and therapeutic procedures may be used when there are no thoroughly established scientific guideposts to follow. The clinician does not necessarily hold that what he does could not benefit from scientific verification; it is merely that he cannot always wait before proceeding.

All clinicians share an interest or focus on the individual child. The nature of the professional activity calls for attention to the child as a person in his own right. Work is centered around individual sick children, and diagnostic decisions and plans for treatment are made on an individual basis. The clinician is also interested in the general. This interest in the general is as a guide to the particular. Hence, interest in diagnosis and classification, a reflection of this general interest, is a device to use other clinical experiences with the single case. There is no contradiction between placing primacy upon the unique, because in order to know the unique, one needs to know the common background—that is, that from which the individual case stands out as unique.

The clinician is interested in the individual child, whereas other specialists in child study are more concerned with development of generalizations about children as a group. This, however, is a matter of degree and some exceptions to these trends should be noted. The child psychologist studies individual differences, the educator, the causes and nature of school difficulties in individual deviant children. Conversely, medical men and clinical psychologists sometimes use larger groups of patients as research subjects. Nevertheless, such instances as these are exceptions to the general definition.

The clinical approach may be used for this service function and it may be used for research. In fact, in the clinical setting, research and practice are hard to distinguish, in that the noting of similarities and differences leads to both individual diagnostic and therapeutic skill and to the adroit formulation of fruitful hypotheses. In the course of ministering to his patients, the clinician may originate many promising ideas for research from what the patients reveal about themselves, from the professional contacts through colleagues as in seminar, and from his readings in the literature. Though vague and ill-formed at first, his idea will serve to sensitize him to other instances he finds in these same sources pointing in the same direction as his "hunch." The primary source is his contact with individual patients.

A specific illustration is to be found in David Levy's account of how his work in maternal overprotection came about. He reports that in listening to case reports being given at a staff meeting of the Institute of Child Guidance, someone discussed a woman having a child after ten years of sterility. The record also showed that she was very solicitous and indulgent toward this child. These two events were not in any way considered interrelated at this point. They were merely aspects of a voluminous case record. Levy raised the question to himself: Assuming she wanted the child, would not this ten years' wait cause her to be very solicitous toward him? The idea intrigued him and he began to search the case records of the clinic for cases showing maternal over protectiveness and then to study the case records to see what other attitudes were shown by the same mother.

The clinical approach, as well as other ways of studying the child, is used to obtain information about children. In the course of his daily work, the clinician develops hypotheses ("hunches") which may be tested against other patients seen subsequently. Thus, there is always a ragged advance guard of knowledge in that no man's land between pure speculation and scientific verification of knowledge. As a clinician, he finds that certain ways of viewing the patient strike him as true, and this apparent truth is accepted until verification of its truth or falsity can be brought about. Some clinicians, to be sure, hold that no verification by scientific procedures, in the sense we have described them, is necessary. They would argue that purely clinical procedures are all that are necessary. For example, the clinical procedure that Freud followed to formulate hypotheses was to draw upon his experience with patients, and then to test these hypotheses against later cases. If, in these later cases, consistency with the hypothesis was observed, he considered the hypothesis verified. As Boring puts it:

Freud's technic lay somewhere between that of the experimental psychologist, who alters an independent variable and observes the result, and the philosopher-psychologist, who induces generalization about human nature from the reservoir of his experience. Freud made his generalization from a wealth of specialized experience and then tested his hypotheses out against particular cases, increasing his assurance about the validity of each induction as the number of consistent cases grew. He had, however, no control, either in the sense of the rigorous constraint of contributing factors or in the sense of adding the method of difference to the method of agreement. Indeed, he seems to have been restricted to Mill's method of agreement, pure and simple, a method which by itself is clearly unsafe.

Boring emphasizes the necessity of *controlled* research. In examining the studies of children to be reported later, appeal to controlled research will be made whenever it is available. It is now possible to present a classification of the research studies considered in this book. It was demonstrated earlier that the scientific method embraced both experimental and differential methods. This was done in a setting primarily of the *laboratory approach* to child psychology. Now it is seen that there is also a second, the *clinical approach*. Studies using the experimental method and the differential method may be done either through a laboratory approach or through a clinical approach.

The clinical approach often does not offer as much opportunity for use of the experimental method as does the laboratory approach. Often, although not always, the differential method is used clinically. Frequently, clinical research is concerned with tracing back into the past for that which has made the child (or adult) patient what he is today, and thus depends upon the differential method. The effects of psychotherapy is a distinguished, although barely explored, area in which experimentation may be used.

Clinical research is by no means as fully developed as is laboratory research, because the clinician is usually confronted by a complex situation in which variables are more numerous and more uncontrollable than in a laboratory setting. He strenuously objects to attempts to simplify prematurely the task by experimental control of these variables. His objection may be stated in the form of an aphorism, "Research contamination is clinical enrichment." The clinician wants as much information about his patient as possible in reaching a decision. Since he is dealing with a patient in a complex, everyday setting, all sources are used. But allowing all these factors to vary without the control called for by scientific research, in effect, contaminates the situation so he cannot trace down the precise effect of each variable.

Greater rapprochement between traditional laboratory and clinical research has been made possible by the development of research methodology which permits concomitant variation in several variables being investigated simultaneously. The classic methods of experimental and differential research called for varying systematically a single factor and restraining all other factors which might affect the dependent variable. This way of studying children ran counter to the deeply held conviction of clinicians that the interaction among the various factors of the personality of his patient was important. As Klein puts it:

In clinical practice it is a commonplace that similar symptoms may arise from quite different origins; or even that the same cause can give rise to very different symptoms. This observation is crucial for the clinician. Expressed conceptually, it tells us that the most basic attribute of an interacting set of variables is not the component variables themselves but the *interaction*. Now that statistical techniques are available to permit simultaneous study of several variables used by both laboratory and clinical workers, this source of difference is disappearing. Thus, laboratory and clinical work share a common aim. Using different means to secure this information occasionally created a situation wherein those individuals or experimenters in one or the other tradition denied the value or even the respectability of the other. Arguments from the traditionalists center upon what they believe to be the lack of exactitude of the clinician, while those of the clinician seize upon what they consider to be the sterile rigor focused upon trivial problems of the more traditional researcher. It is neither profitable nor relevant to continue this line of discussion, except to state that the position taken in this book attempts to draw upon both methods for information. In so doing, the validity of both the charges of lack of exactitude of one and the incompleteness of knowledge of the other are tentatively accepted with this important reservation—that instead of rejecting one or the other, both are accepted with, it is hoped, some recognition of both the merits and deficiencies of each.

It is recognized that the psychology of the child is not a finished body of knowledge, but a very vital and rapidly changing field. All approaches have something cogent to say about the child. It is mandatory to use both the most accurate and the most meaningful contributions to a given problem. It does not follow, however, that accuracy and meaningfulness always reside to an equal degree in the same finding. Experimental-differential evidence found in the traditional fashion will be chosen when such is available and when it appears to be the appropriate method for a particular problem. There will be no hesitation, however, in using clinical findings when they are more meaningful and relevant than data obtained from laboratory investigations.

The frontiers of scientific knowledge of childhood behavior and experience are irregular. Sometimes our thinking about problems in this area can be based upon firm scientific foundations. But for other problems, our knowledge is as yet very incomplete and must be based, if we are to say anything at all, upon incompletely verified findings. Unfortunately, this is true concerning many important problems of the child personality. Dependence upon only that which has firm experimental foundation would result in a small but by no means compact structure. If a continuation of the analogy be permitted, many vital rooms and hallways (not to mention the plumbing) would be completely missing. Here, the structure we are building will be filled out by dependence upon clinical findings when they are appropriate and of value.

This intention to use clinical findings is reinforced by the conviction that many of the more vital problems of child behavior and experience have not as yet been investigated in the laboratory. What, for example, can we say about the infant's first experiences in this shining bauble of a world into which he has just been born? How does he "see" it? What are the effects of these first impressions? These and related problems are interesting and important, but there is a lack of information based upon experimental verification of hypotheses. What little is known or speculated about them will be presented. It is important, however, to recognize that the charge of inexactitude of such findings has merit. The reader with an awareness of the importance of method can to some extent decide for himself, as the source of information will be identified.

Increasing the accuracy of predictions concerning child behavior is the aim of the scientific study of the child.

Pursuing this aim, principles or laws are derived under which are subsumed a variety of facts. The crucial test of these laws is their predictive accuracy. However, these tests are not those of certainty of occurrence but of probability. Despite this uncertainty, they are still of value in advancing our knowledge of child behavior.

The methods of study used by the child psychologist are those he shares with other scientists—experiments in which he controls to some degree the independent variables; and observations in which he has no control over these independent variables, but, instead, depends upon their prior differential effect upon children. Both the experimental and the differential methods have their place and their particular advantages and disadvantages.

Specific techniques—instruments and procedures by which to secure the relevant data—are applied to the children. These techniques may be used with either the experimental or differential methods. They may be classified into three major categories: objective techniques involve the noting of the child's behavior by the psychologist; subjective techniques depend upon the child reporting his observations about himself to the psychologist; projective techniques depend upon the child giving his own meaning and organization to the material to which he is exposed, which is noted and then interpreted by the psychologist. Each of the three categories of techniques and the particular instruments included in these categories have their particular advantages according to the problem being investigated.

The clinical approach is used for helping disturbed individuals, including children. In the clinical approach diagnostic evaluation of the individual is carried out and a course of treatment followed. In addition to its service function, the clinical approach is also used in connection with scientific research. When used for research functions, the clinical approach most often involves applying the differential method, although the use of experimental method is not impossible. From clinical setting the psychologist often arrives at fruitful hypotheses which he then proceeds to investigate in this setting. For a variety of reasons, but particularly because of lack of appropriate controls for all relevant independent variables, sometimes (but not always), research done in clinical settings lacks precision and exactitude in contrast to research done in a laboratory setting. Choice among research efforts for presentation in the chapters to follow will depend not only upon their exactitude but also their relevance to the problem at hand. On this basis of this last criterion there will be no hesitation in using clinical findings when clinical research is judged important and relevant.

10

Problems and Methods of Child Psychology

PROBLEMS OF CHILDHOOD

The Significance of Childhood. An individual's first twelve years are more significant to his ultimate happiness and welfare than is any other interval of his life. The childhood years are learning years, during which the most important patterns of behavior are developed. It has been recognized for many centuries that motor skills, language habits, and knowledge about the world are acquired during childhood. Many such habits, especially those relating to oral language, become increasingly difficult to modify as time passes. Modern research has brought about an even greater realization of childhood's importance by revealing that many other aspects of development, not well understood in the past, depend on the learning during the early years. The emotional responses of the individual, which are important modifiers of his traits of character and personality, are largely determined by childhood experiences. Social adjustments throughout life are greatly influenced by the nature of the child's training and by the success or failure of his early reactions to difficulties. These considerations indicate that the scientific study of childhood has great value in relation to the individual's entire life.

Parallel to the increasing realization of the significance of childhood in the whole scheme of life has been an emphasis on the worth of this period for its own sake. The present century has sometimes been termed "the age of the child" because of its interest in the welfare of the young. Although this tendency may have been sentimental and based on inaccurate conceptions at the outset, it is now clearly recognized that the guidance of children for their own enjoyment, as well as for their ultimate good, must proceed from reliable information. The child deserves the same consideration that an advanced social philosophy deems desirable for all persons.

The Field of Child Psychology. Child psychology seeks to obtain reliable facts about the nature and development of behavior. By gathering adequate information concerning the nature of children, certain uniformities of development can be discovered that make possible the prediction of the outcomes of various causal circumstances and of various methods of guidance. From, this knowledge of the most likely results of courses of action, the control of behavior can be achieved by bringing favorable factors to bear, and by avoiding the more unfavorable ones. Many features of child behavior cannot be forecast with any adequate precision at the present time. because accurate information is lacking on many important problems. Much useful knowledge, however, is now available, and further gains may be expected from an extension of the research procedures that thus far have proved effective.

A more specific conception of the field of child psychology may be obtained from an enumeration of its chief problems. The psychology of childhood seeks to systematize information on the origin and beginnings of child behavior, and on the ways in which behavior is modified in the course of development and learning. Because of the important relationships between physique and behavior, the studies of growth in bodily size, of the development of physical, sensory, and motor capacities, and of the hygiene of childhood receive much attention. The child's intellectual, emotional, and social development, his motives and interests, his moral and religious development are examined in considerable detail. An aspect of this field of growing importance concerns the development of the child's traits of personality and his adjustments to his physical and social environments. All of these topics shed light on the primary problems of the prediction, guidance, and control of child behavior.

Inadequate Older Methods of Studying Children

The Importance of Sound Methods. The value of the theories and applications of any subject is dependent on the soundness of the methods by which its primary data are obtained. All sciences have progressed from the crude, approximate, and often positively erroneous methods used in the past toward a greater precision of observation. Throughout the entire field of psychology, there has been an unfortunate tendency to depend on methods long ago discarded by most other sciences. The principal reason for this lag has been the widespread interest in human behavior and the universal opportunity for observing it, which made each man feel competent to judge and to theorize in this field. Many fallacies concerning childhood that are widely believed today are the result of uncritical methods of observing and interpreting behavior. Only by approaching the subjects without these traditional prejudices and misconceptions can an effective understanding of the child be gained. The most common error of method in child psychology, both in the past and the present, is *superficial, uncontrolled observation*. Several more specific unsuitable, methods, once widely used in: the earlier days of child study, also deserve a passing comment. Prominent among these are *anecdotal biographies*, *reminiscences*, and *questionnaires*.

Superficial, Uncontrolled Observation. Everyone observes child behavior, but few observe it under conditions suitable for scientific purposes. Popular conceptions of the nature of the child are founded largely on superficial observations of children in the home, or on memories of one's own childhood. These are unreliable methods of obtaining data, for a number of pertinent reasons. Common observations are defective because of *inadequate perception* of the facts of behavior. Keen attention is not given to the most important activities, and many significant factors escape notice. Closely allied is the error of *failing to control causes* of behavior. In uncontrolled situations child behavior is the result of many causes, and the really important ones may not be detected or isolated. Home observations are faulty because they are based on *too few observations* and because *standards of comparison are lacking* between the child observed and other children.

A common error of superficial observation is to note and to remember the *unusual or abnormal* in behavior, ignoring the more frequent occurrences. Of course, careful observations of unique or rare phenomena have a distinct value in promoting an understanding of child behavior, provided that they are made under properly controlled conditions. The mistake is often made, however, of basing generalizations on unusual occurrences and incorrectly applying them to all children.

Ordinary observations also lack precision because the *results are not recorded* at the time that the observations are made. To depend on remembering a complex occurrence, even for a few hours, is unreliable, as a great bulk of psychological experimentation has proved. Persons are likely to report what they think should have happened, often forgetting or ignoring important parts of the actual evidence. Another serious error is the introduction of *personal bias* into observations. Fond parents are likely to interpret the actions of their children in a favorable light, thus overlooking the truth. Persons who are interested in some theory of childhood easily see only the events that support their preconceptions, ignoring those which are contrary. Usually they do this without any deliberate attempts at deception.

Anecdotal Biographies. For many years much dependence was placed on biographies of children as data for child psychology. Many of the earlier biographies are useful today only as illustrations of all of the faults of superficial, uncontrolled observation. Their more common defects include meager observations, failure to verify the facts observed, and failure to record data at the time of observation. Bias and prejudice were common, since the biographies were most frequently written by parents or others with a special interest in the child, or else by persons desirous of proving the merits of some special theory of training or education. Some of the more recent and more carefully prepared biographies have distinct value, as is shown presently.

Reminiscences. Accounts of child behavior given from memory a long time after the events have occurred may be interesting or entertaining, but they have little value as a source of reliable information on child behavior. Reminiscences of childhood appear in a number of guises. Some are parental accounts of behavior occurring at a time long past. Others are autobiographical records made at an even later date relative to the real occurrences. In all reminiscences, bias and the tendency to remember the striking, the pleasant, and the favorable are serious handicaps. As someone has said, "We are usually kind to a fault, especially our own." Fiction concerning childhood, some of which has attained great fame for its supposed insight into child nature, is usually based on the author's reminiscences. In all of these sources, a mixture of solid truth with error causes undue dependence to be placed on the account as a whole. Information about children secured through reminiscences sometimes has a limited value. The results need corroboration, however, but not by using other reminiscences as a check, since agreement may be only the coincidence of errors. Facts secured by a faulty method cannot be verified by using the same method, even though different persons employ it.

Questionnaires. During the early days of the Child Study Movement (thirty or forty years ago) questionnaires of various kinds were widely used, especially by G. Stanley Hall, and his students. Recognizing the need for more adequate information on child behavior, they believed that they had found a ready way to secure masses of data by asking questions of children and adults. Some *questionnaires of direct facts* gave information of value and were the forerunners of today's tests and experimental techniques. Thus, teachers asked questions orally of young children, and used supplementary questions whenever the child's answers indicated the need for it. If the question, "Have you seen a sheep?" was answered in the affirmative, it was followed by such questions as, "How large was it?" and When and where did you see it?" Later, questionnaires were printed, with spaces provided for writing the answers. Questionnaires of this direct sort were of some merit, but they often suffered from the failure to secure answers from a sufficiently large or representative group, and from errors in the interpretation of the results.

Far less reliable were *questionnaires of reminiscence and opinion,* sent chiefly to adults, which were also widely used. These suffered from all of the errors of inadequate method. They seemed to be based on the assumption that faulty observation could be corrected by the bulk of great numbers. Thorndike's classic criticism of this type of questionnaire, first made when the technique was widely used, is still pertinent today. " . . . The ignorance of a thousand people is no better than that of one; truth cannot be manufactured from constant errors by getting a great number of them."

Unreliable Theories of Child Nature

How Fallacious Theories Arise. Early in the history of human thought, we find man formulating theories which seem to make his world of experience more coherent and intelligible. Since man has long been interested in the education and training of children, theories of child nature have been formulated by many. Most of the broader theories are unsound and unreliable. Their lack of merit has been caused principally by two factors. One shortcoming has been dependence on superficial observation and unreliable methods of obtaining data, as described in the last section. The other chief cause of error is the use of *uncritical speculation*. Many conceptions of childhood have been based on adult philosophies, qualities being ascribed to the child to make him fit into some larger system of thinking. Often this was done with an almost complete disregard for actual observations. The satisfying quality of a coherent theory was such as to cause its supporters to gloss over its improbabilities and to be blind to contradictory facts.

Many fallacies concerning childhood that persist in popular thinking even today are based on theories long since discredited. At the risk of digging up old ghosts, it is perhaps worthwhile to describe a few of the more common fallacious theories of child nature. The reader is warned that these are without any great merit. Only by approaching the subject without these traditional preconceptions can an effective understanding of the child be gained.

Some Early Theories. One theory of child nature, resulting from a purely speculative approach (and still widely believed), regarded the child as *inherently sinful*. In a past age dominated by gloomy theological conceptions, the dogma of the original sinful state of man easily became twisted into a notion of the innate waywardness of the child. While modified from its earlier theological connotations, the assertions that children are naturally mischievous, that stern discipline is of general benefit, and that "boys will be boys," reflect essentially the same basic attitude. The doctrine of childhood's badness also offers a plausible rationalization to parents who refuse to accept responsibility for the guidance of a child's conduct.

Disbelieving the widely accepted doctrine of sinfulness, Rousseau advanced the theory that child nature was essentially *good and pure,* until spoiled by contact with adult society. This doctrine was based, not so much on observation, as on agreement with a preconceived general philosophy concerning democracy and the worthwhile character of mankind. Many persons since Rousseau's time have proposed that education should be entirely governed by the child's natural tendencies, because of their essential goodness. In a certain sense, this theory has been a useful antidote to the much worse preceding one, but it often has led to sentimentally motivated excesses, and it is not based on sound methods of observation. Other early theories that were derived from speculation are numerous. John Locke's theory of the child's mind as a *tabula rasa* or blank page, until impressed by experiences, was made to fit his philosophical system and was not a result of systematic observations. Another implicit view regards the child as an *adult in miniature,* but it is not borne out by the facts.

The Recapitulation Theory. No erroneous theory concerning childhood has appealed to a wider audience than the doctrine of recapitulation. Because of its comparative recency and because of the existence of a few mistaken advocates even today, it is a particularly important cobweb to clear from the reader's mind. The theory of recapitulation held, in general, that "ontogeny recapitulates phylogeny"; that the child in its development repeats, in abbreviated form, the history of the race. The theory includes two chief propositions, one or both of which have been advocated by various proponents. First, that the human embryo passes through the same stages as did the race in its evolution from simpler forms of life. Second, that the child in its development repeats human history, from the barbaric to the civilized stages. This latter has been termed the "culture-epochs" theory, and school curricula have sometimes been based on it.

The recent opinions of embryologists, who are most competent to speak, are definitely opposed to the first proposition. Except for the very general fact that the embryo develops from simple to complex, as did the race, and shows certain other resemblances, there is little basis for it. As Lewis points out, the embryo possesses a brain unduly large for its skull and for the rest of the body. Exactly, the opposite was true of our remote animal ancestors. The whole structure of the embryo is as characteristically human in all stages as are the adult body and its organs. The second parallelism between the behavior of the child and the development of the species has never been better reduced to its essential absurdity than by Thorndike's quotations from Hall on the "fish stage," and by his comments on the selections. Said Hall: A babe a few days old made peculiar paddling or swimming movements. . . . In children and adults . . . we find swaying from side to side or forward and backward, not infrequent. This suggests the slow oscillatory movements used by fish. . . . Children . . . after the first shock and fright, take the greatest delight in water. . . . Others older and less active can sit by the hour seeing and hearing the movement of water in sea or stream.

Thorndike's comment is: The fish stage is thus paralleled all the way from four days to forty years, even if we doubt the existence in fishes of anything like the elderly contemplation of water by one sitting on the bank. This theory, as stated by its over-enthusiastic, non-biologically trained proponents, has no significance for the problems of predicting and controlling the behavior of children and adolescents. Knowledge adequate to these tasks is best sought, not by the application of dubious parallels, but by careful, extended, and quantitative observations of the actual subject matter — the behavior of children. A vastly greater knowledge of boys and girls may be obtained by studying their interests, impulses, and habits, than by reading the fullest possible account of the racial past or of histories of civilization.

Other Speculative Theories. A number of other speculative theories have attempted to cope with the problem of the relationship between individual and racial development, but without spectacular success. Thorndike's *utility theory* states that variation and selection account for both types of development, the behavior more useful in assisting the individual to cope with his environment being selected. Hollingworth advances the related view that the individual develops as he does, not because of the race's development, but *"for the same reason,* namely, because of the limitations of skill, intelligence, and knowledge." Koffka supports a cautious *correspondence theory,* that both individual and race develop from more primitive to more highly developed forms of reaction.

The theory of *catharsis,* which relates, strangely enough, both to the theory of the child's sinfulness and to that of his goodness, deserves little support. It holds that early wrongdoing is useful in immunizing the child against later wrongdoing. The "baser instincts" were supposed to be worked out of the system during childhood, to the good of later life. All of the speculative theories described in this section may be regarded as examples of an inadequate approach to child behavior. Only by discarding preconceptions and armchair methods, and by observing the child in the same manner as the scientist observes any other event in nature, can effective progress in child psychology be made.

The Scientific Approach to Child Psychology

Scientific Method. The extension and improvement of child psychology in recent years are caused chiefly by the use of scientific methods in this field. The conditions of science in general include the employment of more precise methods of observation and the interpretation of the data by the inductive method of *generalization*. These processes result in the accumulation of a body of scientific *knowledge* which enables the prediction and control of natural events.

An essential of scientific observation is that facts shall be accumulated in a *systematic* manner, according to a planned mode of attack. The methods used should be subject to *verification* by other observers. This necessitates an exact description of the conditions of observation, so that others can repeat them under similar or definitely varied conditions, record their findings, and make valid comparisons with the original results. The methods of science are *precise*, using carefully defined descriptive terms, or quantitative results often obtained by the use of instruments and apparatus. Scientific observations must be made under *controlled conditions*, so that all of the principal influences affecting the results are known and measured, and so that disturbing factors are eliminated.

From the data obtained by scientific observation, conclusions may be drawn, by the use of the inductive method of generalization. First, a wide range of data is systematically tabulated, making it possible to detect orderly sequences and uniform occurrences. Second, an hypothesis is formed to account for the results and to include a number of observations in a common category. Third, this hypothesis is checked or tested by further observation, and experimentation, leading to its rejection or to its more definite acceptance. Generalizations obtained in this manner furnish a more secure basis for a unified conception of natural phenomena than do the speculative methods condemned in the preceding section.

When observations have been made with the proper precautions and have been subjected to critical scientific thinking, they emerge as the body of scientific knowledge of their designated field. Scientific knowledge at any one time represents the solutions of problems for which effective methods have been found. This body of established facts is constantly being revised in the light of new research and is extended from time to time as new methods overcome older difficulties. Science is therefore continually in a state of flux, its essential characteristics being change and progress. Tomorrow's science may differ from yesterday's, not because the earlier generalizations were untrue, but because the later ones are truer. Any scientific treatise is necessarily a compendium of the present status of a subject that will change as new areas of research are developed.

It would be impossible to describe in detail all of the methods of scientific observation that have contributed to child psychology. A selected number of the most significant types of research include: *systematic biographies, case studies, directed observations, measurement, statistical methods,* and *experimentation*. The principal features of these are described in the paragraphs following.

Systematic Biographies. The beginnings of scientific method in child psychology are found in some of the more systematic of the early biographical accounts of the mental and physical development of children. Shortly before 1800, Tiedemann published in Germany his "Observations on the Development of the Mental Faculties of Children." In 1882 a German physiologist, Preyer, published his influential *Die Seele des Kindes (The Mind of the Child)*, giving detailed observations of the development of his son from birth to the age of three years. This, work is still an example of scientific effort in biography. Extensive notes were taken at the very time the observations were made, and from them the biography. Was later written. The topics treated, including such observations as the reflexes present at birth, the appearance of the first reaction to light, and the course of the grasping reaction, show the difference between this biography and non-scientific anecdotal accounts. Writings such as Preyer's foreshadowed the later use of directed observation and experimental techniques. During the two or three decades following, several other adequate biographies of infants were published.

Observations made by intelligent parents and others today may be of psychological value, if systematic and unbiased procedures are followed. Biographies in general, however, suffer from the inevitable handicaps of poor control of the situations studied and of the observation of too few instances. They are of greater value in suggesting problems for study than for settling issues with any finality.

Directed Observation. When observations of the child's responses to certain naturally occurring events are made according to a prearranged schedule, the technique may be termed directed or systematic observation. Situations are selected that occur repeatedly under normal conditions, and the behavior of children of various ages and with various kinds of previous experience is carefully recorded. A prepared schedule or outline for making observations is used, so that the trait may be noted uniformly and so that attention will be directed in a systematic manner. Because of the freedom of this technique, it is the most useful one for investigating the spontaneous behavior of children.

Many excellent examples of systematic observation may be cited. Piaget studied the development of children's language, judgment, and reasoning by recording observations as they were made, according to a predetermined plan. Thomas applied the method to problems such as that, of children's social relationships. McCarthy and others have investigated vocabulary and language usage by this technique. Gesell has been, one of the most important contributors, often using motion picture records to preserve evidences of behavior for detailed analysis, and to compare the responses of the same child at various ages.

A modification of the observational method is to note the occurrence of a particular type of behavior during selected periods of time, known as the technique of *time sampling*. By the use of this method it is possible to determine the reliability of a limited observation, and hence by the use of appropriate statistical techniques to know what length of observation must be employed in order to secure results that accurately characterize the child. It is but a short step from such careful observations of naturally occurring behavior to the experimental methods in which conditions are artificially controlled and modified to discover the resultant change in response.

Measurement. The method of measurement is employed by making quantitative observations of children's responses to certain tasks presented under standard conditions. Measurement is one of the most widely applicable methods, being included in most of the other techniques here described. Physical measurement was one of the earliest developments in the field. Height, weight, the dimensions of various parts of the body, various aspects of muscular strength, and other features of motor response have been measured with instruments of considerable precision. Measurement has also been successfully applied for many years in the investigation of relatively simple psychological functions, such as rate of tapping, memory for diverse sorts of materials, reaction time, and various types of sensory discrimination.

More complex functions, such as intelligence and honesty, have been measured with moderate success only in recent years. Following the pioneer work of the French psychologist, Alfred Binet, the measurement of intellectual characteristics advanced with great strides. In this country, Edward L. Thorndike and Lewis M. Terman have been especially influential among the large number of persons engaged in the development of mental tests. Psychological testing has become a complex technology which is concerned constantly with the improvement of the reliability and validity of the various types of measurements employed.

In investigating still more complex traits of personality and character for which exact measures have not been devised, methods of *rating* are used. Ratings supply a means for making the observation and judgment of traits quantitative, but are to be regarded only as stop-gaps pending the invention of more refined methods.

Statistical Methods. The development of measurements in child psychology has coincided with the invention of appropriate mathematical methods for manipulating the data obtained so as to make their meaning clearer. Without the aid of statistical techniques, the crude results of measurement would be difficult to interpret appropriately. Some problems that are attacked by statistical methods include the determination of the relationship between two sets of measures, the significance of a difference discovered between two groups, and the degree to which a measure can be depended upon to produce the same results when applied more than once. Statistical methods do not furnish an independent 'means of obtaining facts, but are the chief tool for manipulating and interpreting the results of testing, directed observation, rating, and experiment.

Experiment. An experiment is a special kind of observation made under controlled conditions. The situations are set by the experimenter without waiting for them to arise in the child's natural environment, and the responses are noted or measured. In the ideal conception of an experiment, all factors or conditions that might affect the result are held constant except one, which is varied deliberately. Under this arrangement, any variation in responses can be ascribed to the operation of the variable factor which is now regarded as causal. Of course, it is possible only to approximate this ideal in many problems of child psychology. All of the factors that might influence the result are not always known, and only the factors that are suspected to have the greatest effect on the outcomes are controlled. Because of this fact, experiments vary widely in merit and conclusiveness.

A simple example of an experiment will make the concept of control clearer. If we are investigating the relative honesty of boys and girls in a certain situation, many other variables must be excluded. If the boy and girl groups are of the same age, of the same race, of the same intelligence, from the same kinds of homes, and have had essentially the same school and other out-of-school experiences, then these factors are removed from consideration as causes. Any difference now found between the, groups can be considered as caused by sex alone and not by differences in age, race, education, intelligence, or social status. Even with these precautions care must be taken to avoid the influence of still other factors upon the results.

A common type of experiment is carried out by selecting two carefully matched groups of children, and subjecting one (the "experimental") group to some definite procedure which is withheld from the other (the "control") group. The influence of the specific procedure being investigated is inferred from the resulting difference between the groups, since they are alike in all except the critical factor.

Experimentation and exact observation also are facilitated by the use of instruments and apparatus for controlling the situation and for recording responses. Photographic records are frequently used. Adult observers watch children's reactions through one-way vision screens that enable them to watch the child while he is unaware of his being observed. A vast inventory of standardized materials is used to provide the situations presented to children, while mechanical instruments may record his responses with great precision.

Progress in Methods. The ultimate goal of method in child psychology is the extension of valid experimentation. Although its subject matter makes experimental control more difficult than in most other fields of science, new problems are being brought within the realm of exact study every year. The child psychology of the present is a compilation of the results achieved in approximately fifty years of progressively refined research. The child psychology of the future will include an extension of knowledge into areas now inadequately investigated.

Bibliography

Amber Haque (2004), "Psychology from Islamic Perspective: Contributions of Early Muslim Scholars and Challenges to Contemporary Muslim Psychologists", *Journal of Religion and Health* 43 (4): 357-377 [361]

Aslin, R. (1993). "Commentary: The Strange Attractiveness of Dynamic Systems to Development." In L. Smith, E. Thelen (Eds.), A Dynamic Systems Approach: Applications. Cambridge, MA: MIT Press.

Barrett MD, Harris M and Chasan J (1991). "Early lexical development and maternal speech: a comparison of children's initial and subsequent uses of words". *Journal of Child Language* 18: 21–40.

Berk L (2005). *Infants, Children, and Adolescents*. Boston: Allyn & Bacon.

Berk, Laura E. (2009). *Child Development*. 8th ed. United States of America: Pearson Education, Inc.

Bjorklund, D. F. & Pellegrini, A. D. (2000). Child Development and Evolutionary Psychology. *Child Development, 71,* 1687-1708.

Bornstein, M. H. & Lamb, M. E. (2005). *Developmental science: An advanced textbook*. Mahwah, NJ: Erlbaum, 2005.

Bradley Steffens (2006), *Ibn al-Haytham: First Scientist*, Chapter 5, Morgan Reynolds Publishing,

Bronfenbrenner, U. (1979). *The Ecology of Human Development: Experiments by Nature and Design*. Cambridge, MA: Harvard University Press.

Bronfenbrenner, U. (1979). *The Ecology of Human Development: Experiments by Nature and Design*. Cambridge, MA: Harvard University Press.

Bruce J. Ellis, Child Development May/June 2003, 74:3, pp. 801-821

Bruner JS (1990). *Acts of Meaning*. Cambridge MA: Harvard University Press.

Bruner JS and Lucariello J, "Monologue as narrative recreation of the world", in Nelson K, *Narratives from the Crib*, Cambridge MA: Harvard University press

Buchwald J (1987), "A comparison of plasticity in sensory and cognitive processing systems", in Gunzenhauser N, *Infant Stimulation*, Skillman NJ: Johnson & Johnson

Children with active, involved fathers have better social skills, are healthier, and do better in school", according to Duane Wilson, the Proud Fathers, Proud Parents program coordinator for the Michigan Department of Human Services

Cultural, Communication, and Cognition: Vygotskian Perspectives. Cambridge University Press. 1985.

David W. Tschanz, MSPH, PhD (August 2003). "Arab Roots of European Medicine", *Heart Views* 4 (2).

Erikson E (1968). *Identity, Youth, and Crisis*. New York: Norton.

Gleitman LR (1990). "The structural sources of verb meaning". *Language Acquisition* 1: 3–55.

Greenough W, Black J and Wallace C (1993), "Experience and brain development", in Johnson M, *Brain Development and Cognition*, Oxford: Blackwell, pp. 319–322

Hart B and Risley T (1995). *Meaningful differences in the everyday experience of young American children*. Baltimore: P.H. Brookes.

Ingram D (1999), "Phonological acquisition", in Barrett M, *The Development of Language*, London: Psychology Press, p. 73–97

Johnson-Pynn, J., Fragaszy, D.M., & Cummins-Sebree, S. (2003). Common territories in comparative and developmental psychology: The quest for shared means and meaning in behavioral investigations. *International Journal of Comparative Psychology, 16*, 1-27.

Kail RE (2006). *Children and Their Development* (4 ed.). Prentice Hall.

Kegl J, Senghas A and Coppola M (1999), "Creation through construct: Sign language emergence and sign language change in Nicaragua", in DeGrafs M, *Language Creation and Language Change: Creolization, Diachrony and Development*, Cambridge, MA: MIT Press

Lemma A (2007), "Psychodynamic Therapy: The Freudian Approach", in Dryden W, *Handbook of Individual Therapy* (5 ed.), Sage publications

Lerner, R. M. *Concepts and theories of human development*. Mahwah, NJ: Erlbaum, 2002.

Mercer J (1998). *Infant Development: A Multidisciplinary Introduction*. Pacific Grove, CA: Brooks/Cole.

Mind in Society. Cambridge, MA: Harvard University Press. 1978.

Mind in Society: The development of higher psychological processes (Translation by Michael Cole). Cambridge, MA: Harvard University Press. 1978 (Published originally in Russian in 1930).

Moerk E (1996). "Input and learning processes in first language acquisition". *Advances in Child Development and Behavior* 26: 181–229.

Moerk EL (1986), "Environmental factors in early language acquisition", in Whitehurst GJ, *Annals of child development*, 3, CTJAI press

Moerk EL (1989). "The LAD was a lady and the tasks were ill defined". *Developmental Review* 9: 21–57.

Morford JP and Kegl J (2000), "Gestural precursors to linguistic constructs: how input shapes the form of language", in McNeill D, *Language and Gesture*, Cambridge: Cambridge University Press

Pan B and Snow C (1999), "The development of conversational and discourse skills", in Barrett M, *The Development of Language*, London: Psychology Press, pp. 229–50

Patterson C (2008). *Child Development*. New york: McGraw-Hill.

Piaget, J. (1977). "The essential Piaget" ed by Howard E. Gruber and J. Jacques Voneche Gruber, New York: Basic Books

Pinker S (1994). *The Language Instinct*. London: Allen Lane.

Rebekah Levine Coley and Bethany L. Medeiros, Reciprocal Longitudinal Relations Between Nonresident Father Involvement and Adolescent Delinquency, *Child Development*, 78:1, pp. 132-147, Jan 2007

Sameroff, A. (1983). "Factors in predicting successful parenting." In Sasserath, V. (Ed.), Minimizing High-Risk Parenting. Skilman, NJ: Johnson & Johnson.

Schlinger, H.D. (2008). *The long good-bye: why B.F. Skinner's Verbal Behavior is alive and well on the 50th anniversary of its publication*.

Smith PK, Cowie H and Blades M. *Understanding Children's Development*. Basic psychology (4 ed.). Oxford, England: Blackwell.

Smith PK, Cowie H and Blades M. *Understanding Children's Development*. Basic psychology (4 ed.). Oxford, England: Blackwell.

Stern DN (1990). *Diary of a Baby*. Harmondsworth: Penguin.

Tanner JM (1978). *Fetus into Man*. Cambridge MA: Harvard University Press.

The first three of these stages, which correspond closely with Piaget's later-described stages of childhood, were first presented in Steiner's 1911 essay *The Education of the Child*.

Thought and Language. Cambridge, MA: MIT Press. 1962.

Waters E, Kondo-Ikemura K, Posada G and Richters J (1991), "Learning to Love: Mechanisms and Milestones", in Gunnar M and Sroufe L, *Minnesota Symposia on Child psychology*, 23, Self-Processes and Development, Hillsdale, NJ: Erlbaum, pp. 217–255

atson, J.B.(1926). What the nursery has to say about instincts. In C. Murchison (Eds.) Psychologies of 1925. Worchester, MA: Clark University Press.

Vhite, S.H.(1968). The learning maturation controversy: Hall to Hull. *Merrill-Palmer Quarterly, 14,* 187-196.

Wood SE, Wood CE and Boyd D (2006). *Mastering the world of psychology* (2 ed.). Allyn & Bacon.

Wood SE, Wood CE and Boyd D (2006). *Mastering the world of psychology* (2 ed.). Allyn & Bacon.